Introduction to
political science

Introduction to political science

People, politics, and perception

Hendrik van Dalen
University of Georgia

L. Harmon Zeigler
University of Oregon

Prentice-Hall, Inc., Englewood Cliffs, New Jersey 07632

Library of Congress Cataloging in Publication Data

ZEIGLER, LUTHER HARMON (date)
  Introduction to political science.

  Includes bibliographies and index.
  1. Political science. I. van Dalen, Hendrik,
1939–   joint author. II. Title.
JA66.Z44   320   76-49598
ISBN 0-13-493205-6

To Amanda and Joan

Printed in the United States of America

10 9 8 7 6 5 4 3 2 1

Quotations on pages 78, 81, 84–85 copyright © 1969, 1970 by Gary Wills.
Reprinted by permission of Houghton Mifflin Company, and by permission
of the author and his agents, Scott Meredith Literary Agency, Inc.,
845 Third Avenue, New York, New York 10022.

Prentice-Hall International, Inc., *London*
Prentice-Hall of Australia Pty. Limited, *Sydney*
Prentice-Hall of Canada, Ltd., *Toronto*
Prentice-Hall of India Private Limited, *New Delhi*
Prentice-Hall of Japan, Inc., *Tokyo*
Prentice-Hall of Southeast Asia Pte. Ltd., *Singapore*

Contents

7

**Components of the political system:
a functional approach** *179*

8

**Politics and crisis: political system types
in the modern world** *213*

Acknowledgments

We wish to acknowledge with gratitude the contributions of the following colleagues: James C. Davies and Arthur Hanhardt of the University of Oregon, and Robert Clute and Robert Golembiewski of the University of Georgia.

Additionally, we are grateful to Jane Feldman and William Griffith for assisting in the research and writing of chapters 1 and 5. JoAnn Wilson made extensive editorial contributions.

Introduction to
political science

1

An outline of political process

At the beginning of this century, a Tammany ward boss by the name of George Washington Plunkitt offered this advice to aspiring political leaders: "You must study human nature and act accordin'." [1] To Plunkitt, knowledge of politics meant knowledge of people: what they think of themselves, how they see the world and their place in it, what in life is most important to them. People's needs, people's values, people's beliefs—this is the stuff of politics. To understand the political world, we must seek to understand why people behave politically as they do.[2]

Plunkitt's dictum is the premise of this book. Political analysis must be grounded in the study of individual political behavior. None of those institutions, processes, and outcomes we call political—legislatures and parties, lobbying and revolution, constitutions and corruption—exist apart from the political behavior of individuals.[3]

Our approach to the study of politics focuses on the individual as the basic empirical unit of analysis.[4] When we look at political phenomena from this perspective, we see institutions—such as parliamentary cabinets, political parties, legislatures—not as disembodied entities spewing forth policies, candidates, or laws, but as groups of individuals interacting with each other in a setting that is created and shaped by the preferences, expectations, and actions of individuals. If we want to understand a particular outcome of political processes, for example, federal housing policy, what kind of information would we collect? We would undoubtedly want to know about the legislation relating to this area. How much money has been appropriated? What is the form of this federal action: underwriting mortgage loans, grants-in-aid to the states, matching funds? What agencies are charged with implementing the pro-

---

[1] William L. Riordan, *Plunkitt of Tammany Hall* (New York: E. P. Dutton, 1963), p. 25.

[2] Heinz Eulau, *The Behavioral Persuasion in Politics* (New York: Random House, 1963), pp. 3, 24.

[3] Ibid., p. 16.

[4] Ibid., pp. 13–14.

1

grams? How ambitious are the goals set forth in the enabling legislation, that is, how many units are to be constructed in what period of time? What kinds of housing are provided for—single-family homes or low-income "projects"? In what ways are state and local governments and nongovernment groups involved?

Such an inventory would provide us with a good deal of information. But how full, how satisfying, is our understanding of federal housing policy after these questions are answered? The study of politics is more than *description;* it seeks *explanation.* Because there is, presumably, some purpose for all this research, there are other questions we want to answer. Why are federal housing programs structured as they are? Why does this policy fall so far short of providing adequate housing for all citizens? Why is the federal government even involved in providing housing? Why is it that preambles to housing laws affirm the desirability of providing decent housing for everyone, yet there is no federal legislation providing for a minimal level of health care?

It is when we try to answer such analytic questions about politics that we are compelled to direct our inquiry to the behavior of individuals. "The goal is the explanation of why people behave as they do, and why, as a result, political processes and systems function as they do." [5] If we look for factors that determined the existence and the character of housing policy, we begin to ask questions like these: What was the political philosophy of the president(s) under whose administration(s) these programs were created? What was the presidential part in the policy-making process? What is a president's conception of his role? How has congressional leadership handled such legislation, and to what constituencies is it attentive? Who has given political voice to the needs of the poorly housed? Why are those who live in substandard housing not as effective in influencing such policy as those in the construction and banking industries, who are fewer in number and whose needs are less desperate? Who administers these programs? Are these people corrupt, hostile, bureaucratically neutral, or activists concerned with social change? Does public opinion support energetic federal action in the area of social welfare? As we begin to comprehend the significance of individual behavior for analyzing and explaining political phenomena, the need to seek explanation for human behavior becomes clear.

Given this emphasis on individual behavior, what may not be so apparent is how this is an introductory text in *political science* and not in psychology. Political scientists are concerned with the *political consequences* of human action; it is the political order we want to understand. The task we have chosen for ourselves does not encompass the entire

[5] Ibid., p. 24.

range of human behavior. Our chosen problem is to explain what goes on in one sector of human life—the political arena. Thus, we are concerned with behavior that is *politically relevant;* relevance is defined by *context,* the setting in which behavior occurs or on which behavior has a perceptible impact.

But political science is an *eclectic* discipline in its methods of inquiry. Having staked out our intellectual bailiwick—the study of politics—we are not inhibited from exploring other academic domains for tools that will be useful in tackling the problems the political order presents. Social psychologists, economists, anthropologists, and sociologists have developed concepts and analytical techniques that can contribute to our understanding of politics.

THE PERSONAL BASIS OF POLITICS

We begin our inquiry into politics at the micro (individual) level of analysis, with an examination of what Heinz Eulau terms "the personal basis of politics." [6]

When we deal with personality as a factor in political behavior, the eclecticism of political inquiry is apparent. We shall refer to the work of a number of psychologists who propose different ways of thinking about the dynamics of the human mind, because their research and thinking provide political scientists with concepts and perspectives that contribute to our analysis and understanding of political phenomena. We are not committed to *a* theory of personality any more than to *a* theory of human action. There is, after all, no consensus on a single general theory of either personality or human behavior. But of more immediate significance is the fact that, as political scientists, our concern is with problems of *politics,* not with the problems of *personality.*

We must keep in mind that we cannot directly observe "personality"; we can only *infer* its contours and content from behavior. What we call "personality" is a *construct:* The meaning we ascribe to the notion of "personality" is constructed from the interpretations we give to its manifestations in behavior. Abstracting personality from the very patterns of behavior it is intended to explain and interpret is an inductive process.[7] Thus, in our analysis of the personal basis of politics, we focus on those aspects or those expressions of personality that seem most useful for explaining political behavior.

Perception is critically important in this task, for people *act* on the

---

[6] The title of Eulau's chapter on personality and politics, ibid.

[7] Ibid., p. 86.

basis of what they "know." A person's response to a situation is guided
by his definition of that situation. Variety in human behavior is related
to variety in the way people perceive "reality." Don Quixote tilted at
windmills, but because he perceived them to be knights on horseback
who had besmirched the lady Dulcinea's honor; Quixote, "knowing"
himself to be a knight pledged to live by the code of chivalry, acted
accordin'. In *Dr. Strangelove,* a United States Air Force general is con-
vinced that the purity and essence of the natural body fluids of the
American people are being polluted and diluted by the Russians; to put
a stop to this pernicious emasculation of the American race, he devises
a way to bomb the polluters with the American nuclear arsenal.

Such extreme cases of aberrant and bizarre behavior most readily
exhibit the interaction between a person's perceptual apparatus and
the situation itself that leads to the behavior. But the same principle
operates in the more normal range of human behavior, specifically, in
that scector of human behavior that is politically relevant. If a voter
sees "not a dime's worth of difference" between the Democratic and the
Republican parties, it is not surprising if he registers as an Independent
or under a third party; if he perceives even that effort as meaningless,
he will likely not vote at all. If an individual sees the world as engaged
in a monumental struggle between communism and democracy, it is likely
that he would have supported continued American involvement in the
Indochina war and in Angola, as necessary for the preservation of freedom.

If, then, differences in individual behavior can be explained by differences in individual perceptions of reality, how do we account for variety
of perception? In the following chapter, we present two theories that root
perceptual diversity in patterns of basic uniformities of human behavior.
To explain differences by commonalities is not as paradoxical as it might
first appear. The study of human behavior assumes that some regularity
of pattern underlies the variety of behaviors we observe. Theories are
organizing devices; they set up conceptual frameworks within which we
can order and relate and interpret specific and diverse observations.

One theory proposes that a person's self-conceptions, his views about
the nature of society and his relation to it, and his ideas about what is
important in life, depend on how much his physical and psychological
needs have been satisfied. These perceptions, in turn, shape the character
of his political behavior. Those people in the sub-Saharan nations who
are suffering through a terrible drought and famine are not involving
themselves in the political life of their countries, not even in revolutionary activity; their overriding concern is to have enough food to live.
A person who enters public life with a solid sense of self-esteem is not
compelled to use the opportunities of public office to gratify his need

for a feeling of self-worth; having confidence in himself, he can develop his abilities to achieve goals that are less self-centered.

The other theory argues that a person's behavior is determined by the scope and the character of his moral orientation, by his definition of desirable relationships with other people. As a person's moral capacities develop, he moves to more demanding and abstract conceptions of human relations—from an obsession with coercion and punishment, to conformity, to tolerance, to ideals of justice, equality, and human dignity. At each successive stage of moral growth, his "moral universe" expands, from a concern with self to the inclusion of more remote others—family, associates, the society, humanity. The crux of this theory is the proposition that an individual's behavior is shaped by his beliefs about how he ought to behave.

We can enhance the value of "perception" as an analytic concept by refining it to take account of the *forms* of perception. The facets of perception most useful for interpreting political behavior are beliefs, values, attitudes, and opinions. *Beliefs* are basic assumptions about reality, ideas that describe the world to us; we can think of them as organized into *systems.* A person's belief system provides the basic structure through which he defines and interprets his universe. *Attitudes* and *opinions* are formed on this structure; they predispose a person to respond to an object or a situation in a particular way. Attitudes are enduring general orientations, whereas opinions focus on immediate and specific issues.

We can further refine our analytic framework by looking at various characteristics of belief systems. Thus, we can describe systems of beliefs by their contents; by how logically and consistently beliefs are related and organized; by the importance a person attaches to various beliefs. Using such dimensions, we can construct *typologies* of belief systems. A typology is a conceptual device which establishes criteria by which phenomena are classified according to their most significant similarities and differences; "most significant" means the most relevant for the purposes for which the typology is being constructed.

One such construct that has contributed to the interpretation of political behavior is "the open and closed mind," developed by Milton Rokeach. The notions of "open mind" and "closed mind" are categories of cognitive structures; they designate two radically different ways in which people organize their perceptions and use their perceptual apparatus to "know" the world. The open mind is marked by belief in the basic goodness of human nature and the nonthreatening nature of society, and the belief that authority is not absolute, but subject to questioning and judgment. It is characterized by knowledge of those things that are not believed in by the particular individual as well as of those that are; by ability to consider other, different ideas and beliefs; by a

high degree of integration among beliefs. The closed mind is the an-
tithesis of the open mind. A person who is "closed-minded" holds misanthropic views of people and society, and regards authority as absolute.
He is intolerant of different ideas and opposing beliefs, although he
knows little about them. His belief system is "compartmentalized": He
holds to beliefs that are not logically consistent, but does not recognize
that inconsistency. Each general structure of belief undergirds a set of
attitudes and opinions about specific political issues. A "closed-minded"
person, for example, tends to give only weak and selective support to
civil liberties: Although "believing" in the abstract ideal of freedom of
speech, he may oppose having the works of Marx and Lenin on the
shelves of the town library. An "open-minded" person who supported
the American war effort in Indochina would have recognized the legitimacy of dissenting opinions, and would not have labeled antiwar dissi-
dents "unpatriotic" or "un-American" because they did not agree with
him in supporting government policy.

The chapter on presidential character demonstrates how the methods
and tools of the study of personality might be used to deal with one
important problem in the study of politics: Why do presidents behave
politically as they do? Here we can follow the indirect and inductive
process of exploring the personal basis of political behavior—abstracting
"personality" from the observed behavior it is intended to explain and
interpret.

James Barber has constructed a typology of presidential personalities
based on two dimensions. One characterizes a president's performance of
his political role by how much energy he invests in it; this is labeled the
active–passive dimension. The other describes a president's "affective"
response to his role performance; it indicates, in other words, how he
feels about what he does. Specifically, it is a register of *felt satisfaction* [8]
about his presidential experience; this is the *positive–negative* dimension. These simple dimensions are dichotomous; that is, each has only
two categories into which a president may be classified: he is either active
or passive, positive *or* negative.

Combining these two dimensions yields four *types* of presidential
personality: active–positive, active–negative, passive–positive, passive–
negative. Each type represents a "style" (a way of acting), and a "worldview" (a way of seeing the world). "Style" refers to a pattern of behavior,
the manner in which a president goes about doing what his role requires. "Worldview" is a configuration of beliefs, values, and attitudes
about the nature of people, society, and politics; it includes a person's
moral orientations or outlooks. Each type also connotes a person's orien-

---

[8] James D. Barber, *Presidential Character: Predicting Performance in the White
House* (Englewood Cliffs, N.J.: Prentice-Hall, 1972), p. 12.

tation toward himself and his interpretation of his experience of life.[9] By a person's self-understanding and the meaning he attaches to his life, we mean, then, his structure of motives, of fulfilled and unfulfilled psychological needs; we are talking about how he feels about himself.

Barber argues that there is a close, coherent relationship between personality and behavior: from observations of patterns of behavior one can infer structures of personality; in turn, our observations of presidential behavior are enriched by a new dimension of meaning. The perspective of "personality" reveals patterns and aspects of behavior that might otherwise go unseen. How a president organizes his office and structures the decision-making process in the White House can be seen as a reflection of his personality; understanding personality factors can unveil relationships between the processes and the results of decision-making. Indeed, Barber argues that by studying how these personality types are formed and by interpreting observed behavior in this light, we can *predict* how presidents will act in office.

The critical position of the presidency in the American political order in turn makes the problem of analyzing and explaining presidential behavior critical to political science. *How* political scientists go about doing this—the analytical method chosen—is also determined by the nature of the problem. Intensive psychological inquiry is a more fruitful approach for understanding politics when it is applied to the behavior of individual presidents (or other leaders) than when it is used for analyzing the behavior of other classes of political actors having less individual impact on the functioning of the political system. The institution of the presidency provides a context for the full play of personality traits— a fluid, open-ended environment that places a minimum of restraint on personality as a determinant of behavior. The elasticity of the office makes it particularly susceptible to being shaped by the character of the individual who occupies it. Thus, we are concerned with the problem of presidential personality because of the significant *political consequences* of presidential behavior.

How, then, shall we approach the problem of the political behavior of "the masses"—the vast majority of people whose individual political contexts allow far less potential for influencing the political arena? A different question calls for a different method for tackling it. It is clear that the construction of thorough individual psychological profiles would have a very low yield of political insight for a very high investment of effort. We can gain far more understanding of the conditions and consequences of the behavior of "lesser" political actors by aiming for less depth and greater breadth.

9 Ibid., pp. 7–8.

The political significance of the behavior of each person "in the mass" is quite limited when compared to that of a political leader. Similarly, an "average" person's "political" behavior is far more limited than that of a member of a political elite. These two statements seem so self-evident—indeed, almost tautological—that it might be wondered why we bother to make them. But these axioms indicate why our methods and our perspectives change. Our concern here is not with the political behavior of individuals considered one by one, but with the political behavior of *collectivities* of individuals. This is the form in which the behavior of people "in the mass" has the greatest impact on the political order.

In trying to analyze and explain such behavior, we are aiming for general but meaningful statements that are applicable to broad classes or categories of people. We are asking, What kinds of people are characterized by what kinds of cognitive structures? And further, What cognitive structures are related to what kinds of political behavior? We are looking for correlations among these variables that define behavioral tendencies that are valid for particular types of individuals. Such generalizations are not intended to explain completely and precisely the political behavior of each individual per se in the category we are making statements about—nor does the nature of the problem we are studying require this.

In the chapter called "Popular Images of Politics" we will continue to expand our repertoire of concepts and constructs about the personal basis of politics. A number of theoretical formulations about perception and personality have proved useful for studying political behavior: for example, ideological constraint, the authoritarian personality, participant–subject orientation. There is a good deal of overlap among these; each conceptualization is devised to tap some pertinent aspect of "personality." There are similarities between the closed mind and the authoritarian personality, and between the open mind and the participant orientation. There is a high level of "co-incidence" of anomie (the sense of exclusion from societal norms), lack of self-esteem, "subject orientation," misanthropic views of people and society, and other characteristics of the closed mind. Where we find evidence of one, we will very likely find evidence of the others—they tend to "co-occur," for there is a logical as well as an empirical relationship among them.

Let us consider some of the ramifications of this last cluster of variables (anomie, low self-esteem, and so forth). Research indicates that people with such variables have consonant political attitudes: predisposition to think of politics in terms of dark conspiracies, to rely on stereotypes and prejudices in relating to others, to search for scapegoats. How do such individuals behave in the political arena? They tend to respond to the political world with apathy, but are highly susceptible to being activated by emotional and irrational appeals to support the use of the state as an instrument of suppression and control. We have here in outline a portrait of "the mass man."

Such a pattern of thought and behavior has important consequences for the functioning of the political system. As we emphasize in this book, there is a fundamental consistency between the characteristics of a political system and the prevailing constellation of political ideas and behavior. In a sense, the predominant beliefs, values, and modes of action keep the political system on a short tether; the structure and substance of political life cannot stray very far from what people believe is acceptable and appropriate in politics. Popular expectations define the parameters of political activity. "The masses" can be "manipulated" only to the extent that they are manipulable. An ascendant belief in the absolute nature of authority is congenial to the establishment of an authoritarian regime. The prospects for systematic oppression of minorities are dim in a society in which the value of equality is firmly and widely cherished and colors other social relationships. The stability of any political regime depends upon the degree of "fit" between it and the underlying "political culture" in which it is embedded.

MACRO-LEVEL POLITICAL ANALYSIS

We have stated that the essence of politics lies in human action, and that our study of politics must therefore be grounded in the study of people's behavior. We have, however, delimited the scope of our inquiry to include only behavior deemed "politically relevant." The criterion of relevance is the *context* in which behavior occurs or in which it has consequence; for us, the context is "the political order." Although in this text we examine "behavior" and "the political order" in sequence, we cannot wrench one from the other in theorizing about politics. Our perspectives and our methods of inquiry change, but we do not jettison the insights we have gleaned from examining individual political behavior.

If we define *political* behavior by its context, by what criterion do we define a context as political? What is this sector of human experience we call "the political order?" Politics can be defined generally as the means by which "authoritative allocations" of societal values are made. In this definition, values are those scarce symbolic and material goods with which people's needs are satisfied. Because such values are not in sufficient supply in society to satisfy all needs and demands, there is inevitable competition and conflict. "Authoritative allocation," then, involves the resolution of such conflict; choices must be made among competing demands for societal goods—choices that are binding on society as a whole. Politics necessarily implies *power*—power to make allocative decisions and to implement those decisions for society.

Although power is at the heart of politics, there is no consensus on a single theory of power—just as there is no general agreement on a single theory of personality or of human action. Political scientists have developed a number of differing conceptualizations of the nature of power, and one might wonder about the usefulness of such a plenitude of ideas.

Political scientists resort to a variety of *empirical* tools—methods and techniques for gathering and interpreting data; similarly, we employ a variety of *conceptual* tools. We noted earlier the wealth of constructs and concepts used in the study of the political behavior of "the masses." There is purpose to all this variety: Each concept, construct, and theory is an instrument of analysis designed to tap a particular aspect or dimension of the general phenomenon under study—whether it be personality, perception, or power. Each conceptual variant sheds a rather different light on that phenomenon, revealing a facet that is not brought out by any of the others. This is essentially what we mean by "insight": some significant contribution to understanding, a discovery of meaning. Conceptualizations furnish perspectives, ways of looking at things, that direct us to objects of observation, organize gathered information into some coherent and manageable form, and provide criteria for interpreting what we see.

In chapter 6 we shall present some of the more insightful and theoretical formulations about the nature of power. One is the very basic distinction between "power" and "authority." The concepts represent two very different, independent realities, for power may be exercised without authority and authority may be invoked without the power to enforce. Such a distinction alerts us to the difference between a role or office and the individual who performs that role or occupies that office. A visible case in point is the institution of the American presidency. Consider the possible consequences of identifying *a* presi*dent* with *the* presiden*cy;* if we confound the two, we may deny ourselves (and others) the right to criticize a president—because we accept as legitimate the authority invested in the presidency, dissent becomes synonymous with disloyalty. Consider another example of the distinction between power and authority: During the Senate Watergate hearings, Senator Sam Ervin and attorney John J. Wilson engaged in a spirited debate about whether, under the Constitution, a president may authorize "illegal" acts. Specifically, does a president's authority (and duty) to safeguard national security justify breaking into Daniel Ellsberg's psychiatrist's office to obtain information about the man who "leaked" the Pentagon Papers, or was it a violation of the Fourth Amendment guarantee against unlawful search and seizure? The legality or constitutionality of such action is at issue, but whatever the judgment of its legitimacy, *the act was done.*

In the wake of Watergate, there has emerged a host of issues and events revolving around questions of authority. Our recent national political life has been dominated by the notion of "constitutionality." We have invoked provisions of the Constitution to fill the office of the vice-presidency when it was vacated by resignation, and to institute impeachment proceedings against the president. We have debated the constitutional validity of presidential claims of executive privilege, and the meaning of "high crimes and misdemeanors." The judiciary has come to the forefront of our political life, repeatedly required to decide upon lawful procedures. Our intense concern with the constitutionality of acts reflects the pre-eminence given to written rules and "the rule of law" as the sources of authority in our political system.

Max Weber's typology of authority defines three distinct sources of political legitimacy, and, thus, three types of authority: the traditional, the charismatic, and the rational–legal (or bureaucratic). The prevalence of one of these types of authority in a polity mirrors the dominant belief and value systems of its people, for legitimacy represents a conception of what is rightful and proper in politics. Each has different consequences for the process of governance and for the outcomes of the political process. The refrain, "a government of laws, not of men," expresses the essence of rational–legal authority. The constitutional consciousness just noted reveals the significance the American people attach to the rational–legal as a basis of political legitimacy. "Bureaucratic" is an alternate label for this type of authority, because bureaucracy is organized on the same principle of orderly and consistent procedure based on written rules. In contrast, charismatic authority derives from the extraordinary qualities of a particular individual—personal magnetism, charisma: "a gift of grace." Traditional authority draws on custom or tradition, not on written rules; unlike charismatic authority, it is transferable to other persons.

We can begin to see that "power" is not a simple matter to explain—no more than are "personality" and "perception." As we refine and elaborate and multiply sets of analytic concepts, we may find our analyses becoming more complicated and less clear-cut than expected. How does this help us to understand politics? We should keep in mind that good political analysis does not obscure complexity, but reveals it. The process of understanding does not mean constricting the scope of knowledge, or reducing a rich and complex reality to a comfortable simplicity. To do so is self-deceiving. Explanation and comprehension are open-ended processes of continual discovery and expansion of knowledge.

THE POLITICAL SYSTEM AND ITS FUNCTIONS

Having identified the political order as inseparable from the realities of power and authority, how do we begin to map the political world, to locate power and authority within the political system? Such a task requires some framework that will help us to identify the components of the political system and to explore the relationships among them. We require a conceptual apparatus that will enable us to observe and interpret political activities, for the object of our inquiry is to understand what *goes on* in the political arena.

These needs are met by *systems theory,* and by a closely related theory, *structural-functionalism* (or as we shall call it, functionalism). This analytic approach focuses on the *functions* of the political system, that is, on political activities and their intended and unintended consequences. The "political system" is conceived as a set of individuals, institutions, and processes interacting on a regular basis to make binding decisions on the allocation of symbolic and material resources for society as a whole. There are two primary kinds of inputs into the political system—demands and support—which are influenced by the outputs of the political system, as well as by what happens in the nonpolitical environment. "Input functions" are activities associated with the formation and transmission of demands and support. "Output functions" are activities associated with policy-making and implementation. This functional approach will be developed in greater detail in chapter 7, but it may be useful at this point to indicate how it contributes to our analysis.

Political socialization is the learning process by which people acquire political beliefs, values, and attitudes; it is the process by which individuals come to share a common "orientation" toward politics, a *political culture.* Political socialization is designated an "input function" because of its role as a major determinant of the content and form of the demands and support tendered the political system. It is not difficult to see the relationship between a person's experience of his needs, his value system, his expectations of society's response to him—and the kinds of demands he makes on the political system. Similarly, it is apparent that the manner in which his political demands are communicated, and the character of the support he gives to the political system, are heavily dependent upon his beliefs about how people ought to and do behave politically, and his ideas about authority.

Political culture defines the context of political activity; it establishes the "rules of the game" in the political arena. This is a theme we will develop and emphasize in this book: How a society structures its political life is consonant with its prevailing pattern of political orientations. A society that is deeply divided on fundamental beliefs, values, and attitudes, and that renders only weak legitimacy for its political institutions, will be unstable and, alternatively, repressive. In contrast, a consensual political system requires a society in which characteristics of the "open mind" are widely shared: trust in individuals, emphasis on the values of equality and freedom, belief in the conditional nature of authority, and so on.

Just as the substance of political socialization varies, so do the forms of the institutions that perform this function. In American society, the family, school, peer groups, and the media are major socializing agents, although inculcating political orientations is not their primary purpose. But in the People's Republic of China, the burden of political education falls on work and study groups—institutions created specifically for that purpose, for which there are no counterparts in our society.

Similar observations can be made about other functions. "Rule-adjudication" (an output function) is the process whereby disputes that arise from the framing and implementation of allocative decisions are resolved. In the United States, the civil court system is the primary agent of rule-adjudication for both the content and the administration of policies and laws. In France, a separate, independent administrative court system specifically deals with conflicts over the implementation of government policy and with administrative malfeasance. The office of the ombudsman in Sweden is invested with similar authority to oversee the bureaucracy. "Rule-making" (another output function) refers to the actual process of making binding choices among competing demands. This function is performed primarily in the legislative arena in parliamentary democracies. In the Soviet Union, the party leadership is the rule-making institution; in Brazil, it is the military junta; in Uganda, President-dictator Idi Dada Amin.

Political systems may also differ in the effectiveness of function performance. If we judge success in political socialization by degree of consensus on political beliefs and values, England—the only democracy without a written constitution—may be deemed more successful than Pakistan, where massive refusal to accord legitimacy to its political institutions resulted in civil war and the creation of Bangladesh. The input function of "interest articulation" furnishes other examples of this point. In the United States, an extraordinary emphasis is placed on expressing political demands. The freedoms of speech, of the press, of association, and to petition the government, are not only among the most hallowed of our civil liberties, but probably are also the most exercised. In many countries (North and South Korea, the Philippines, Spain, Russia, Taiwan, China, East Germany) such activities are severely restricted or prohibited outright.

The utility of the functional approach for political analysis is that it allows us to examine diverse political systems within one general conceptual framework. By constructing a set of generic functions that define the common denominators of political systems, we can compare a number of very different systems and thereby reap the insights offered by the display of contrasts and similarities.

We are brought again to typology construction as a method of analysis: interpreting observed political phenomena on the basis of an organizing principle that formalizes a set of significant likenesses and differences. In chapter 8, we examine more closely several kinds of political systems. The typologies to be presented go beyond *structural* points of comparison (that is, institutional forms) to differentiate political systems by the *conditions* conducive to the establishment and continuing viability of various systems. Most significant are those conditions that relate to political culture. Thus, we will consider in greater detail the relationship between a political system and the underlying pattern of political orientations that prevails in a society. The substance and distribution of beliefs, values, attitudes, and expectations about politics are, as we have argued, critical determinants of the form and functioning of the political system.

Here (as throughout this text) we shall include in our discussion those aspects of the nonpolitical environment that play an important part in shaping people's political predispositions, such as the structure of the economy and the character of social relationships in a society. We shall, for example, look at the relationship between political instability and transition from a traditional to a modern society. We shall see how a profound and sustained crisis—such as economic depression or a prolonged state of war—can erode the political-cultural foundations of democracy, and how it can give birth to and nurture a totalitarian political system.

In this book, we view the political world from the vantage point of individual political behavior—a perspective that offers two windows on that world. From one, we can see politics as a context which influences the whole character of individual orientations toward political life. A person's experience of politics shapes his ideas about what political life is and what it should be, and thus in large part determines how he shall act politically. If, in his contacts with government institutions, he finds that authority is wielded arbitrarily and that he has no avenue to seek redress, he will come to distrust authority and avoid entering the political arena. If, when he voices his political opinions and makes his political demands, he finds he is listened to and even encouraged to speak out, he will be emboldened to continue making his views known, and come to value the tolerance extended to him and adopt it toward others.

From the other window, we can see the political realm as fundamentally influenced by individual political orientations and behavior. The structure and the functioning of political institutions depend on the thinking and behavior of individuals, considered singly or collectively. For example: American presidents who have held activist conceptions of the office have contributed mightily to expanding the role of the presidency to what it is today. In taking on more and more wide-ranging responsibilities, they have expanded popular expectations of presidential duties. We have come to hold presidents accountable for whatever goes on in our economy, for urban riots or quiescence, for campus activism or "quietism." Concurrently, the actual powers of the office have mushroomed; the president today has greater means to accomplish greater ends than his predecessors of a century ago. The actions of presidents and the reactions of the American people have together radically transformed the institution of the presidency as it actually functions. Only when the powers of the office were flagrantly abused did Congress attempt to constrain the president.

In considering the political system as both context and consequence of political behavior, and in examining several types of political systems, we are drawn ineluctably to the question: Which is the *best* one? Robert Dahl points out that answers to such questions can be sought at different "levels of generality." [10] In its most general form this question can be rephrased as: Which political system is the *ideal* one? The problem is thereby framed within the domain of political philosophy, for "ideal" indicates that our concern is not with conditions as they actually obtain. Rather, we are dealing with an *abstract* situation, constructing an ideal within a set of assumptions that are not necessarily realized or realizable. The Republic envisioned by Plato is one such conceptualization of the ideal political order; the final stage of Marx's historical dialectic, in which the state has "withered away," is an equally famous formulation. The significance of such ideal political models does not rest in the likelihood of their actual occurrence. Their meaning is "ideological," rooted within the belief and value systems of individuals, the patterns of perception and thought that may guide political action.

At a far less general level, we may restate the question so that it falls more squarely within the realm of political analysis—that is: Which is the *optimal* political system? [11] By substituting "optimal" for "best,"

10 Robert A. Dahl, *Modern Political Analysis* (Englewood Cliffs, N.J.: Prentice-Hall, 1963), p. 94.
11 Ibid.

we are indicating that our focus is on specific, concrete situations. We are working not within a framework of assumptions of "most favorable" circumstances, but within the constraints that are imposed by the actual situation. Because conditions are "given," our judgment as to the optimal political system must depend upon those particular actual circumstances. Although an optimal political order cannot be delineated without reference to individual values, its significance rests primarily upon the likelihood of its realization in a given context. Our concern is not with defining what we *believe should be,* but with determining the best that *possibly could be.* To operate effectively in the realm of the possible and the likely, adequate relevant knowledge about what does go on in the political order is essential. This kind of judgment requires knowledge about the range of alternative political systems, the conditions that must be present for the effective functioning of each system, the conditions that are in fact present in the situation under study, and the possible and probable consequences of each political system.

This text does not attempt to tackle the question of the ideal political order. The purpose of this book is to introduce the student to some of the most prominent and widely used theoretical tools of political analysis. As we have stated, the utility of such analytical tools lies in their potential for expanding our comprehension of the political sector of our lives. With these, we can begin to lay the groundwork for rational determinations of important political questions. The ultimate purpose of the ideas presented in this book is realized by the individual student. Dahl points out that analysis is a necessary prelude to the evaluation of things political: "Factual knowledge is not a *substitute* for moral judgment, but it *is* a necessary prerequisite." [12] To judge the desirability of particular political forms and processes, one must apply his personal values to what he knows about the political world. Our intent is to help the student fulfill that prerequisite of knowledge.

SUMMARY AND CRITIQUE

No single paradigm—that is, no one philosophy, set of questions, or research tradition—characterizes all of political science.[13] It is an eclectic, but not necessarily disorganized, discipline. For every major point of

---

[12] Ibid., p. 106.

[13] For further consideration of the concept of paradigm, see T. S. Kuhn, *The Structure of Scientific Revolutions* (Chicago: University of Chicago Press, 1962), and Margaret Masterman, "The Nature of a Paradigm," in *Criticism and the Growth of Knowledge,* ed. I. Lakatos and A. Musgrave (Cambridge, England: Cambridge University Press, 1970), pp. 59–89.

view there is likely to be a counter-conception that some will consider equally plausible. This state of affairs may frighten those who hope to find a single correct answer to every question. To others it will offer the challenge to think independently, along with an opportunity for creativity and debate. To reflect the diversity of the discipline and alert the student to opposing conceptions, each chapter will conclude with a summary and critique.

Politics has been defined as the art of the possible. It is the means by which a working consensus on issues of concern to all is forged out of the immense diversity of interests and outlooks prevalent in any society at any time. The alternative to politics is not harmony, but chaos. As long as politics is an art, it will remain a preserve of those who have developed, by whatever means, the talent, skill, and wisdom necessary to fathom its great complexity. As an art it resides in the realm of intuition rather than reason. That which is subject to reason and thought is conscious and basically controllable. Intuition is not. The systematic study of people and politics, the main thrust of this book, is one attempt to come to grips with forces so great that they can either cause or prevent chaos. It is doubtful that we can control forces of this magnitude unless we understand them. An ignorance of politics therefore not only leads to a great deal of anxiety, but also makes us subject to the whims of those who have mastered the art—and if history is any indicator, there is no rule that these people have to be motivated by good intentions.

The emphasis upon a systematic understanding of people and politics places this text in line with the behavioral tradition in political science. This is neither a new nor an outmoded approach, and its strengths and weaknesses have been the subjects of a long and continuing debate. Behavioral political scientists are associated with the empirical, or quantitative, orientation to the discipline. They collect data that can be statistically analyzed in an effort to determine the important laws of politics. This approach is subject to a number of criticisms.

First, it is frequently argued that a concern with laws and the regularities of human behavior leads to an emphasis upon facts rather than upon values, upon what *is* rather than upon what *ought to be*. This lends a conservative tinge to behavioralistic endeavors. After all, if we can provide a "scientific" explanation for a particular set of events—for example, America's involvement in the Vietnam war—does this not in effect become a rationalization for the events themselves? Further, even if *why* the event occurred is explained, is the explanation of any use in helping us decide whether it *should* have occurred?

Second, the attempt to use quantitative techniques in research may favor ease of analysis rather than relevance as the criterion for choosing questions for inquiry. Unfortunately, the issues most amenable to precise measurement are indeed not always of the greatest import. Hence it has been argued that behavioralists devote much attention to trivial questions while ignoring truly pressing concerns, or considering them only after they have overwhelmed the body politic and created an immense social crisis. Behavioralists are often accused, not without reason, for coming on the scene with too little, too late. Many political scientists have tired of hearing that the big questions will be tackled after a sufficient body of systematic theory has evolved from extensive analysis of smaller matters; this provides little consolation when we are already facing the big questions. The riots and social dislocations of the 1960s, the problems of poverty amid plenty in a society that preaches equality of opportunity, the immense disenchantment with a government that produced the Vietnam war and Watergate, the rape of the environment, and the host of problems brought on by the worst economic downturn in forty years are frequently cited as examples.

Like any other new idea, especially one that entered the discipline under the guise of "the behavioral revolution," more was no doubt promised by the behavioralists than could be delivered in a relatively short time. But the critics are not always consistent. While they point to the trivial nature of some behavioral research, they also appear at times to stand in fear, if not awe, of its potential. Science, they say, serves no master. Understanding carries with it not only the possibility of control, but the possibility of manipulation as well. Who is going to ensure that the results of systematic political analysis will be put to good use rather than evil? Indeed, given the scientist's concern with facts rather than values, can the behavioral approach distinguish between right and wrong?

There are several ways to respond. We could decide that it is best to remain in ignorance, thereby admitting that we cannot be trusted with knowledge of ourselves. Of course, this will not benefit us if an unscrupulous leader comes to power, for without knowledge of the laws and regularities of political behavior we can never know when we are being manipulated. We could continue to do research but treat it as an intellectual exercise and so restrict the circulation of findings that it would be impossible to employ them in the political arena. This solution is not without problems, however, for if the findings were put to use by politicians concerned with improving the lot of mankind, they might go a long way toward that end. Hiding the results of research or limiting their dissemination would be tantamount to obstructing change for the better. A political scientist who held back his findings might therefore be contributing to a status quo that provided less than optimal living conditions for large numbers of people.

To respond to the arguments concerning the value neutrality of science, we must look closer at what appears to be the root of the problem:

the assumed existence of a distinction between facts and values. It has long been true that certain scientific facts were not even perceived until theories were developed that enabled people to discover them. We see as facts what our presuppositions about reality tell us should be there. These presuppositions are based upon our values and goals, which in turn are built into the theories that form our picture of the world. To an efficiency expert viewing an auto assembly plant, it is a fact that coffee breaks are too long. The sociologist next to him sees as fact the extensive division of labor that is part of the productive process in modern society. The Marxist looking over their shoulders notices that people who do not hold stock in the enterprise are putting the cars together.

There is no such thing as "immaculate perception." We never " 'see everything that is there to be seen.' An observation is *made;* it is the product of an active choice, not of a passive exposure." [14] No choice is ever value-free. We see what our values tell us is important. What separates science from ordinary perception is the care with which observations are made and the conscious effort to specify how various measures were derived, what was done with them and why, and what the implications are for the theory concerned. The last-mentioned will be of particular importance to anyone who accepts the theory and therefore bases his goal-seeking behavior upon it.

Behavioralists begin by studying people, because they feel that knowledge of people *as individuals* is important, indeed vital, to an adequate understanding of politics. This would be a revolutionary thought in a communist political system, where the *impersonal forces of production* as they affect *classes* of people are the central concern. It should be no surprise that where belief in *impersonal* forces predominates, so does a tendency to rely on the heavy hand of physical coercion to keep the population "in tune with the forces of production" regardless of anyone's view to the contrary. The behavioralist emphasis, in turn, developed in the United States primarily out of the efforts of social psychologists to apply the tools of scientific observation and analysis to elections in a democracy, a form of government that clearly elevates the individual to a position of prominence—at least in theory if not always in practice. In fact, so much of behavioral research is related to the actions of people in a democratic context that some critics question its utility outside that context. Obviously, in view of such criticism, we shall not argue that behavioralists are value-free. Their assumptions and values are basically humanistic and therefore similar to those written into the American Constitution.

The debate that began with the inception of the behavioral revolution

---

14 Abraham Kaplan, *The Conduct of Inquiry* (San Francisco: Chandler, 1964), p. 133.

has resulted in a healthy skepticism. Behavioralists can no longer hide in their statistical ivory towers. The search for explanation *and* relevance has broadened the scope of inquiry from an examination of that which is easily measured to a wider-ranging concern with conceptualization—the building of theoretical structures designed to sketch in the major factors involved in a problem and to offer suggestions about how to effect a solution, even though important aspects of the problem may not always be readily subject to precise measurement. Conceptualization will be emphasized in the chapters that follow. Although the results of empirical studies will be brought in from time to time, the major emphasis will be upon broad concepts of general import to an analysis of political behavior and upon some ways in which they may be fitted together to form explanations of human events. There is a link, however indirect it sometimes is, between explanation and prediction.

We hope that the material in this book will help you understand some of the forces that will affect your future. Today's students are often told that tomorrow will belong to them. If we fail to understand the forces at work in the political arena, there may not be much to inherit.

Selected Bibliography

BAY, CHRISTIAN, "Politics and Pseudopolitics: A Critical Evaluation of Some Behavioral Literature," *American Political Science Review,* 69 (March 1965), 39–51.

DAHL, ROBERT A., *Modern Political Analysis.* Englewood Cliffs, N.J.: Prentice-Hall, 1963.

DAHL, ROBERT A., "The Behavioral Approach to Political Science: Epitaph for a Monument to a Successful Protest," *American Political Science Review,* 55 (December 1961), 763–72.

EULAU, HEINZ, *The Behavioral Persuasion in Politics.* New York: Random House, 1963.

GRAHAM, GEORGE J., JR., and GEORGE W. CAREY, eds., *The Post-behavioral Era: Perspectives on Political Science.* New York: David McKay, 1972.

KAPLAN, ABRAHAM, *The Conduct of Inquiry.* San Francisco: Chandler, 1964.

KUHN, T. S., *The Structure of Scientific Revolutions.* Chicago: University of Chicago Press, 1962.

2

Politics and a hierarchy of human needs

We have stated that politics is people: their loves, hates, prejudices, and especially their behavior. It is not enough for the student simply to be able to describe political events comprised of multitudes of people acting together or against each other. Political science is better viewed not as a discipline designed merely to *describe* a situation, but as a body of knowledge and technique that enables one to *analyze* the political scene, to systematically disassemble the components of an event and put them together in such a fashion that one can answer the question *why*. Why was Senator George McGovern defeated in the 1972 presidential election? What lessons can be learned from that which will enable the Democratic party to have its candidate elected again? What can the Republican party do to rebuild itself and retain the office of president in a post-Watergate era, when trust in government officials is at an all-time low? Will America possess a functioning democracy in the year 1984? What kind of a world will our children face? What will things be like as we approach middle age? What can we do to encourage the trends we think are good and to hinder the ones that are not?

Our explanations will be built on the methods and contents of a number of the social sciences. At the individual level, much of our theoretical perspective will come from works primarily social-psychological in nature. For groups and group interactions, we will draw upon significant works from the field of sociology. Where society-wide *decisions* are made, we will operate at what is formally considered the political level of analysis. In this chapter we will look at the significant factors in individual motivation that directly relate to the broader questions of political analysis.

Before going any further we must confront two major dilemmas: the nature of science and the nature of man. It may be surprising that while many people are concerned with developing a science of politics, we do not all agree on the make-up of this science. There are at least two basic conceptions: the universal-generalization paradigm and the developmental paradigm.

The *universal-generalization paradigm* seeks after universal laws, truths that are valid for all people at all times and places. Researchers holding to this view believe that there is an objective reality, a world that can be uncovered and understood by experiments and the gathering of data. The findings from each experiment are cumulative, adding up to the unfolding of more objective information—information free from observer bias. Hence all experiments can be replicated and the findings confirmed.

The *developmental paradigm* includes the notion that reality and truth change with the individual's knowledge of himself and the world in which he lives. What is accepted as true today may not be part of what is considered reality tomorrow. Far from being fixed and cumulative, knowledge is often made obsolete by new conceptions. In due time these new concepts may themselves be overturned and replaced by others more suitable to the needs of people in an era that evolved out of the old, a world that may even have been vaguely envisioned by it, but which now operates according to a different set of assumptions and rules. Accordingly, those who adhere to the developmental paradigm contend that it makes little sense to apply generalizations based upon the behavior of twentieth century Americans to people who lived in the Greek city-states in Aristotle's time, for example—or, as is more commonly the case, to generalize from the latter to the former. Because of the vast differences in environment, history, and intellectual world, any rule that purports to apply to both sets of people must overlook so much and be so general and all-inclusive that in effect it explains everything and therefore nothing.

The second dilemma concerns the individual. Do human beings have unique individual natures, or are they products of their environment? Does some invariant natural pattern exist in every individual, regardless of environment—regardless of what we are taught by our parents, our teachers, our schoolmates and peers, our boss, and even the very language in which we think and speak? Or is each of us "society's child," the result of a socialization process that began with a blank slate, our experiences determined and defined by others, and put together by the influence of others into a combination we call "personality"? Perhaps you have encountered this question before—the "nature–nurture" controversy.

The question is important because it is at the heart of political dynamics. If there is a human nature, it will be reflected in the political institutions that exist at any time, else the polity will become unfit for human habitation, as it were, and problems will arise. In extreme cases revolution may result. If there is no human nature per se, then the political system that is best able to socialize the population, to train citizens to accept its ways without question, and to convince them that it represents the only correct form of government will be able to survive indefinitely. Where problems arise, proponents of the human nature view will look for the causes in a lack of fit between human nature and political institutions. Those who fall on the nurture side of the controversy will be inclined to seek answers by searching out areas where the individual is taught to experience life in a manner that leads to behavior out of tune with the maintenance of the existing regime. The former will advocate changing the polity to match human nature. The latter may espouse (although this is not the only conclusion) changing the individual's learning environment so that he comes to behave in a manner that supports or at least does not threaten the polity. Obviously, the theory we accept will bear on the manner in which we respond to political problems.

Consider the two dilemmas as they relate to the following hypothetical situation. Suppose that in 1984, an observer from the West asks, "Does the Soviet Union have a government?" The question is relevant to orthodox Marxists, who hold that the final stage of history following the proletarian revolution is the "withering away of the state," a situation in which each "gives according to talent or ability and takes according to need." At this point in the evolution of history the individual is neither grasping nor exploitive. There is no need for the state to enforce authoritative allocations of value, for there is no scarcity; there are no "haves" and "have nots." Hence the state, no longer necessary, "withers away." To the non-Marxist observer, the question is also relevant, if he contends that Marxism is simply a myth and the notion of a stateless society nothing more than an unreachable utopia. But he wants to be sure, so he arranges for a trip to the Soviet Union.

He defines the political system as that portion of the society that authoritatively allocates values, that is, formulates and executes policy wherein "certain things are denied to some people and made accessible to others." [1] He carries with him a set of computer cards that he punches for each observation he makes: Does the Soviet Union have a political system—a system for authoritatively allocating values? Yes/No. He punches the cards and labels them with each observation.

The first thing he sees upon leaving the airport is what looks like a department store. Customers ask the clerk for a form headed "Statement of Need," which they fill out, sign, and return. The clerk then goes to the shelf and retrieves the requested items. On the basis of this observa-

[1] David Easton, *The Political System* (New York: Alfred A. Knopf, 1953), p. 130.

tion, our visitor determines that a state exists. The clerk is acting as a state functionary; the statement of need is a record of allocations made, which the government will use in equating available supply with existing demand. Yes, the observer says, the Soviet Union has a political system. He next visits a large auditorium where a number of people in blue coveralls are congregated. He watches one man on the stage pin a gleaming medal on another, similarly attired individual. The medal reads "Creative Abilities Development Award." The crowd applauds the worker, who has developed his talents to a high degree. Again, the researcher asks himself: Does a state exist? Yes. Obviously, the individual pinning the medal on the worker represents authority. Allocations of values are being made in that only one individual is awarded the medal. Besides, they all appear to be dressed in uniform—the uniform of the worker's state. Again he punches the card, "yes."

After observing a number of similar activities, the researcher returns to the United States, conducts some statistical tests with his punched cards, and finds that indeed the Soviet Union has a political system.

A representative of an American television network is in Moscow at the same time. To add a dimension of human interest to his description of life in Russia, he asks a woman in the street if the Soviet Union has a political system. "Why, of course not," she answers. "Don't you know that Marx predicted the withering away of the state following the stage of socialism? Look over there—you see people going into the store to receive according to need. At that factory you see people working according to ability. Everyone is now able to develop his talents to the fullest. My brother even received a medal for the extent to which he succeeded in this endeavor." For the people involved, the state has withered away. For the Western observer, the state still exists. Who do *you* think is correct?

Proponents of the universal-generalization paradigm of science would logically conclude that the Soviet Union in 1984 does indeed have a political system. They have formulated a universal definition and applied it to a specific situation, which it fits nicely. This conclusion has been bought at some expense, however, as you may have noticed: In the process the opinions of the population have been completely overlooked. If, in fact, what people think and believe is important to an understanding of politics (or the lack of politics, as it were), then the universal-generalization paradigm is not very helpful, at least in this example. We should also note that the universal-generalization paradigm implies that explanations of human behavior are to be found on the *nurture* side of the nature–nurture dilemma. That is, two conceptions of human nature are compatible with the universal-generalization paradigm, and it does not matter much in practice which one the researcher holds. Either human nature is a fixed, constant element that is everywhere the same, therefore making it possible for the scientist to formulate universal laws, or human nature is not important, perhaps even nonexistent. If human nature is constant, then it can be overlooked because it never varies. It makes no contribution to the *differences* between people and political systems that we want to explain. Hence we need not take it into account. And if it is nonexistent, of course, then it is of no import whatsoever.

The developmental paradigm aims at explanations that are more individual and context-specific. The variation in American and Soviet perspectives could be explained by differences in opinions, attitudes, beliefs, and perhaps even human nature. Political scientists whose views incline toward the developmental paradigm do not eschew the concept of human nature per se, but they are more favorably disposed towards a dynamic interpretation of it. Nature as well as nurture is likely to be a part of their explanation. Human nature may be perceived as a *process of growth or evolution*. The process itself may conceivably be fixed and invariant, but a rich variety of behavior could be induced by human nature because of the many different points on the evolutionary continuum. Each of these points may involve a particular way of behaving and relating to the political system. Again alluding to the above example, it could be argued that Soviets and Americans are at different *stages of evolution*.

The Americans in this example are operating in a world where their needs can be fulfilled only by items that are in short supply; or, perhaps more correctly, they are at a stage where they *believe* these items are in short supply. They *act* accordingly, competing with each other for these allegedly scarce resources. Some obtain more than others. The political system comes into existence and maintains itself by stabilizing the situation. It keeps the "have nots" away from the throats of the "haves." It provides a rationale which makes the existence of "haves" and "have nots" appear to be in the natural order of things. This usually, but not always, keeps the latter quiescent; where conflicts arise, peaceful settlement is sought through recourse to the legal arm of the polity. If this fails, government can use its monopoly on the legitimate (widely accepted as right and just) use of force, suppressing those who threaten to breach the peace.

The Soviets in the example are at a "higher" stage of human evolution. Scarcity does not exist and people no longer believe that it exists. Hence there is no need to compete; people cooperate with each other. The main concern is not to do your neighbor out of something, but to develop your intrinsic talents and capabilities to the maximum in an atmosphere free from the need or belief in the need to work at unful-

Copyright, 1973, G. B. Trudeau/Distributed by Universal Press Syndicate.

filling tasks in order to survive. The differences in conception are evident in the cartoons above.

In a society without "have nots," the Soviets would argue, there is no need for government to enforce anyone's will. Cooperation rules: People do what is best for all not because they *have* to, not because they are *afraid of breaking the law,* but because they *want* to do what is best for all. At this point in human and social evolution, the individual acts in both his and society's best interests. Hence there is no need for a traditional political system. There are, of course, any number of reasons why the Soviet Union today does not match the image of a communist utopia envisioned by Karl Marx, but we should not let that detract from another point illustrated by this example: Differences in human nature may lead to divergent conceptions of politics and the need for different kinds of political structure. In the discussion that follows, we will take a position that is consonant with the developmental paradigm and the importance of nature as well as nurture.

IN SEARCH OF HUMAN NATURE

Our discussion of human nature will center on two themes: needs and consciousness, or perception. Needs can be viewed as motivators: They induce the individual to engage in behavior aimed at their satisfaction. We can speak of innate and acquired needs. Innate needs involve inherent aspects of the human organism. Acquired needs are learned from the environment or the nurture side of the nature–nurture continuum. The need to satisfy the biological demands of the body for food may be viewed as innate. Knowledge of the items that it is "proper" to consume to satisfy this need is acquired by nurture. We learn what to eat and how to eat it in our relations with others. Consciousness and perception involve the manner in which we define a situation and what we see. Until the results of our actions prove contrary to our expectations, we act upon a situation as we define and see it. Needs and perceptions are interrelated. When we are hungry and driving along the highway, we are more likely to spot the distant flashing neon sign of the hamburger stand than if we had just eaten. Perceptions can also affect the organism's response to needs. To cite an extreme example, a group of people may starve together on a desert island because they do not perceive each other as sources of food. A cannibal would not have this perceptual problem.

To develop a satisfactory basis for analyzing political behavior, we must consider needs *and* perceptions. Needs provide the impetus that sets us in motion; perception supplies the "roadmap for action." Both working together in a concrete situation produce the kind of behavior that is relevant to political scientists. In this chapter we shall concern ourselves with what the humanistic psychologist Abraham Maslow considered innate human needs. A discussion of acquired needs and wants would take us too far afield at this point, given their infinite number and close association with the innate needs as well as with perception, a topic that will be discussed in the next chapter.

Maslow envisioned a hierarchy of needs, the progressive fulfillment of which described an individual's *healthy developmental pattern*. Maslow was not concerned only with an individual's being (with what someone is at the present time), but also with becoming—with the manner and means by which an individual could turn his potential into actuality. The universal-generalization paradigm of science can deal only with the "is" and the "what has been." How in the world, a scientist enamored of the above paradigm would say, can you gather any empirical data on states of mind and conditions that are in the future rather than in the present or in the past?

Maslow wanted to investigate the future—what we could and should be. This puts his work in tune with the developmental paradigm of explanation. Its use here blunts the edge of the antibehavioralist critique, which contends that by dealing only with the "is" and the "what has been," those concerned with a systematic analysis of politics possess an inherently conservative bias. It also returns values to the central focus. If we can describe a healthy developmental pattern, we can also describe an unhealthy one. Political systems that function well will move a society in the direction of healthy development; those that do not will either halt development or force it to regress.

After a great deal of clinical experience and observation, Maslow concluded that every person has "the impulse toward full development of humanness." The great paradox, he said, is that so few ever attain it. As you read this book, keep that paradox in mind and ask yourself why? and *what can be done about it?* Maslow put it nicely:

> *I remember an old textbook of abnormal psychology that I used when I was an undergraduate, which was an awful book but which had a wonderful frontispiece. The lower half was a picture of a line of babies, pink, sweet, delightful, innocent, lovable. Above that was a picture of a lot of passengers in a subway train, glum, gray, sullen, sour. The caption underneath was very simply, "What happened?"* [2]

MASLOW'S HIERARCHY OF NEEDS

The first and most basic needs are physiological (food, water, sleep). In the extreme case the individual is completely dominated by the search for their satisfaction. "Freedom, love, community feeling, respect, philosophy, may all be waved aside as . . . useless, since they fail to fill the stomach." [3] Individuals at this level of the need hierarchy have

[2] Abraham H. Maslow, *The Farther Reaches of Human Nature* (New York: Viking, 1971), p. 26.

[3] Abraham H. Maslow, *Motivation and Personality*, 2nd ed. (New York: Harper & Row, 1970), p. 37.

neither the desire to engage in political activities nor the energy for them. They are depoliticized and withdrawn from the set of people who either act as politicians or influence them. The starving person is at best a sad pawn in someone else's political game. Sometimes he serves as cannon fodder for the elites in a regime threatened by war or revolution; at other times he is manipulated by demagogues in search of power for personal ends. In all instances he is a passive player on the political stage, at best a follower but never a leader.

When the physical needs are sufficiently and regularly supplied, other needs emerge and "dominate the organism." Next in the hierarchy are the safety needs, which engage the organism in a search for "security; dependency; protection; freedom from fear, from anxiety and chaos; . . . structure, order, law, limits; strength in the protector," and the like. The functions that many view as unique to government are grounded in the safety needs. Governments *must* maintain order, ensure the security of persons and property, and protect the individual against external enemies.

Life just below fulfillment of the safety needs corresponds to what philosopher Thomas Hobbes called the state of nature. In the state of nature nothing is secure. The law of the jungle rules; its servants are brute force and blind cunning. A war of all against all ensues and life is "nasty, brutish and short." Under these conditions people are happy to trade absolute freedom for the "erection of a power which might oppress individuals, demand the fruits of their labor, and even require the sacrifice of their lives." [4] But freedom without order is meaningless, and even an out-and-out dictatorship is preferable to the intolerable uncertainties of life in the chaos and anarchy of a Hobbesian state of nature.

Thus, at the heart of government lies the citizen's exchange of loyalty and obedience to the polity in return for security and fulfillment of the safety needs. Government in turn depends upon this allegiance for survival. With allegiance comes voluntary compliance with the law, hence the domestic peace and tranquility that ensure continued loyalty and support. The polity must be able to draw upon at least a certain minimum of allegiance from its citizens. A government that must rule by force alone will not last long. The world has yet to see a government that is able to command the human and material resources necessary to enslave its own people and at the same time remain secure from the threat of revolution or domination by foreign powers.

After the safety needs are satisfactorily met, the needs for love and belonging emerge. The individual is motivated by the desire to gain

[4] Sheldon S. Wolin, *Politics and Vision* (Boston: Little, Brown, 1960), p. 263.

acceptance from his peers and to obtain a firm, legitimate status in society. He seeks close contact with others and is inclined to "feel sharply the pangs of loneliness, of ostracism, of rejection, of friendlessness, of rootlessness." An individual at this level of the need hierarchy may derive a great deal of gratification from membership in a close-knit group that makes him part of a common cause. Groups tend to be particularly cohesive when they face a real or imagined threat from an out-group, be it a foreign nation, a rival gang, the communists, or the devil. Such groups prove especially attractive to people with strong needs for love and belonging. Examples abound. Street gangs may fulfill this need for ghetto youths reared in an atmosphere of desperation and an environment where parental love is often noticeable primarily by its absence. The philosophies of fanatical political movements like the Nazis in Germany and the Ku Klux Klan and John Birch Society in America are founded upon a bedrock belief in the existence of an enemy that is omnipresent, insidious, cunning, powerful, and dangerous. Ready converts for such groups can be found among those who are threatened with a loss of position in the existing status hierarchy. Such people are mortified by the fear of giving up their toehold on legitimacy, and with it the feeling that they *belong*, that they are valued, accepted, and important parts of society.

Generally, the more desperate the need for belonging, the more extreme the group is likely to be and the more aberrant the members' behavior. It is certain that much of the motivation behind the radical political activity in the 1960s was a desire to gratify this level of need by interacting in close personal associations of groups that are in motion— groups with a cause. One leader of Vietnam Summer, 1967, noted, "The kind of people who get involved in the Movement are really people who have a strong need for friendship." [5] Another leader expressed hesitation about returning to college or taking up a typical eight-to-five job where he felt he would have to manipulate others or be completely on his own:

> But I don't want to be isolated. . . . I just don't like to get the
> feeling that I'm all alone and I'm doing something to everybody
> else. I like to have the feeling that there are fifty of us or five
> hundred or ten thousand that are doing it together. And I want to
> feel that I have friends and that I'm in a spirit of comradeship
> with them. . . .[6]

[5] Quoted in Kenneth Keniston, *Young Radicals* (New York: Harcourt Brace Jovanovich, 1968), p. 26.

[6] Ibid., p. 38.

However, many and perhaps most of the movement radicals of the 1960s came from affluent families with a secure social status. Their parents were well educated; they transmitted a minimum of status anxiety and a maximum of social consciousness to their children. The need for belonging that was met by membership in antiwar groups composed of these upper-middle-class, college-age individuals could not have been extraordinarily great. If worse came to worst, most of them could return to families where they were accepted and loved. This was reflected in the moderate, mostly nonviolent activities they engaged in and their emphasis upon equalitarian rather than authoritarian forms of leadership (excepting the Weathermen faction that broke away from Students for a Democratic Society). The groups themselves tended to be ad hoc and transient. Organizations rose and fell with the tide of events and the various phases of the schol year while members came and went at will.

The Manson Family stands in marked contrast, illustrating the extremes to which people can go when the need for love and belonging is very great. Charles Manson, the leader, evolved an eschatological philosophy for his group that consisted of a grotesque combination of revolution, racism, and revelations.[7] His rule was absolute, exerting a magnetic hold over Family members. Those who sought to leave or were not trusted found themselves terrorized and in some cases dead.

Manson did not appear overly worried about safety, a concern that would have been manifested in a strong fear of arrest. He had been in and out of reformatories and penal institutions all his life and knew what to expect. Incarceration did not frighten him. Indeed, in 1967 he completed a ten-year term and as he was being released "begged the authorities to let him remain in prison. Prison had become his home, he told them."[8] He was not granted the request. Shortly thereafter he gravitated to the Haight-Ashbury section of San Francisco and started the Family. Similarly, the large number of weapons possessed by the Family served more as symbols of resentment, hatred, and aggression directed against a society members believed rejected them, than as instruments of defense and safety. That the group called itself the "Family" could also be viewed as a sign of a strong need for acceptance and belonging.

A glance at significant parts of the lives of two major characters in this group may convey some idea of the conditions and behavioral manifestations associated with intense deprivation of this level of need.

---

[7] Vincent Bugliosi and Curt Gentry, *Helter Skelter* (New York: W. W. Norton, 1974), pp. 245–46.

[8] Ibid., pp. 145–46. Quotations from *Helter Skelter* on this and the following pages are reprinted by permission of Vincent Bugliosi and W. W. Norton & Co., Inc.

Manson was an illegitimate child raised in an environment that was anything but warm and affectionate. He never knew who his father was. His mother "would leave the child with obliging neighbors for an hour, then disappear for days or weeks. Usually his grandmother or maternal aunt would have to claim him." [9] By the time he was in his early teens, Manson was well on the way to a life where the cycle of crime, arrest, and incarceration was repeated with monotonous regularity. Prison reports noted that he had "a tremendous drive to call attention to himself" and "tends to involve himself in various fanatical interests." [10] One of these interests was music, and through this medium he sought to gain acceptance from society. He did not get very far: No one seemed to understand his music, no one took a serious interest in recording and marketing it, and some did not even want to hear it. On the night of August 5, 1969, Manson took his guitar to what he described as a "sensitivity camp" where "rich people went on weekends to play at being enlightened." An ex-Family member recalled hearing him say that he

> *played his guitar for a bunch of people who were supposed to be the top people there, and they rejected his music. Some people pretended that they were asleep, and other people were saying, "This is too heavy for me," and "I'm not ready for that," and others were saying, "Well, I don't understand it," and some just got up and walked out.* [11]

Three days later the infamous Sharon Tate murders took place.

Lynette "Squeaky" Fromme, who took command of the Family after Manson went to prison for involvement in the Tate murders, came from a middle-class background much less extreme than Manson's but apparently lacking in love and belonging. People who knew the Frommes remembered young Lynette

> *"as a little doll" who failed to get the love she needed from her family. "I don't know what's wrong," she once told . . . [a] teacher. "My dad won't speak to me. He won't let me eat with the rest of them." As she grew older, Lynette was regularly thrown out of the house until, finally, she stayed away for good.* [12]

9 Ibid., p. 137.
10 Ibid., pp. 144–45.
11 Ibid., p. 275.
12 *Newsweek,* 22 September 1975, p. 30.

Under the title "The Story of Squeaky," it was reported in *Newsweek:*

> *One night in 1967, a puffy-faced, scraggly-haired girl of seventeen*
> *sat on a sidewalk in Venice, California. She had always thought*
> *she was ugly and unloved, and she was crying. "A man walked up,"*
> *she later recalled, "and said, 'Your father kicked you out of the*
> *house.' . . . He asked me to come with him. I said no . . . and*
> *he said he'd like me to come but couldn't make up my mind*
> *for me. No one had ever treated me like that—he didn't push me*
> *—so I picked up all I had and went with him. That was Charles*
> *Manson. . . . A dog goes to somebody who loves it and takes*
> *care of it," she later explained.*[13]

Such groups, however bizarre, are not insignificant to an analysis of politics. Group members are highly intense, closely knit, and encapsulated in a "with us or against us," "our group against the world" outlook that disposes them to engage in extreme forms of behavior. At minimum they have a great capacity for mischief and the disruption of domestic tranquility. Should group members ever set their sights on politics and succeed in obtaining high public office, one can expect enormous abuses of power. The Nazi regime in Germany, which held a particular fascination for Manson, is a prime example. Squeaky Fromme provided recent evidence of the potential for trouble such groups possess. She pointed a .45 caliber pistol at President Gerald Ford in Sacramento, California, and was subsequently convicted of attempting to assassinate him.

When the needs for love and belonging are satisfactorily met, the need for self-esteem emerges. Maslow distinguishes two varieties of this need. The first relates to the individual's view of himself—his strengths, talents, ability. The second involves the way others look at him. At this level the individual has a "desire for strength, for achievement, for adequacy, for mastery and competence, for confidence in the face of the world, and for independence and freedom." He also wants "reputation or prestige, . . . status, fame and glory, dominance, recognition, attention, importance, dignity, or appreciation." [14]

At this point on the need hierarchy the person, interacting with others, comes to view himself as an individual—someone unique, with special talents, capabilities, and skills that make him competent in a particular field and enable him to accomplish tasks of importance. With this comes recognition from others and a place in society. At this level

---

[13] *Newsweek,* 15 September 1975, p. 18.

[14] Maslow, *Motivation and Personality,* p. 45.

the person is both a unique individual and a part of society. He is not "on the outside looking in," he has no need to control others to show that he is either as good as they are or better.

The individual who satisfies needs for self-esteem has confidence in himself. He feels no need to prove himself repeatedly to gain recognition and acceptance. He is also wiling to accept responsibility and the risks that go with it. He does not attempt to avoid responsibility, to "let someone else do it" out of fear that he will fail to measure up to what others expect of him.

The person with self-esteem is not easily threatened because he feels accepted by others and legitimate in society. Furthermore, in the process of obtaining self-esteem he comes to develop his own conceptions of success and failure. Because he can make up his mind about things of importance, he is less dependent upon the opinions of others than are people who have not attained this level of the hierarchy. The person with self-esteem is therefore not inclined to follow leaders blindly or seek out authoritarian, extremist groups every time an obstacle comes between him and a goal.

With self-esteem comes a coherent, positive identity. The individual, we might say, *knows who he is and loves and respects himself.* He therefore wishes to be treated with dignity *as an equal.* Only with self-esteem can one really feel the hurt that comes from being treated by others in an unequal fashion. Because he loves and respects himself, he can also love and respect others. Hence he is in a position to treat others as equals. Any position below this level of need in the hierarchy places the individual in an unequal, asymmetric relationship where he is dependent upon others. Dependent relationships involve modes of interaction that are characterized by inferiority–superiority and submission–dominance. These modes carry with them an orientation toward life that is basically authoritarian rather than democratic. If, as we argue in this text, the nature of government is rooted in the nature of the individual, then the basis for democracy resides in those members of the population who have at least attained a minimum degree of self-esteem.

The individual attains self-esteem by making decisions and bearing their consequences—by venturing into the world, perhaps failing at first, but trying again until, on his own, he achieves success. No parent can give self-esteem to a child, and no political leader can bestow it upon a population. The individual must develop it on his own; to do this he must have the freedom to decide on matters of importance. He must also, of course, have a sufficient degree of safety and feel that he has a home port, a place where he belongs and can return if need be—a secure base, as Maslow puts it, from which he can venture into uncharted waters in the quest for self-esteem. Freedom without safety, or freedom with safety but without love and belonging, is not sufficient. Assuming that the physical needs are met, only with safety, love and belonging, *and* freedom has the individual a real opportunity to attain self-esteem.

To attain self-esteem is to take a large step toward developing one's unique individuality. If human nature is developmental, then those who do not reach this level will never be as individuated—we might even say as "human"—as they could be. Gaining self-esteem is not always easy, and many pitfalls along the way can arrest progress, sometimes permanently. For example, we noted that the individual whose love and belonging needs are intense may gravitate to an extremist group in search of their fulfillment. He may be more than happy to give himself totally to the group with a cause. "Total giving" is synonymous with "total dependence," however, and once in a fanatic, authoritarian group the individual may soon become trapped. The fear of venturing out on his own (and getting caught in the evil that the leader says exists outside the group) may now be so great that the person ceases to think for himself. In effect he has purchased love and belonging at the expense of a higher need—self-esteem—although the tragic dilemma is not directly apparent to him at the time, because those primarily concerned with gratifying lower needs are not in a position to worry about the higher ones. Nevertheless, in such a trade both the individual and the nation suffer a loss in terms of what might have been. For the individual, the "real self"—the self that begins to emerge strongly and clearly through the achievement of self-esteem— never emerges and the cycle of development is short-circuited. The person settles for a concept of self that is not his own and a level of intellectual and emotional existence far below that which he could have aspired to and more than likely attained. The nation in turn loses a citizen who could have been relied upon to support a democratic government. Slavish dependence is antithetical to the healthy self-love that manifests itself in a willingness to treat others equally and fairly, and it does not lead to self-reliance, which carries with it the independence of thought and use of individual judgment that characterize informed voters and capable politicians.

At times the results of thwarted development are amply, and sadly, apparent. Vincent Bugliosi describes some of them in his initial impressions of "Squeaky" Fromme and another Mansonite, Sandra Good:

Nothing seemed to faze them. They smiled almost continuously, no matter what was said. For them all the questions had been answered. There was no need to search any more, because they had found the truth. And their truth was "Charlie [Manson] is love."

Although [in 1969] Squeaky was twenty-one and Sandy twenty-five, there was a little-girl quality to them, as if they hadn't aged but had been retarded at a certain stage in their childhood. Little girls, playing little-girl games.

I sensed something else. Each was, in her own way, a pretty girl. But there was a sameness about them that was much stronger than their individuality. I'd notice it again later that afternoon, in talking to other female members of the Family. Same expressions, same patterned responses, same tone of voice, same lack of distinct personality. The realization came with a shock: they reminded me less of human beings than Barbie dolls.[15]

A similar phenomenon is observable in some members of religious sects like the Reverend Sun Myung Moon's Unification Church. Active members of this sect, dubbed "Moonies," find their best source of converts among people who are lonely. As one official of the sect put it: "If someone's lonely, we talk to them. There are a lot of lonely people walking around." Once he is a member, every effort is made to see that the individual is totally immersed in the group. Everything, including marriage, is subject to the regulation of the leader. A sampling of the Reverend Moon's quotations conveys some idea of the amount of intellectual freedom that exists for members of the sect:

I am your brain.

What I wish must be your wish.

The time will come . . . when my words will almost serve as law. If I ask a certain thing it will be done.

The whole world is in my hand, and I will conquer and subjugate the world.

Our strategy is to be unified into one with ourselves, and with that as the bullet we can smash the world.[16]

---

15 Bugliosi and Gentry, *Helter Skelter*, pp. 132–33.

16 Berkeley Rice, "Messiah from Korea: Honor Thy Father Moon," *Psychology Today* (January 1976), 36–47.

Other freedoms are also restricted. In the Moonie communes there are

> . . . *no drugs, no drinks, no sex, no money, no problems, no choices,*
> *no decisions. From the team leader's cheerful "Rise and shine!"*
> *in the sexually segregated dormitories to the last group songs and*
> *prayers at midnight, the Moonies rarely have to think for themselves.*
> *Full of religious fervor and new-found purpose, they follow orders*
> *and perform chores with gusto.*[17]

According to a former member of the sect, "It was like being taken care of. . . . The people were very friendly, and you really thought they did love you. . . . Also, I was kind of afraid of going out into the world. . . ." The external manifestations of this and similar cults are the same:

> *Those who observe Moonies closely often notice a glassy, spaced-out*
> *look in their eyes, which, combined with their everlasting smiles,*
> *makes them look like tripped-out drug freaks. . . .*
>
> *The mother of [a member of another such cult] gave this description*
> *of her son's cult-mates: "Their eyes are fully dilated, and they*
> *glitter. . . . Although they talk to you, and they smile at you, you*
> *don't feel that it's the whole person."* [18]

According to Maslow, once self-esteem is attained, the individual desires to put this self into action and bring it to fullest fruition, to develop his talents and skills to the greatest extent possible. He desires *self-actualization*. At this point the individual seeks to "become actualized in what he is potentially." Motivation based upon a desire for *growth* begins with self-esteem and emerges fully in self-actualization. Below the self-esteem level the individual is motivated by necessity to overcome *deficiencies*. The deficiency-motivated person is busily engaged in *preparing* to live; the growth-motivated person wants to live and develop. With growth motivation comes a desire for challenge, improvement, change; with deficiency motivation comes a general fear of the unknown, rigidity of thought, stereotyping of behavior, and a strong attachment to the familiar. The growth-motivated individual

[17] Ibid.
[18] Ibid.

enjoys the present and looks forward to the future. The deficiency-motivated person clings to the past, is anxious about holding on to what he has in the present, and fears that he may lose it in the future.

Enormous political implications follow from these two types of motivation. Unlike the deficiency-motivated individual, the growth-motivated person has a strong, resilient personality that enables him to undergo a great deal of deprivation or crisis and still retain an optimistic outlook, a concern for humanity, a belief in himself, and a willingness to make up his mind about political matters. He remains confident and hopeful even in adversity. Because he retains a sense of direction and is not easily frustrated, he needs no scapegoat. In short, the growth-motivated person is not inclined to surrender his fate with reckless abandon in a time of troubles to a charismatic political leader who promises heaven for the good tomorrow and hell for everybody else the day after. For the deficiency-motivated individual the reverse applies, more often than not.

THE NEED HIERARCHY AND DEMOCRACY

If a democracy is to be feasible, a good proportion of its citizens must have satisfied their lower needs. A reasonably high standard of living is symptomatic of this. Therefore we could say that the higher the standard of living, other things being equal, the greater the probability that a country will have a democratic government. This relationship is evident in table 1.

Table 1 *Distribution of 32 Democracies by Level of Socioeconomic Development* *

	Democracies		
Per Capita Income	*Total (N)*	*Percent of Total*	Percent of All Democracies
$ 56	0	0	0
87	1	6.7	3
173	3	9.7	9
445	14	25.6	44
1330	14	100	44
	32		100

* Robert A. Dahl, *Modern Political Analysis*, 2nd Edition, © 1970. By permission of Prentice-Hall, Inc., Englewood Cliffs, N.J.

The reasons for this relationship are not obscure. Democracy is a form of government based upon a number of assumptions, one of which is the equal voting power of eligible citizens. "President or plumber, newspaper publisher or lettuce picker, middle-aged political scientist or eighteen-year-old novice student of politics—each casts only one vote at the polls." [19] While the amount of influence an individual wields is likely to vary with income, education, social position, and financial resources, the "power of the ballot" is given to everyone, irrespective of economic status. To use this power effectively, the individual must theoretically be able to evaluate competing sources of information and make his own reasoned, informed decision. Such an act requires a sense of obligation to participate and a willingness to pay the costs of voting to gain the benefits it provides. The costs in terms of time, energy, and effort to keep informed are immediate and highly visible. Competent leaders and satisfactory public policy are the benefits, but they usually come later, after the costs have been incurred, and are not always as directly evident as the costs.

Another basic postulate of democratic theory as it has evolved in the United States is stated clearly in the Declaration of Independence: "All men are created equal." This concept is primarily responsible for the extension of the suffrage in the United States. Clearly, however, the mere legal extension of suffrage will have marginal effects upon actual participation unless those to whom the suffrage is granted see any advantage in political equality. The desire for political equality can emerge fully only when the physical, safety, and love needs have been adequately fulfilled. Until this point is reached, it may be futile to expect the individual to take part in the political process or to act on motives other than immediate gratification and the satisfaction of individual, as opposed to social or cooperative, goals. It is plausible that it was less out of selfishness and elitism than out of doubts about the masses below the level of self-esteem that the country's founders limited suffrage to those who possessed a degree of property and income. They believed that the masses thought only of short-term gratification and were likely, should the opportunity arise, to mortgage the future for the present. Given the low interest in the abstractions of democracy, the framers of the Constitution feared that the masses of people would, if given political opportunities, sacrifice individual freedom in favor of an authoritarian political system that promised to provide immediate gratification. The power of long-range thinking is rarely found among those accustomed to living on the lower rungs of the need hierarchy.

[19] James MacGregor Burns and J. W. Peltason, *Government by the People*, 8th ed. (Englewood Cliffs, N.J.: Prentice-Hall, 1972), p. 8.

Nations crippled by poverty possess great numbers of individuals engaged primarily in fulfilling physical needs. These people are much more likely to accept existing authority as legitimate, for they have neither the desire nor the energy to question the government. Locked into a situation that demands their total effort simply to survive or at best to find satisfaction at the level of the love needs, such individuals are willing to accept the dictates of the existing political and social system, whatever they might be.

SUMMARY AND CRITIQUE

According to Abraham Maslow, human beings are motivated by a hierarchy of needs: physical, safety, love and belonging, self-esteem, and self-actualization. Needs lower on the hierarchy must be satisfactorily fulfilled before the higher ones emerge to be attended to. If an individual undergoes a particularly intense deprivation of a need, or if the deprivation occurs in especially traumatic circumstances, higher needs may never be able to emerge. A healthy developmental pattern is one that brings the individual up to self-esteem and then finally to self-actualization. Unhealthy patterns block the individual and make him defense-motivated. The extended franchise and strong emphasis upon equality in democracies demand many growth-motivated people in politics and in the population if the government is to function properly.

Criticisms of a basic need approach to political behavior generally revolve around two areas of dispute: (1) the components of the set of supposedly innate needs, and (2) whether indeed truly innate needs actually exist. With regard to the latter, strict *behaviorists* (not to be confused with behavioralists) see the individual in effect as the sum total of his learning experiences. Man has no nature per se. He is shaped by the environment according to laws of conditioning similar to those observed in learning experiments using animals and birds.

The extreme relativism involved in this position creates major difficulties. If people in an aggressive authoritarian regime bent upon total control over the individual can be conditioned to live just as happily as they can in a democracy encouraging freedom and self-expression, then who is to say that one government is better or worse than another? And if the individual is completely a product of his environment and the learning process, then who is to be allowed to control the environment and shape the learning process, and why? And what checks are to be put upon the controllers? Must they act in the citizen's interest? Can there in fact be an individual *self*-interest apart from that which the environment *teaches* is the self-interest? Further, if people learn through some principle of selection and reinforcement, be it even so simple as pleasure and pain, then it would appear that indeed some inherent nature is at work from the beginning that provides the individual with a basic selection and filtering process that makes learning possible. The behaviorist approach presents other problems. If the individual passively responds to the environment, amoeba-like, ingesting what is pleasurable and spitting out what is not, then how do we explain the activities of people who can dream up societies and environments that have never existed, and through human volitional acts attempt to create them—and sometimes even succeed?

This is not to say that the physical and social environment is of little or no importance. Indeed, the reverse is true. If the environment is not supportive, a person's development will be stifled at the lower levels of the need hierarchy. An individual subjected to a loveless, always-threatening environment, for example, would not be able to attain self-esteem. Far from being easily overlooked, the power of the environment, especially in one's early years, may be so awesome that we are led to believe that it is the only important factor involved in human behavior—at which point we lose sight of the little self that is struggling for development. If everyone existed at the lower rungs of the Maslow hierarchy, environmental determinism might provide a reasonably satisfactory account of behavior. But with self-esteem and then self-actualization come a sense of confidence in one's ability to deal with the environment and behavior that is not, in a predictive sense, determined by it. The self-actualizer is not *independent* of the environment—it always exerts certain influences upon him—but he is in a very real sense *free* from it. *He* determines how he will interact with it, rather than the other way around. The behavioristic approach is a patently inadequate means by which to explain the actions of self-actualizing people.

Just what *are* the truly innate needs presents another problem. James Davies contends that the safety need, while important, is not truly a basic need, actually gratifying in itself, but is instead a precondition for fulfillment of the needs above it. It is a means to an end rather than an end in itself.[20] Other needs, like knowledge and power, could be viewed in a similar light, as could what one author describes as a need for *personal control,* or "control over the forces and experiences that impact upon and shape our lives." [21] At the upper levels of the hierarchy one could also say that needs for *freedom* and *responsibility*

[20] James C. Davies, *Human Nature in Politics* (New York: John Wiley & Sons, 1963), pp. 9–10.

[21] Stanley Allen Renshon, *Psychological Needs and Political Behavior* (New York: Free Press, 1974), p. 43.

are present. The lack of precise agreement on innate versus ancillary needs is not an indication of a deep rift between scholars working in this general area, however. All concede that we have far to go to a "definitive" theory of human behavior—if such is possible—and most agree that human nature is essentially developmental—an idea that is in its own way optimistic, even revolutionary in its implications for the future of the species.

The needs discussed in this chapter may be viewed as motivators of the human organism; they provide the impetus that leads to behavior. Other factors are also important, however; the environment plays a large role, as we have noted, and so does perception. Perception provides both a "roadmap for action" and a process for revising it after each trip so that the individual can start with an up-to-date picture every time he ventures into the world. Political perception will be the subject of the next chapter.

Selected Bibliography

BAY, CHRISTIAN, *The Structure of Freedom*. Stanford, Ca.: Stanford University Press, 1970.

BETTELHEIM, BRUNO, *The Informed Heart*. New York: Avon, 1971.

DAVIES, JAMES C., *Human Nature in Politics*. New York: John Wiley & Sons, 1963.

DAVIES, JAMES C., "Where From and Where To?" in *Handbook of Political Psychology*, Jeanne N. Knutson, ed. San Francisco, Ca.: Jossey-Bass, 1973.

KNUTSON, JEANNE N., *The Human Basis of the Polity*. Chicago: Aldine Atherton, 1972.

MASLOW, ABRAHAM H., *Motivation and Personality*, 2nd ed. New York: Harper & Row, 1970.

MILLER, EUGENE F., "Positivism, Historicism, and Political Inquiry," *American Political Science Review*, 66 (September 1972), 796–817.

RENSHON, STANLEY ALLEN, *Psychological Needs and Political Behavior*. New York: Free Press, 1974.

SKINNER, B. F., *Beyond Freedom and Dignity*. New York: Bantam, 1971.

SKINNER, B. F., *Walden Two*. New York: Macmillan, 1962.

THORSON, THOMAS LANDON, *Biopolitics*. New York: Holt, Rinehart and Winston, 1970.

3

People, politics, and perception

Perception involves how people look at the world, the assumptions they make about it, how they respond to new situations, and how they arrive at a conclusion when faced with a difficult moral decision. Perception is relevant to an understanding of political behavior because people act upon the world as they perceive it and believe it to be. If we know how a person views himself, those around him, and the world in general, and if we have familiarity with his basic beliefs and how he puts them together in his mind, then we know much about his perception—we might even say his personality. This puts us in a reasonably good position to predict how he might behave in a particular situation. We will begin our considerations of perception with a stage theory of morality.

THEORIES OF MORAL GROWTH

Dynamics similar to those of the Maslow hierarchy are postulated in a sequential stage theory of moral growth developed by Lawrence Kohlberg. Kohlberg postulates six stages carrying man from the point of strict self-centered concern with avoiding physical pain and deprivation to the highest reaches of human intellectual experience where "conscience is a directing agent" and people view each other in terms of "mutual respect and trust."[1]

In developing the stages of moral growth, Kohlberg asked people how they would act in a situation that posed a moral dilemma, and why. For example, one such dilemma is contained in the following story:

In Europe, a woman was near death from cancer. One drug might save her, a form of radium that a druggist in the same town had

[1] Charles Hampden-Turner and Phillip Whitten, "Morals Left and Right," *Psychology Today* (April 1971), cited in *Annual Editions: Readings in American Government '72–'73* (Guilford, Conn.: The Dushkin Publishing Group, Inc., 1973), p. 11.

recently discovered. The druggist was charging $2,000, ten times what the drug cost him to make. The sick woman's husband, Heinz, went to everyone he knew to borrow the money, but he could only get together about half of what it cost. He told the druggist that his wife was dying and asked him to sell it cheaper or let him pay later. But the druggist said, "No." The husband got desperate and broke into the man's store to steal the drug for his wife. Should the husband have done that? Why? [2]

The object of such dilemmas is to stimulate the individual to describe his general theory of personal morality. While Kohlberg's moral problems were used with children, they are equally challenging to adults. It is from the responses to these challenges that the six stages of moral growth were developed. We shall apply Kohlberg's stages of moral growth to the response to political events. The application is speculative, merely suggesting possible interpretations.

At the lowest level, stage one, the individual seeks to avoid punishment by a superior power or "significant other"—another individual with influence over him. A person with this moral outlook possesses:

a punishment and obedience orientation. *To the child [or adult who has not progressed beyond this stage] the* consequences *of action determine the goodness or badness of the action. . . . Avoidance of punishment and unquestioning deference to power are valued in their own right, rather than in accordance with an underlying moral order that employs punishment and authority.*[3]

This level of moral judgment may lie behind some of the more destructive examples of political repression and the tactics of certain opposition groups. One example that comes readily to mind is the German *Freikorps*—reconstituted military forces made up of demobilized German soldiers who could not adjust to German civilian society after their defeat in World War I. The level of destruction in terms of human lives and political assassination that resulted from their rampages has seldom been

[2] Lawrence Kohlberg, "Stage and Sequence: The Cognitive-Developmental Approach to Socialization," in *Handbook of Socialization Theory and Research,* David A. Goslin, ed. (Chicago: Rand McNally, 1969), p. 379.

[3] Lawrence S. Wrightsman, *Social Psychology in the Seventies* (Monterey, Ca.: Brooks/Cole, 1972), p. 112.

equaled.[4] In the *Freikorps,* at stage one of the morality scale, the insecure and frustrated could find:

> *new confidence and exhilarating strength by identifying . . . with the victorious march of the Freebooter Army. The Free Corps spelled power and he gloried in it. . . . The precisely constructed military machine [of the Free Corps] rolled on blindly and without any concern whatsoever for ideological [or higher moral] purposes. And like a machine it rolled over and crushed everything which tried to oppose it. . . .[5]*

The *Freikorps* were organized around the *Führerprinzip,* the "leadership principle," in which absolute loyalty and obedience were given to the leader, and orders were carried out without question. "The war could not release them from its grip. . . . The most active part of the [Free Corps] . . . marched simply because it had learned to march. It marched through the cities enveloped in a cloud of sullen rage—a cloud of vaulting, purposeless fury—knowing that now it had to fight, to fight at any cost." [6]

We should not be surprised to find that many of the statements uttered by Adolf Eichmann, an operative of the Nazi security forces engaged in tracking down and murdering Jewish civilians during World War II, fall at level one of Kohlberg's Moral-Judgment scale. For example:

> *In actual fact, I was merely a little cog in the machinery that carried out the directives of the German Reich.*

> *Yet what is there to "admit"? I carried out my orders. It would be as pointless to blame me for the whole final solution of the Jewish problem as to blame the official in charge of the railroads over which the Jewish transports traveled.*

> *But to sum it all up, I must say that I regret nothing. Adolf Hitler may have been wrong all down the line, but one thing is beyond dispute: The man was able to work his way up from lance corporal in the German army to Führer of a people of almost 80 million.*

[4] See Robert G. L. Waite, *Vanguard of Nazism: The Free Corps Movement in Post-war Germany 1918–1932* (New York: W. W. Norton, 1969).

[5] Ibid., p. 30.

[6] Ibid., p. 29.

I never met him personally, but his success alone proves to me that I should subordinate myself to this man.[7]

The second stage of moral growth in Kohlberg's theory corresponds with the position of people on the physical needs level of the Maslow hierarchy. The focus shifts somewhat from a concern with power and force to one of self-interest. The second level is illustrated by what Edward C. Banfield found characteristic of a small rural town in the Italian countryside. In his book *The Moral Basis of a Backward Society,* he describes how individuals viewed themselves and their society. He called this mode *amoral familism,* its chief tenet being to "maximize the material, short-run advantage of the nuclear family; assume that all others will do likewise." [8] People with such a moral outlook cannot be expected to be active in politics, nor perhaps even to lend assistance to others, although the community might gain thereby. As Banfield puts it: "In a society of amoral familists, no one will further the interest of the group or community except as it is to his private advantage to do so. In other words, the hope of material gain in the short-run will be the only motive for concern with public affairs." [9] Indeed, one of the local teachers, when interviewed, stated, "Even the saints, for all their humility, looked after themselves. And men, after all, are only made of flesh and spirit." [10]

Lawrence Wylie describes a similar situation that he encountered in a small French town. *Les autres,* meaning all the other people of the village except one's own family, "are a nuisance." Under the conditions of threat and possible denunciation that occurred during the German occupation of France in World War II, *les autres* "became a menace. . . . Whenever anyone received a special gasoline or clothing or food ration there were always *les autres* who started a rumor that it was obtained illegally. It seemed that no one could do anything without arousing the antagonism of someone else." [11] Wylie describes the atmosphere as one of "bitterness, deprivation, and distrust"—an environment not conducive to the politics of collective action.

Kohlberg categorizes the first two stages as comprising the *preconventional* level. That is, an individual's behavior is governed not by society's norms and conventions but by power, fear of punishment, and a desire to

[7] Adolf Eichmann, cited in Wrightsman, *Social Psychology,* p. 115.

[8] Edward C. Banfield, *The Moral Basis of a Backward Society* (New York: Free Press, 1958), p. 83.

[9] Ibid., pp. 83–84 (italics removed).

[10] Ibid., p. 20.

[11] Lawrence Wylie, *Village in the Vaucluse* (New York: Harper & Row, Colophon Books, 1964), pp. 28–29.

gratify oneself and immediate others. The attempt to act in accordance with society's norms occurs at the *conventional* level, stages three and four. At stage three the individual's moral outlook stresses "conformity to stereotypical images of what is majority or 'natural' behavior." [12] A person at this level attempts to follow the dictates of the crowd and to avoid disapprobation for behavior that violates group expectations. An individual's moral judgment is no more than the judgment of the group, with little thought of possible long-range effects of a particular judgment. Stage four differs from stage three in the model for conformity; thus, whereas in stage three the individual's moral orientation conforms to the attitudes of those with whom he is in close proximity, for example, family, peer groups, and friends, in stage four conformity is to the authority structure of the society as a whole, particularly with regard to the political system. The stage-four person is oriented "toward authority, fixed rules and the maintenance of the social order. Right behavior consists in doing one's duty, showing respect for authority and maintaining the given social order for its own sake. One earns respect by performing dutifully." [13] The stage-four individual will place a strong emphasis upon maintaining and reinforcing the *status quo.*

Stage five occurs at the *postconventional* level of moral development. At this point the individual's moral structure moves him beyond mere conventions and into considerations regarding relative values, the purposes of the social and political system, and the need for a system of resolving disputes in a reasonable and just manner. According to Kohlberg,

> *Right action tends to be defined in terms of general rights and in terms of standards which have been critically examined and agreed upon by the whole society. There is a clear awareness of the relativism of personal values and opinions and a corresponding emphasis upon procedural rules for reaching consensus. Aside from what is constitutionally and democratically agreed upon, right or wrong is a matter of personal "values" and "opinion." The result is an emphasis upon the "legal point of view," but with an emphasis upon the possibility of changing law in terms of rational consideration of social utility rather than freezing it in the terms of stage four "law and order." Outside the legal realm, free agreement and contract are the binding elements of obligation. This is the "official" morality of*

12 Lawrence Kohlberg, "The Child as a Moral Philosopher," *Psychology Today* September 1968), 26.

13 Ibid.

American government, and finds its ground in the thought of the
writers of the Constitution.[14]

At stage six, the highest stage, individual conscience is the guiding
principle. Decisions are made according to guidelines provided by

ethical principles appealing to logical comprehensiveness, universality
and consistency. These principles are abstract and ethical (the
Golden Rule . . .); they are not concrete moral rules like the Ten
Commandments. Instead, they are universal principles of justice,
of the reciprocity *and* equality *of human rights, and of respect for the*
dignity of human beings as individual persons.[15]

A POLITICAL EXAMPLE OF STAGES OF NORMAL GROWTH

One study conducted among college-age adults in Boston and the San
Francisco Bay Area analyzed the relation between levels of moral judgment and political subgroups in the United States. The researchers found
that subjects describing themselves as political conservatives "consistently
referred to law, order, authority maintenance (Stage 4) and conformity
to stereotyped roles (Stage 3) in making their moral judgments." [16] In
talking about the Vietnam war, they admired members of the armed
forces for carrying out their prescribed roles and meeting the expectations
of the loyal citizenry—"especially by comparison with 'campus bums.' " [17]
They also stressed adherence to the "lawful authority of the Commander
in Chief," the president, as opposed to those who seek to make their
own decisions on matters of national interest and policy. On the other
side of the political spectrum were the radicals, who desired rapid change
in the U.S. social, economic, and political situation and U.S. withdrawal
from active military involvement in Southeast Asia. Here the authors
found "an interesting division. Although most radicals had Stage 6 con-
sciences and principle orientations, a large minority made egocentric
Stage 2 judgments." [18] Such statements expressed a judgment of the war
as damaging domestic economic concerns or threatening the individual
through the draft and the like. In their general conclusion, the findings

14 Ibid.
15 Ibid.
16 Hampden-Turner and Whitten, "Morals Left and Right," p. 10.
17 Ibid.
18 Ibid.

"correspond to the image of a fairly homogeneous silent majority of conservative Americans confronting a disparate array of left-of-center ideal-
ists (Stage 6) and opportunists (Stage 2). Between these poles are the
Stage-5 liberals, desperately urging the two groups at least to agree on
the methods of disagreement." [19]

Kohlberg's conception provides some basis for hypothesizing about the
anomalies frequently encountered in radical movements, both left and
right: the apparent contradiction between idealistic radical leaders and
writers and their frequently less than idealistic followers. The true revolutionary leader is not only at stage six of Kohlberg's hierarchy, but is also
more than likely to be at the top level in Maslow's scheme as well—motivated
to improve the lot of mankind, to realize his full potential, and to
achieve satisfaction of self-actualization needs. The opportunist, on the
other hand, may join the movement only because he perceives it as a
path of self-aggrandizement and a way of "getting ahead." Thus, on
occasion the leader whose moral values may be above reproach can be
seen alongside people motivated by self-interest and a desire for personal,
manipulative political power. Similarly, given the consistent, all-encompassing view of people and human nature held by the individual at
Kohlberg's sixth stage of moral development, it should not be too surprising to find the revolutionary idealist frequently misjudging the
actual intent and real motivations of the stage-two members of the radical
group.

V. I. Lenin, a consummate tactician and a strong-willed man of considerable intellectual power, believed like Marx that

> *the goal . . . is freedom—freedom from the forces of nature and
> society, freedom for the unhampered development of all potentialities
> inherent in man as an individual and as a species, most specifically,
> freedom of man from exploitation by his fellow men. Lenin in
> his first major work set himself the goal to help "the proletariat
> put an end to all and any exploitation as quickly and as easily
> as possible."* [20]

He therefore sought the overthrow of the traditional Russian social and
political order—an order that degraded the workers and alienated him
from himself.[21]

[19] Ibid.

[20] Alfred G. Meyer, *Leninism* (New York: Frederick Praeger, 1971), p. 11.

[21] Cf. the Marxist interpretation of alienation in Karl Marx, "Alienated Labour," in
Alienation and the Social System, Ada W. Finifter, ed. (New York: John Wiley, 1972),
pp. 12–18. Also see Erich Fromm, *Marx's Concept of Man* (New York: Frederick Ungar,
1961).

The reported differences between the outlooks of Lenin and Stalin are illustrative. Stalin appeared to be much more self-centered; one author describes him as "grim and heartless." His early training taught him that survival depended upon "distrust, alertness, evasion, dissimulation, and endurance." [22] Endurance and survival were important to Stalin not in terms of the human condition so much as in terms of himself, as was amply evidenced by the terrible purge trials of the 1930s. Stalin was not an idealist. Rather, he was a bureaucratic plodder and a man of nationalistic as opposed to universalistic principles.

He was interested in the practical use of the Leninist gadgets [of administration], not in the Leninist laboratory of thought. His own behavior was . . . dictated by the moods, needs, and pressures of the vast political machine that he had come to control. His philosophy boiled down to securing the dominance of that machine by the handiest and most convenient means.[23]

The stage-two opportunist frequently finds a place for himself in the social and political changes fostered by the stage-six idealist bent upon major alterations in the status quo. The stage-two "outcast," having no chance for a position of status, power, prestige, or acceptance under the existing situation, finds the urge for personal survival and aggrandizement consonant with the actions of a movement that, in its idealism, may mistakenly perceive the outcast's dissatisfaction with the status quo as evidence of his adherence to the humanistic goals of the group.

It should be clear that a person's behavior—that is, the way he relates to others, views himself, and responds to the political system—depends considerably upon his level of moral development. What can be said at this point about the forces influencing an individual's level of moral development?

LEVEL OF MORAL DEVELOPMENT AND FAMILY BACKGROUND

There is a definite correspondence between Maslow's need hierarchy and Kohlberg's levels of moral development. We suggest that it is not too simplistic to say that the lower classes in any society tend to actualize the middle and lower clusters of both hierarchies. Masses mobilized by

[22] Isaac Deutscher, *Stalin: A Political Biography* (New York: Vintage Books, 1960), p. 3.

[23] Ibid., p. 235.

elites to maintain the status quo, for example, would be found primarily
at stages three and four. Table 1 outlines a hypothetical classification
scheme illustrating six political types corresponding to the six moral
stages in Kohlberg's schema. The classification is also based upon membership in a sociopolitical status group, ranging from the elite (those
who are some distance above the mean in income and education) to
the masses (those below the mean on these variables). In this scheme
the mass types are either politically passive or are motivated in their
political behavior by others. They tend generally to look to significant
others rather than themselves for authority and direction. This tendency
is something that researchers have found developing early in the childhood training of working-class offspring. Research on child rearing has
generally indicated that

> *middle-class parents provide more warmth and are more likely to
> use reasoning, isolation, show of disappointment, or guilt-arousing
> appeals in disciplining the child. They are also likely to be more
> permissive about demands for attention from the child, sex behavior,
> aggression to parent, table manners, neatness and orderliness, noise,
> bedtime rules, and general obedience. Working-class parents are
> more likely to use ridicule, shouting, or physical punishment in
> disciplining the child, and to be generally more restrictive.*[24]

A study of middle- and working-class mothers [25] revealed significant
class-correlated differences in the *values* that are emphasized and imparted to the young. In one sample, middle-class mothers were found
to emphasize the values of *happiness* for the child, the need for him to
be *considerate of others* and to possess self-control and to be *curious
about things*—that is, to ask questions, not to take things for granted,
and to attempt to understand how things work. Working-class mothers,

[24] Wesley C. Becker, "Consequences of Different Kinds of Parental Discipline," in
Review of Child Development Research, Vol. 1, Martin L. Hoffman and Lois Wladis
Hoffman, eds. (New York: Russell Sage Foundation, 1964), p. 171. Becker is summa-
rizing the work of U. Bronfenbrenner, "Socialization and Social Class Through Time
and Space," in *Readings in Social Psychology*, E. E. Maccoby, T. M. Newcomb, and
E. L. Hartley, eds. (New York: Holt, Rinehart and Winston, 1958), pp. 400–425; M. L.
Kohn, "Social Class and Parent–Child Relationships: An Interpretation," *American
Journal of Sociology*, 68 (1963), 471–80; M. L. Kohn and E. E. Carroll, "Social Class
and the Allocation of Parental Responsibilities," *Sociometry*, 23 (1960), 372–92; D. R.
Miller and G. E. Swanson, *Inner Conflict and Defense* (New York: Holt, Rinehart and
Winston, 1960); R. R. Sears, E. E. Maccoby, and H. Levin, *Patterns of Child Rearing*
(Evanston, Ill.: Row, Peterson, 1957).

[25] Presumably the results are generalizable to the seldom-researched upper-middle-
and upper-class families.

Table 1 *Moral Development and Political Behavior*

Level of Moral Development	Socio-political Status	Basis for Behavior	Characteristic Political Behavior
1	Mass	Individual is manipulated on the basis of power and force alone.	Follower of whatever faction wields the greatest amount of power in an area immediately affecting his needs. Follows regardless of legality or legitimacy of faction issuing the orders.
2	Mass	Politically apathetic, or self-centered follower of political activist.	Narrow range of ego-centric interests. Suspicious of others; lacking in community spirit. Motivated for personal ends of self-aggrandizement and/or self-protection. Stays out of politics unless need fulfillment immediately threatened or immediate economic or political (power, status) rewards are forthcoming.
2	Mass	Political activist out for own ends. Actually a "man of and from the masses" (e.g., Stalin, Hitler, Huey Long).	Seeks power in an attempt to dominate and manipulate others—in this endeavor uses appeals at Kohlberg-scale moral stages one and two.
3	Mass	Individual anchoring behavior specifically and emphatically upon group norms.	Follows the political tide of opinion expressed by those he associates with. Easily manipulated by opinion leaders.
4	Mass	Duty-bound patriot.	Follows his government's policy without question; votes out of duty; tends to reinforce status quo.
4	Marginal elite	Political conservative whose elite status is threatened by socio-economic change (e.g., members of John Birch Society).	Analyzes political choices on basis of degree of threat to social and economic position; decides in favor of the least threatening (most conservative) alternative.
5	Elite	Moderate.	Attempts to reconcile competing factions within the rules of the political game; willing to compromise.
6	Elite	Independent; self-motivated and self-assured leader.	Attempts to bring political situation into line with his view of the ideal.

on the other hand, stressed the values of obedience to *authority* and *neatness*, or external appearance. While both sets agreed upon a number of values, it was found that "middle-class mothers give higher priority to values that reflect *internal dynamics*—the child's own and his emphatic concern for other people's. Working-class mothers, by contrast, give higher priority to values that reflect *behavioral conformity*." [26]

These differences are further accentuated by looking higher or lower in the class structure; thus, the higher the socioeconomic status of the mother, the greater the emphasis upon internal dynamics. The lower the socioeconomic status, the greater the emphasis upon behavioral conformity.[27] A similar situation obtains regarding the father's values, with the major exception that working-class fathers emphasize the *ability to defend* oneself to a significantly greater extent than in the other group. Defense, however, means physical self-defense rather than a longer-range economic survival or advancement in prestige, economic security or power, and the like.[28] The author of the study concludes that "middle-class parents are more likely to value self-direction; working-class parents are more likely to value conformity to external authority." [29] By these terms, the author means that

> *self-direction focuses on* internal *standards for behavior; conformity focuses on* externally *imposed rules. (One important corollary is that the former is concerned with intent, the latter only with consequences.) Self-direction does not imply rigidity, isolation, or insensitivity to others; on the contrary, it implies that one is attuned to internal dynamics—one's own, and other people's. Conformity does not imply sensitivity to one's peers, but rather obedience to the dictates of authority.*[30]

It may be said, then, that in general the middle- or upper-class individual is predisposed toward internalizing a set of values that will allow him to *empathize* with others—to understand their plight and think about ways of doing something to improve the human condition. The *conformity* that is characteristic of the lower classes, on the other hand, results not from an *understanding* of the other fellow's situation, but rather from recognition that the other person "has the power"; "he makes

---

[26] Melvin L. Kohn, *Class and Conformity: A Study in Values* (Homewood, Ill.: Dorsey Press, 1969), pp. 20–21.

[27] Ibid., p. 29.

[28] Ibid., p. 23.

[29] Ibid., p. 35.

[30] Ibid.

the rules, and I don't have any power to do anything about it." A conformist outlook is inimical to the tendency to question laws and policy and to formulate major alternatives and seek systematic ways of implementing them.

If we could divide the population into elites and masses, we would probably find that individuals classified as elites tend to look to *themselves* for motivation and direction—to their inner sense of values, of right and wrong. After all, to lead demands precisely that—an ability to act without *always* having to make reference to one's peers. It also involves the ability to size up (to empathize with) one's following and thereby to perceive the hopes, the fears, the aspirations, and the frustrations of the rank and file. The leader is thus better able to satisfy the desires of his following before its members begin looking for someone else to do the job. Responsibility is also an element here, and this, too, is imparted to the middle- and upper-class individual through family training.

PERCEPTION AND POLITICAL PERSONALITY

One major aim of research on the individual, or micro level, of political analysis, has been to discern particular types of *political personality*. A pioneering effort along this line is Harold Lasswell's *Psychopathology and Politics,* first published in 1930, and a subsequent (1948) work, *Power and Personality.*

Power seeking, or the desire to influence decisions and the subsequent behavior of others,[31] is a major characteristic of the political personality. It results, Lasswell argues, from an attempt to compensate for a "low estimate of the self," particularly in cases where the conception of self is ambiguous, containing both high and low estimates.[32] A balance between these opposite estimates places the individual above the low-estimate point at which feelings of helplessness and inactivity would prevail, but below the high-estimate point at which the goals of the individual's actions would exceed what is possible in reality and would lead to consequent failure. Such a balance produces a likely candidate

---

[31] The concept of power is relatively complex and cannot be dealt with in detail here. A more complete discussion is reserved for chapter 6. For other sources, consult Harold D. Lasswell, *Power and Personality* (New York: Viking, 1963), pp. 7–19; Robert A. Dahl, *Modern Political Analysis,* 2nd ed. (Englewood Cliffs, N.J.: Prentice-Hall, 1970), pp. 14–34; Harold D. Lasswell and Abraham Kaplan, *Power and Society* (New Haven, Conn.: Yale University Press, 1963); and Alexander L. George, "Power as a Compensatory Value for Political Leaders," *Journal of Social Issues,* 24, no. 3 (July 1968), 29–40.

[32] Lasswell, *Power and Personality,* p. 53.

for the label "power seeker." [33] Such an individual develops in an environment where deprivations suffered in the relationships involving the primary unit, the family, are balanced with a "compensating flow of affection and admiration" [34] from others outside the family.

The tendency toward power seeking is not the only characteristic of the political individual, however. After all, people may seek power in the economic, social, even the religious sphere as well as in the political. But the political individual, for Lasswell, is unique in that he has displaced or transferred "private motives from family objects to public objects." [35]

Granting, for the sake of argument and without major contrary evidence, that an individual's current motives stem from basic human drives that are played out in a social context—in interactions with others and in the face of social norms, rules, and sanctions—it may be inferred that Lasswell's political individual exists at the higher stages of moral development in Kohlberg's scheme. It is the person in the higher stages who generalizes from his condition to that of the country, the nation, perhaps to humanity as a whole. For an individual of such moral development it is a short jump to the political system—the institution providing authoritative allocations of moral values and scarce resources for the society—in order to realize his own ends *as they have been generalized by him to society as a whole.* (In his ascent of the Kohlberg stages of moral development, the political individual loses contact with his motives as purely individual drives and comes to identify his own concern as *society's.*) In short, he really believes that his actions are taken in the best interests of the nation, whatever their actual results might be.[36]

Individuals lacking the opportunity or the desire to gain a formal education; or the leisure to study, think, and relate their experiences to "the human condition"; or the time or the chance to develop the verbal skills necessary to engage in informed discourse on the social and political questions of the day—these individuals are not likely to become political. First, the probability of their ascending the Kohlberg stages of moral development is slight, given the constraints imposed by the necessity of making a living and protecting what little has been gained. Second, opportunities and a will to focus on the political system as a means to realizing private motives, other than pure economic or "bread and butter" concerns, are lacking for people in such a situation. Politics

[33] Ibid.

[34] Ibid., p. 44.

[35] See Harold D. Lasswell, *Psychopathology and Politics* (New York: Viking, 1963), p. 75.

[36] See ibid., p. 76.

demands individuals who can astutely assess the relative degrees of power wielded by a variety of competing groups; thus, a politician motivated purely by private gain and private interest would be doomed to failure. Such recent events in the United States as the resignation of a president and a vice-president appear to support this argument. At worst, politicians are adept at mirroring the public interest in terms of their own; at best, they act in terms of what they actually perceive to be the best public interest. Rarely, if ever, do they act purely on the basis of their own self-interest.

Like other endeavors and institutions in modern societies, politics demands and attracts more than one type of individual, since it is characterized by a division of labor.[37] Lasswell distinguishes several political types. One is the *compulsive* personality, an individual who "relies upon rigid, obsessive ways of handling human relations." Another, with a very different political style, is the *dramatizing* character, someone who goes into politics in order to evoke emotional responses from others. According to Lasswell, "The compulsive tends to go by the existing rules without basically questioning them. The dramatizer is attuned to the symbols and emotions that stir the masses." [38] Building upon the compulsive and dramatizational dimensions, Lasswell describes the *bureaucratic* type, an individual with personality characteristics structured on the compulsive type, and the *agitational* personality, structured on the dramatizing type. The bureaucratic personality is prone to follow established authority and existing guidelines while at the same time attempting to avoid responsibility.[39] It would follow that he is generally passive and, except in attempting to avoid responsibility, is inclined to follow the strict dictates of his superiors. The agitator, on the contrary, is not inclined to accept things as they are. He tries to "capture the loyalties of the oppressed," and is of particular importance in times of crisis and the breakdown of traditional social norms, rules, and regulations. The agitator relishes the acclaim of the masses, and manipulates the symbols that hold the key to their emotions. Such an individual is inclined to consider *himself* as the authority; it is he who "has the word." Says Lasswell, "The agitator easily infers that he who disagrees with him is in communion with the devil, and that opponents show bad faith or timidity." [40]

---

[37] For a classic statement on the division of labor, see Emile Durkheim, *The Division of Labor in Society,* trans. George Simpson (New York: Free Press, 1968; first published in France in 1893).

[38] Lasswell, *Power and Personality,* p. 62.

[39] Ibid., pp. 88–90.

[40] Lasswell, *Psychopathology and Politics,* p. 78.

Both the bureaucratic and agitator character types could fit nicely into an authoritarian government—a government of strictly centralized authority and an extensive bureaucracy. Examples of this kind of political system include Nazi Germany and the Soviet Union under the Stalinist regime. In fact, it was the rise of precisely these kinds of systems that made further, more extensive studies of political personality a matter of urgency to political scientists. Rather than attempting to specify in detail the potentially infinite number of political types, studies of political personality began to move toward delineating some of the basic dimensions around which personalities are organized. A pioneering effort in this regard was *The Authoritarian Personality*,[41] a collaborative study published in 1950. "The authors of this study, familiar with the holocaust wrought in Europe by the Nazi movement, sought to determine the characteristics of the *potentially fascistic* individual, one whose structure [of thinking and perceiving] is such as to render him particularly susceptible to anti-democratic propaganda." [42]

From the study several dimensions of an authoritarian personality type began to emerge. The opposite, the democratic personality, was not specified, but may be inferentially defined by dimensions opposite to those of the authoritarian—the nonauthoritarian, or equalitarian, personality being an essentially liberal, unprejudiced individual.

Questionnaire items were combined to yield a scale for each of the major dimensions. Among the scales was the *anti-Semitism scale,* which sought to determine the extent of the individual's "stereotyped negative opinions describing the Jews as threatening, immoral, and categorically different from non-Jews, and of hostile attitudes urging various forms of restrictions, exclusion, and suppression as a means of solving the 'Jewish problem' "; [43] the *ethnocentrism scale,* designed to measure the individual's "rigid . . . acceptance of the culturally alike and . . . rejection of the culturally unlike"; [44] the *political and economic conservatism scale,* included under the assumption that the potential fascist would value "the *status quo,* religion and tradition over science and humanitarianism." [45] Finally, the authors constructed the *implicit antidemocratic trends or potentiality for fascism scale,* which was designed to elicit evidence (or its lack) for an authoritarian, potentially

---

[41] T. W. Adorno et al., *The Authoritarian Personality* (New York: John Wiley & Sons, 1964), 2 vols.

[42] Ibid., vol. 1, p. 1 (emphasis in original).

[43] Adorno et al., *The Authoritarian Personality,* cited in Roger Brown, *Social Psychology* (New York: Free Press, 1965), p. 482.

[44] Ibid., p. 484.

[45] Ibid., p. 485.

fascistic or right-wing "syndrome," or "collection of concurrent symptoms." [46] The major components were:

Conventionalism. *A rigid adherence to conventional values.*

Authoritarian Submission. *A submissive, uncritical attitude toward idealized moral authorities of the ingroup.*

Superstition and Stereotypy. *The belief in mystical determinants of the individual's fate, the disposition to think in rigid categories.*

Power and "Toughness." *A preoccupation with the dominance–submission, strong–weak, leader–follower dimension; identification with power figures; exaggerated assertion of strength and toughness.*

Destructiveness and Cynicism. *A generalized hostility toward and a tendency to downgrade the value of the individual human being.*[47]

Criticisms were leveled against both the methodology and the substantive conclusions of this monumental study. (Nevertheless, a whole subfield of social-psychological literature grew up around it.) One of the criticisms involved the authors' tendency to address themselves to authoritarianism of the *right* and to overlook the authoritarianism of the *left*.[48] Authoritarians of *all* hues, for example, are frequently associated with social movements and "holy causes"—be they proponents of radical change or of a return to the halcyon days of the past. As Eric Hoffer notes in *The True Believer*:

> *There are vast differences in the contents of holy causes and doctrines, but a certain uniformity in the factors which make them effective. He who . . . finds precise reasons for the effectiveness of Christian doctrine has also found the reasons for the effectiveness of Communist, Nazi and nationalist doctrine. However different the holy causes people die for, they perhaps die basically for the same thing.*[49]

[46] Ibid., p. 487.

[47] List and description adopted with minor changes from Roger Brown, *Social Psychology*, pp. 487–88.

[48] Richard Christie and Marie Jahoda, eds., *Studies in the Scope and Method of "The Authoritarian Personality"* (New York: Free Press, 1954). See especially Edward A. Shils, "Authoritarianism: 'Right' and 'Left,'" in ibid., pp. 24–49.

[49] Eric Hoffer, *The True Believer: Thoughts on the Nature of Mass Movements* (New York: New American Library, 1964), p. 9.

Nowhere have Nazi, or fascist, extremism and communist extremism better shown their close similarities than in the 15 years after World War I that led to and followed the downfall of the German Weimar Republic, in 1933, at the hands of the Nazi movement.

Adolf Hitler himself was the first to admit that National Socialism (Nazism) and Communism had much in common. "There is more that binds us to Bolshevism than separates us from it," he once said in a revealing conversation, "there is, above all, revolutionary feeling. . . . I have always made allowance for this circumstance, and given orders that former Communists are to be admitted to the party at once." [50]

After Hitler came to power, many communists in fact entered the Nazi party. "Indeed, there were so many of them that they were given a special name. They were known popularly as the Beefsteak Nazi— Brown on the outside, Red on the inside." [51]

Several additional dimensions are characteristic of the authoritarian political personality. One such dimension is *dogmatism*. The dogmatic individual thinks in terms of power and superior–inferior relationships. He distinguishes sharply between what he believes in and what he does not—and is intolerant of those whose beliefs differ from his, although he knows very little about them. The dogmatic individual considers the world a threatening place. He tends to view authority as absolute. [52] Milton Rokeach adopts the term "party line thinking" to describe how the dogmatic person operates. The "party line thinker" resists change when it does not result from the actions of the authorities to whom he looks for direction, but he will change quickly to conform with any change in their dictates. [53] On the basis of tests designed to measure dogmatic and authoritarian characteristics, Rokeach developed a typology of cognitive types—of types of thought processes—with two different structural configurations: the *open mind* and the *closed mind*. The same structural configuration may exist in people who have very different

[50] Robert G. L. Waite, *Vanguard of Nazism: The Free Corps Movement in Postwar Germany 1918–1932* (New York: W. W. Norton, 1969), p. 273.

[51] Ibid., p. 274.

[52] See John P. Kirscht and Ronald G. Dillehay, *Dimensions of Authoritarianism: A Review of Research and Theory* (Lexington: University of Kentucky Press, 1967), p. 11.

[53] See Milton Rokeach, *The Open and Closed Mind* (New York: Basic Books, 1960), p. 225.

beliefs: for example, the educated liberal and the educated conservative, or the communist or radical leftist and the member of the John Birch Society, who is intent upon destroying what he calls communist subversion in the United States. Rokeach argues that *what* a person believes is less important than *how* he organizes his beliefs, what relations they bear to one another, and how they relate to his disbeliefs—the things he *does not* believe in. Here again, we find ourselves faced with the components of perception.

BELIEFS, VALUES, AND RELATED TERMS

By belief we mean an assumption about reality, a statement describing how the world works. Frequently, the belief is prefaced by a statement saying, "I believe that . . ." [54] In his belief, the individual draws a relationship between an object and a characteristic of it.[55] As long as he holds the belief, he acts as though the relationship postulated is true, whether or not it actually is, objectively.[56] For example, a voter who favors a liberal political position, and who believes that all Democrats are liberals, may well vote for anyone labeled Democrat regardless of the candidate's voting record.[57]

> *Beliefs also represent basic elements of a more or less complex*
> *framework, a belief system, which the individual uses for*
> *understanding and dealing with himself and his environment.*
> *A belief system may be defined as having represented within it,*
> *in some organized psychological but not necessarily logical*
> *form, each and every one of a person's countless beliefs about*
> *physical and social reality.*[58]

In sum, each individual organizes his beliefs, his basic assumptions about reality, in a manner that is logical *to him*—a manner that allows

[54] Milton Rokeach, *Beliefs, Attitudes, and Values* (San Francisco: Jossey-Bass, 1970), p. 113, as cited in James J. Best, *Public Opinion Micro and Macro* (Homewood, Ill.: Dorsey Press, 1973), p. 7.

[55] Best, *Public Opinion,* p. 7. See also Daryl J. Bem, *Beliefs, Attitudes, and Human Affairs* (Belmont, Ca.: Brooks/Cole, 1970), pp. 4ff., as cited in Best, *Public Opinion,* p. 7.

[56] See Best, *Public Opinion,* p. 7.

[57] Ibid.

[58] Ibid.

him to deal with the world and the people in it in what he considers
to be an efficient, reasonable, logical, and entirely "correct" fashion.
A belief system (with its associated set of values indicating how one
should behave and what goals are worth striving for) provides the logical
foundation upon which attitudes and opinions are formed. Attitudes are
"more or less enduring orientations toward an object or situation and
predispositions to respond positively or negatively toward that object
or situation." [59] Opinions are similar to attitudes but lack their persistence in that they are orientations toward "more superficial and transitory issues." [60]

Beliefs and values provide the basic structure through which the
individual defines his universe. The resulting attitudes and opinions
help supply specific cues he picks up in attempting to orient himself
to a new situation. As summed up by James Best, belief systems provide

> *a ready-made set of cues for interpretation and criteria for*
> *evaluation. At the same time the fact that beliefs are structured*
> *forces perceptions of the external world into preexisting and*
> *preformed categories. Without beliefs and values we would have*
> *to spend a large part of each day classifying and evaluating*
> *anew events and objects with which we regularly deal.*[61]

Thus, the belief system "serves for most people as a labor-saving device,
saving the time and energy of continually relearning criteria for judging
their political environment." [62] Identification with a political party and
with its symbolic belief system, for example, simplifies the job of the
voter. He need not spend an inordinate amount of time and energy in-
forming himself of every issue and listening carefully to the rhetoric of
the many rival candidates.[63]

The belief system also protects the individual from discomfort by
filtering out or minimizing the effect of stimuli that tend to threaten
his ego or identity. Stimuli that reinforce his ego are, on the other
hand, quickly perceived and even embellished. "This filtering process
means that a person is most aware of those aspects of his world which

[59] Ibid., p. 6.
[60] Ibid.
[61] Ibid., p. 12.
[62] Ibid., pp. 12–13.
[63] See Anthony Downs, *An Economic Theory of Democracy* (New York: Harper &
Row, 1957).

are compatible with his belief system and least aware of those which are antagonistic." [64]

Not all beliefs are of equal importance to the individual. Some beliefs, such as a religious person's belief in God, may be highly significant to that individual, while other beliefs, such as that the earth is round, may not be of much significance to anyone. Cognitive theorists call this the central–peripheral dimension. Beliefs that are central form the basis for a number of other, more peripheral beliefs. Alteration in a central belief therefore implies a number of changes in its associated peripheral beliefs. It follows that the more central the belief, the more significant it is in determining the individual's response to social and political stimuli—people and events. When politicians touch upon areas involving these central beliefs, and especially those concerned with the person's sense of self, or identity, the individual is often motivated to react in an emotional, defensive manner to protect from challenge a central belief upon which many other beliefs, attitudes, and opinions depend. On the basis of the central–peripheral dimension, political scientists distinguish between "position issues" and "style issues." Position issues involve direct, usually economic or material, self-interest. Style issues, on the other hand, have a more "indirect, subjective, and symbolic appeal involving individual self-expression." [65] While very few individuals will die to protect their income per se, a position issue, any number will die for "democracy," "liberty, equality, fraternity," "the Fatherland," great symbols of style issues that occupy a central—and usually unquestioned—segment of their belief system. Where the foundations of identity are challenged, as, say, by the fear of a foreign power traditionally viewed as an enemy, it is not difficult to recruit people willing to risk themselves. Style issues are capable of evoking strong emotions, especially when they touch upon beliefs that are central to the individual's self-esteem and his hold upon reality. Thus, while

> *an emotionally sensitive issue [may be important] to only a small*
> *segment of the electorate . . . , the capacity of such issues to arouse*
> *fervid response may be such that a Congressman would rather*
> *confront his constituents on a knotty economic matter like revision*

---

[64] Best, *Public Opinion,* p. 25. See also Leon Festinger, *A Theory of Cognitive Dissonance* (New York: Harper & Row, 1957). For an excellent discussion of the many elements involved in belief systems and public opinion, see Best, *Public Opinion,* pp. 5–47.

[65] Bernard R. Berelson, Paul F. Lazarsfeld, and William N. McPhee, *Voting: A Study of Opinion Formation in a Presidential Campaign* (Chicago: University of Chicago Press, 1954), p. 184.

of the tariff affecting the district's principal industry than on . . . a "style issue" like humane slaughtering.[66]

The deeper and more central the belief, the more explosive the response should the belief be questioned or threatened. An example of this may be taken from an analysis of the belief system of the Malagasies, of Madagascar. They were observed by the French psychiatrist O. Mannoni shortly after World War II. At that time, a large segment of their belief system revolved around the concept of "dependence," or the attainment of a vertical—that is, unequal, superior–inferior—relationship with another individual. The dependency relationship provided the Malagasy with a great deal of security, and relieved him of the burden of responsibility. All Malagasies sought to act within the rules and customs their ancestors had evolved. The belief in the efficacy and naturalness of this relationship was so great and so significant a part of the Malagasy personality that Mannoni writes: "To the Malagasies the soul is virtually identical with dependence. . . . It is that which unites the family and the tribe. . . ."[67] When the French colonizers broke the bonds of dependence on them that the semi-Europeanized Malagasy had developed, the Malagasy belief in dependence was challenged. The dependent Malagasies were abandoned by the Europeans before they had the opportunity to replace the belief in dependence with the European concept of human equality. Hence they were placed in a position of literally being threatened with losing the beliefs that defined their basic identity—a situation tantamount to losing their soul. The result was intense psychological insecurity, a fierce hatred of the European, fear, and subsequent political violence.[68]

Peripheral beliefs, attitudes, and opinions are of less importance and evoke much milder reactions when called into question. For example, the president of the United States has traditionally had considerably more leeway in foreign affairs than he has in the domestic arena, in large part because foreign policy concerns do not directly impinge upon the central part of the average American's belief system.[69]

66 F. I. Greenstein, *Personality and Politics* (Chicago: Markham Publishing Co., 1969), p. 59. See also Richard M. Scammon and Ben J. Wattenberg, *The Real Majority* (New York: Coward, McCann & Geoghegan, 1971), p. 30.

67 O. Mannoni, *Prospero and Caliban: The Psychology of Colonialism* (New York: Frederick Praeger, 1966), as cited in *When Men Revolt—and Why,* James C. Davies, ed. (New York: Free Press, 1971), p. 44.

68 Davies, *When Men Revolt,* pp. 45–46.

69 See Lloyd A. Free and Hadley Cantril, *The Political Beliefs of Americans: A Study of Public Opinion* (New Brunswick, N.J.: Rutgers University Press, 1967), pp. 59–60; and Scammon and Wattenberg, *The Real Majority,* p. 40.

Also significant for political analysis is the degree to which belief systems are integrated—that is, are interrelated and consistent with other beliefs. Lacking such integration, the individual is said to *compartmentalize* his beliefs, to cluster them in isolation from others. Isolation of beliefs leads characteristically to inconsistent or illogical behavior. An individual with a compartmentalized belief system may take contradictory stands on an issue or issues without feeling any pressure to reconcile contradictory beliefs or change his position on the issue. Each position relates to a different portion of the belief system—a portion that is isolated from the contradictory segment.

In one study, Lloyd Free and Hadley Cantril divided liberals and conservatives into *operational* and *ideological* classifications. The *operational liberal* responded positively to questions involving the *specific* application of tenets contained in the liberal philosophy, for example, government intervention in fighting poverty, educating the poor, providing medical care for the aged, and the like. The *operational conservative* took a negative stand on these specific, concrete issues. The *ideological* versions of the liberal and conservative were defined by response to *general* questions about philosophy and basic issue evaluation. Was the respondent in favor of the involvement of national government in state and local matters? Was he for or against government interference with property rights? (Did he believe that a trend toward socialism was bad?) How much communist or left-wing influence did he see in government? Respondents were then asked to identify themselves as liberals, conservatives, or middle of the road. The results indicated that there was a considerable degree of difference between operational position, ideological position, and self-proclaimed identification—differences so great, in fact, that one author was led to describe the responses as "schizoid." [70]

As table 2 indicates, the sample divided about equally in terms of self-identification among liberal, middle of the road, and conservative.

Table 2 *Operational and Ideological Spectrums and Self-Identification as
Liberal or Conservative*

	Operational Spectrum	Self-Identification	Ideological Spectrum
Liberal	65%	29%	16%
Middle of the road	21	38	34
Conservative	14	33	50

Lloyd A. Free and Hadley Cantril, *The Political Beliefs of Americans: A Study of Public Opinion* (New Brunswick, N.J.: Rutgers University Press, 1967), p. 46.

[70] Best, *Public Opinion*, p. 156.

But while 65 percent of the respondents fall into the *liberal* category on the operational spectrum, 50 percent of them hold *conservative* opinions on the ideological spectrum. This can be interpreted to mean that many Americans tend to separate or "compartmentalize" the practical and the ideological. An individual practicing cognitive compartmentalization might support a candidate who promised both to "end the current trend toward socialism" and to "support his constituents' requests for an urban renewal program financed by federal funds." Cognitive compartmentalization emerges strongly in questions concerning tenets of democratic philosophy and their practical application. In one sample of the general population it was found that 89 percent of the respondents "believe in free speech for all no matter what their views might be," while fully half the sample believe at the same time that a book with "wrong political views . . . does not deserve to be published." Over half the sample also maintained that "freedom does not give anyone the right to teach foreign ideas in our schools." [71]

Cognitive compartmentalization leads to a discrepancy between theory and practice, a division between the basic philosophical ground rules of the political game and the activities of everyday political life. Where compartmentalization is widespread, the people exercise less control over the government than they would if there were less compartmentalization. Compartmentalization enables elites to adopt inconsistent public policies. The resulting lack of "principles" among elites sometimes makes the masses cynical, and consequently unable or unwilling to do anything to bring the politicians into line with the political ground rules. The most recent U.S. example is the public response to the break-in and the tapping of phones at the Democratic party campaign headquarters in the Watergate complex, in Washington, D.C., during the 1972 election campaign and the subsequent spate of disclosures about shady campaign-financing practices. In a Gallup poll conducted in April 1973, for example, over half of a national sample (53 percent) thought that the whole thing was "just politics—the kind of thing both parties engage in." Many indicated their belief that "the same thing goes on all the time." Others said that "it's a commonplace activity these days." With the philosophy of democracy safely isolated from the practice of democracy in the minds of many citizens, it is indeed not surprising that such an event took place.[72]

---

[71] Herbert McClosky, "Consensus and Ideology in American Politics," *American Political Science Review*, 58, No. 2 (June 1964), 361–82, cited in Thomas R. Dye and L. Harmon Zeigler, *The Irony of Democracy* (Belmont, Ca.: Wadsworth, 1970), pp. 128–29.

[72] Citations taken from a Gallup poll reported in *Athens [Georgia] Banner-Herald and The Daily News,* 22 April 1973.

Other significant dimensions of belief systems involve the degree of their differentiation from corollary disbelief systems (the things people don't believe in); the content of basic beliefs about mankind and the world (for example, are they friendly or threatening?); and the nature of authority.[73]

On these dimensions, belief systems may be classified as "open" or "closed," and their possessors have respectively open or closed minds. Measured on a belief–disbelief continuum, the open mind possesses a high degree of differentiation on both the belief and disbelief ends of the continuum, for example, the open-minded person knows much about democracy, which he believes in, and just as much about communism, which he doesn't believe in. On the other hand, a closed mind with the same basic beliefs and disbeliefs will know much about democracy and very little about communism. He may have a good understanding of the Constitution and be able to discuss intelligently the separation of powers doctrine therein—perhaps he can even recite the tenth article in *The Federalist Papers*—but his understanding of communism will be woefully inadequate.

It follows that the open mind will be less inclined to *reject* someone who holds an idea that he opposes. The closed mind, on the other hand, knowing little about the groups, races, or philosophies that he dislikes or disagrees with, will be much more inclined to reject them—indeed, even to fear them. It is common to fear the unknown and to attribute to it far greater powers than it actually possesses. Those who believe that the communists, under the direction of the Soviet leaders, are taking over America usually know little about the history of the Communist party and even less about the leaders in the Kremlin to whom they attribute such superhuman power. A careful scrutiny of the Soviet political system would reveal examples of the same human failures —and successes—that characterize any polity. For example, the same leaders who apparently negotiated a highly favorable grain purchase from the United States were out-maneuvered in the Middle East by U.S. Secretary of State Henry Kissinger. However, a closed-minded person views Soviet leadership as so malevolent and skillful that nothing short of total ideological war can assure democratic victory or even parity. Realistic analysis is not possible for such a person, since the strong emotional commitment to the skillful malevolence of the Soviet political system filters out any contradictory information.

The open mind possesses a higher degree of interrelationship among the parts of the belief system than does the closed mind, which is more

[73] This and the following discussion rely heavily on Rokeach, *The Open and Closed Mind*.

compartmentalized. For the open mind, beliefs in social equality, for example, will not be isolated from beliefs concerning economic philosophy. Should the two conflict—as in the person who believes that all people are created equal but doesn't want to let blacks into the neighborhood—the open mind will recognize the discrepancy between the two beliefs and either attempt to reconcile them or suffer from the tension, which cognitive theorists call "cognitive dissonance," created by the contradiction. At minimum, the open-minded individual facing a dissonant situation is more likely to compromise, to move toward the middle ground, realizing that both beliefs have merits and that some form of moderation is necessary. The closed mind will be inclined to act as though each of the contradictory beliefs is unqualifiedly true. He will probably compartmentalize, battling, for example, to keep blacks out of his neighborhood while favoring the abstract notion of equality.

The two cognitive types also differ in the general content of their beliefs. The central beliefs of the open mind are such that he views the world as a friendly place, as benign rather than threatening to him. The closed mind, on the other hand, sees the world as a threatening place and views his own situation in the same manner. People are unfriendly; they are not to be trusted; they are "out to get him," "to take advantage of him," and the like.

Finally, the two types differ in beliefs about authority. The open mind holds that authority is not absolute. Laws, for example, are not made simply to be obeyed; rather, they exist to provide benefits for the people, to help rather than hinder the human condition. To an open mind, the spirit rather than the letter of the law is of primary importance. When the letter of the law ceases to accord with the spirit, the law should be changed. People, in turn, are not to be judged on the basis of their relationship to existing authority. Judgments should be based upon merits rather than on appeals to authority. The closed mind adheres uncritically to the dictates of authority, the letter of the law is of primary importance for him, and people are judged by their adherence to or deviation from the behavior advocated by the individual's significant authority or authorities.

Table 3 summarizes the major differences between these two cognitive types.

Obviously, the closed mind is the authoritarian type discussed by the authors of *The Authoritarian Personality,* and his characteristics were described above, under the term "dogmatism." The closed mind is characterized by rigid thinking, a strong bias toward "selective perception"—seeing what he wants to see—and gross oversimplification, especially when he is dealing with people and subjects that fall on the dis-

Table 3   *Differentiating Characteristics of the Open and Closed Cognitive Type*

	Open	Closed
Degree of differentiation	High in belief system High in disbelief system	High in belief system Low in disbelief system
Magnitude of rejection of objects falling on disbelief side of continuum	Low	High
Extent of communication between segments of belief and disbelief system (degree of compartmentalization)	High communication (Low compartmentalization)	Low communication (High compartmentalization)
Nature of people and society	People basically good; society basically nonthreatening	People basically evil; society and situation threatening
Nature of authority	Authority relative; authority a "means" to human "ends"	Authority absolute; people to be judged by extent to which they follow dictates of "the authorities"

Adapted from Milton Rokeach, *The Open and Closed Mind* (New York: Basic Books, 1960), pp. 55–56.

belief side of the continuum. This is manifested in dichotomous, "black–white," "them–us" thinking and reliance on stereotypes for elements of the disbelief system. For such an individual the world is a simplistic but threatening place. Intolerant of ambiguity, he tends to censor, by selective perception, parts of the multifaceted reality. Hence he perceives only a very few of the alternative paths to a goal. Thus he is able to pour all of his energy into its pursuit—to go "whole hog," to jump headlong into something without a full, careful elaboration of alternatives and the likely consequences of each. This gives a tinge of compulsiveness to his behavior. He is a man who is driven—because the world is threatening; because he can throw all of his energies into the single-minded pursuit of a single goal; because with a simple "all or nothing" response to any problem or issue he is terribly vulnerable to *frustration*. For his having censored his perception of the complexity of reality in making his decision in the first place also makes the chances good that he has overlooked or failed to take into consideration some very significant causal variables. Now, throwing everything into a single alternative, he has nowhere else to go should it fail; he has nothing else to draw upon in his response repertoire. Yet, failure is often the very path he is likely to find himself on given the significant forces he missed in choosing the alternative in the first place. The closed mind, then, is especially inept at participation in the political process, since such participation normally requires compromise. We will observe such difficulty in the next chapter, in the *active–negative* presidential character.

SUMMARY AND CRITIQUE

Harold Lasswell was one of the first social scientists to point out the significance of personality in political behavior. His *power seeker* went into politics to make up for an inadequate sense of self; such an individual would be below the *self-esteem* level of Maslow's need hierarchy. Both the dramatizing and bureaucratic personalities that Lasswell discusses could be called, in the language of later studies of personality, closed-minded authoritarians. The open-minded character, on the other hand, could be called a democratic personality type. This kind of person does not force the world into rigid, dichotomous categories of good and evil. He may go into politics because he wants to help others and to self-actualize, instead of to use power to compensate for low self-regard. He understands those who do not agree with him as well as those who do. Instead of creating an "enemies list," as did Richard Nixon when he was president, such an individual would be inclined to follow the path of President Gerald Ford, who in his acceptance speech noted specifically that while he had adversaries in Congress, he had no enemies. The open mind sees the need for accommodation; he is willing to compromise with his opponents. We would find this type of person at stage five of Kohlberg's scheme of moral development.

The concepts used in this chapter are not without problems. As soon as one begins "putting people into boxes"—for example, "He's a power seeker," "there's a Kohlberg stage five," etc.—some injustice is bound to be done to the individual. Because people are complex, and because enough behavior is determined more by circumstances than by personality type or cognitive structure, personality theorists do not claim total powers of explanation. Accordingly, we have noted the speculative nature of the subject matter in this chapter. At one point, for example, it was implied that Lenin was a stage six idealist. Was he? Christ and Mohandas Gandhi could also fit there. Do we want to lump these three together? Have we misclassified Lenin? If he is not a stage six, then where else does he fit? Although these are important considerations, easy answers are not forthcoming.

Students of cognitive and personality theory are sometimes criticized for being "mentalistic," for postulating the existence of concepts that cannot be adequately defined and measured. Critics argue that it is therefore not possible to subject such theories to definitive tests. Proponents of such theories thus appear to be indulging in a self-fulfilling prophecy. The *belief* in the existence of something called a closed mind or a power-seeking personality is so great that when we look for it in the empirical world our selective perception filters out any evidence to the contrary.

On the other hand, many breakthroughs in both social and physical science have come about because researchers were willing to act on hunches and take long shots that departed radically from the conventional wisdom. How much can we progress in our understanding of people and politics if we rely only on the empirically measurable, or on the orthodox commonplace? A personality theorist or a cognitive theorist might argue that science moves forward when people depart from the conventional, not when they let it set their horizons and limit their scope of inquiry.

Another criticism of cognitive and personality theory involves application of the "law of parsimony": when two or more explanations exist for the same phenomenon the simplest is to be chosen over the more complex. Offering positive inducements to engage in new behavior and negative inducements (sanctions) for the old behavior is often an extremely effective way to change a person's behavior. Why should one spend years in psychoanalysis plumbing the depths of personality and cognitive structure in order to change behavior patterns that can be effectively altered without any consideration of personality? The answers to such questions are neither simple nor clearcut. However, a personality theorist might respond by saying that tinkering with reinforcement schedules treats only symptoms, not root causes. In politics, it may be desirable to provide psychological testing for those running for public office.

As a politician's power increases, so do the consequences of his bringing his personality to bear upon the decisions he makes. The personality of a ward boss under the strong heel of a political machine may be of little import to his actions. Either he does his job or he is quickly replaced, with few or no adverse effects filtering down to his constituents. This is not true of people who occupy positions of great power and influence: The president of the United States, for example, is one of the most powerful people in the world. With nuclear weapons at his fingertips and the power of the veto over legislation passed by Congress, the president's personality and character type become extremely important indicators of the probable course of action that will be taken during his administration.

In the next chapter, the personalities of several American presidents will be discussed. Upon concluding that chapter the reader may want to ask himself whether personality type or political party and platform provide the best indicator of a president's behavior once he has attained that high office.

Selected Bibliography

ADORNO, T. W., et al., *The Authoritarian Personality* (2 vols.). New York: John Wiley & Sons, 1964.

BROWN, ROGER, *Social Psychology*. New York: Free Press, 1965.

CHRISTIE, RICHARD, and MARIE JAHODA, eds., *Studies in the Scope and Method of "The Authoritarian Personality."* Glencoe, Ill.: Free Press, 1954.

GEORGE, ALEXANDER L., "Power as a Compensatory Value for Political Leaders," *Journal of Social Issues*, 24 (July 1968), 29–40.

GREENSTEIN, F. I., *Personality and Politics*. Chicago: Markham, 1969.

HARVEY, O. J., D. E. HUNT, and H. M. SCHRODER, *Conceptual Systems and Personality Development*. New York: John Wiley & Sons, 1961.

KOHLBERG, LAWRENCE, "Stage and Sequence: The Cognitive-Developmental Approach to Socialization," in *Handbook of Socialization Theory and Research*, David A. Goslin, ed. Chicago: Rand McNally, 1969.

LASSWELL, HAROLD D., *Power and Personality*. New York: Viking, 1963.

LASSWELL, HAROLD D., *Psychopathology and Politics*. New York: Viking, 1963.

ROKEACH, MILTON, *The Open and Closed Mind*. New York: Basic Books, 1960.

SARTORI, G., "Politics, Ideology, and Belief Systems," *American Political Science Review*, 63 (June 1969), 398–411.

4

Applications of political personality theory: some examples of presidential character

While human behavior appears to be infinitely complex and to display a variety of forms, close president watchers conclude that a relatively limited variety of behavior is exhibited by men in this high office. Some, like Harry Truman, appear to be open-minded; others, like Richard Nixon, appear to be rather closed. Our discussion will begin with the closed-minded type.

Although closed-minded members of the political elite are unusual, since, as noted in the last chapter, they are ill-equipped for political life, they nevertheless appear from time to time. They usually rise suddenly from the lower-middle class or upwardly mobile working class. Their sudden rise to political prominence is frequently followed by an equally rapid decline of catastrophic proportions that brings a nation or a political party down with them. Under pressure, their selective perception tends to blind them to the realities of the situation, and a gross miscalculation or error of judgment leads to their downfall. The case of Richard Nixon is instructive. After a tour of military duty in World War II he ran for a seat in the House of Representatives. He labeled his well-entrenched opponent a front for communist and "un-American" elements and won the election. Shortly thereafter he sky-rocketed to fame as a member of the House Un-American Activities Committee. He worked hard to prove that Alger Hiss, a respected member of the Eastern establishment, was a former member of the Communist party. His efforts paid off, and he became a political celebrity.

By 1952 he was Eisenhower's running mate and from then on a national figure, continuously in the limelight. In 1974 he became the first president to resign, his administration in disgrace, his party in disarray. His obvious blindness to the seriousness of the Watergate affair and his gross miscalculation of opinion inside and outside government were largely to blame for his demise.

Richard Nixon is not unique. He fits the general pattern of people who emerge from the masses and go into politics to fulfill self-esteem needs. These *active–negatives,* as they are called by James David Barber in *The Presidential Character,*[1] are extremely hard workers who derive little intrinsic reward from their strenuous efforts.

Most active–negative political leaders possess four significant characteristics. First, they have a high *need for achievement,* "an enduring personality disposition to strive for success. . . ."[2] Second, they lack a coherent identity, or sense of self, which results from an inability to fulfill the *need for self-esteem.* As a result the active–negative tends to feel inferior. He is therefore inclined to lash out at the world to prove that he is "as good as the next person." Lacking faith in himself, he has little faith in others. At times he thinks people are "out to get him." All of this is indicative of a closed mind.[3]

A third characteristic is a general *inability to introspect,* to turn inward and analyze one's beliefs and behavior in the light of experience. For the active–negative, the locus of control or set of causative elements working in the universe tends to be external rather than internal.[4] He is likely to believe that "luck, chance, fate" and "powerful others" are the determining forces in life.[5] When this is combined with a high need for achievement, we see why the active–negative has trouble deriving satisfaction from his work. As he is driven from one success to another by the need for achievement and self-esteem, his inability to introspect prevents him from rewarding himself for his accomplishments. Hence the need for self-esteem remains unfulfilled and a cognitive or perceptual

---

[1] All of the presidents discussed in this chapter are included in Barber's study. The interested student will find *The Presidential Character* (Englewood Cliffs, N.J.: Prentice-Hall, 1972) worth reading.

[2] Harry J. Crockett, Jr., "The Achievement Motive and Differential Occupational Mobility in the United States," in *A Theory of Achievement Motivation,* J. W. Atkinson and N. T. Feather, eds. (New York: John Wiley & Sons, 1966), p. 191n.

[3] A recent empirical study indicates that individuals deprived of self-esteem are significantly more dogmatic or closed-minded than are individuals either below or above the self-esteem level of the Maslow hierarchy. See Jeanne N. Knutson, *The Human Basis of the Polity* (Chicago: Aldine-Atherton, 1972), p. 209.

[4] See J. B. Rotter, "Generalized Expectancies for Internal versus External Control of Reinforcement," *Psychological Monographs: General and Applied,* 80 (1966), 1–28. For an interesting application of these concepts to political motivation and behavior, see Stanley Allen Renshon, *Psychological Needs and Political Behavior* (New York: Free Press, 1974).

[5] These are Rotter's terms as cited in Renshon, *Psychological Needs,* pp. 90–91.

characteristic, the belief in external control, permanently blocks a psychological need. The result is a compulsive, driven individual who expends prodigious energy in an attempt to reach objectives that, once attained, provide little inner satisfaction. But while the active–negative is caught in this dilemma, he is in a profound sense released from another: Rarely if ever does he blame himself for failure. Rather, his strong belief in external control leads him to blame other people for any plight he might find himself in. Thus, under conditions of frustration we find him heaping blame upon "knee-jerk liberals," "overzealous aides," "pointy-headed intellectuals," a "poisonous and biased press"—in short, upon anyone and anything but himself.[6]

The fourth characteristic is that active–negatives go into politics *not* because they will it in advance or diligently prepare for it, but because the "accidents of fate" bring them close enough to politics for them to perceive that a political career can provide the feeling of power and manipulation that they desire as a means of compensating for low self-esteem. Thus, active–negatives are no more inexorably driven toward politics than individuals at other positions on the Maslow hierarchy.[7] In fact, individuals with strong beliefs in external control are less likely to be self-starters in politics than those who strongly believe in internal control. The latter, perceiving themselves to be largely responsible for their fate, might prepare from early on for a political career with little or no stimulation from the outside. The active–negative, on the other hand, believing in "the fates" or actions of "significant others," will find his path toward or away from politics contingent upon situations and events over which he has little or no control. Richard Nixon, for example, writes in *Six Crises* that the college he attended did not offer any political science courses. He became a "public man," as he puts it, only "because my fate sent me to Congress in 1946."[8]

THE MAKING OF AN ACTIVE–NEGATIVE PRESIDENT: A GLANCE AT THE LIFE AND TIMES OF RICHARD NIXON AND WOODROW WILSON

What makes an active–negative president, and what is he like? These questions are best answered by looking at actual cases. However, the reader should be aware at the outset that the source material that must

[6] While this presents difficulties for an active–negative's adversaries, it strongly reduces the probability that the active–negative political type will commit suicide under conditions of high frustration.

[7] Knutson demonstrates this empirically in *The Human Basis of the Polity*, p. 216.

[8] Excerpts on this and the following pages from *Six Crises* by Richard M. Nixon. Copyright © 1962 by Richard M. Nixon. Reprinted by permission of Doubleday & Company, Inc., and W. H. Allen & Co., Ltd.

be used when dealing with public figures, many of whom are no longer alive, poses certain problems. Inferences drawn from biographical material are made at a distance and cannot be independently validated. We cannot confirm a statement taken from a biography of Woodrow Wilson by having him take a personality-inventory test. Some politicians are extremely upset by psychological explanations of their political behavior, and they can hardly be expected to write anything that might be called a psychological study of themselves. This is true, for example, of Nixon's ghost-written book *Six Crises,* although we shall use it as source material nevertheless. Further, it is always possible to introduce into the analysis a systematic bias by selectively quoting and taking statements out of context.

The inherent subjectivity of the data makes it extremely difficult for anyone interested in political psychology to present an open-and-shut case for the validity of the inferences derived from material written about American presidents. Therefore, until further in-depth research techniques are developed and applied, the analyses of political figures that follow should be viewed as tentative rather than as conclusive and definitive. They are meant to be suggestive of the potential explanatory power of a psycho-historical approach to decision-making behavior. Final judgment rests with the reader. Do the analyses make sense? Do they fit what the reader knows about the people involved, about himself and those around him? Do the analyses raise significant questions for further research? What are the alternatives to these explanations, and how effectively do they answer the question, Why did a particular political event occur? Can we explain political behavior *without* considering individual motivations, perceptions, and social backgrounds?

Richard M. Nixon

We noted that Richard Nixon enjoyed a meteoric rise to political prominence. Such rises are characteristic of active–negative presidents primarily because a slower ascent leaves them open to being "found out" before they attain high office. Or, to put it another way, the slower the political rise of an active–negative, the greater the probability that he will make a major miscalculation that will end his political career *before* he encounters any opportunities to run for high office.

The need for achievement emerges strongly in Nixon's conception of work and his general orientation to life. The tasks that life presents are to be confronted with "tough, grinding" effort to produce a "superior performance." One can't let up; can't "take a break," or else he will stray from the path of hard work and therefore ultimate success. Nixon writes that *"taking a break" is actually an escape from the tough, grinding discipline that is absolutely necessary for superior performance. Many times I have found that my best ideas have come when I thought I could not work for another minute and when I literally had to drive myself to finish the task before a deadline.*[9]

This is not a quote taken out of context. Those who read *Six Crises* will be exhausted by the pervasive feeling that Nixon would like to stop, to rest and catch his breath, but somehow cannot. The reader cannot help but empathize with him in his efforts to climb what always appears to be a political Mr. Everest. The air is thin, he is carrying the heaviest load, the last bit of reserve energy is spent, but he reaches into the depths of his soul to find more. In preparing the Hiss case he "put in longer hours and worked harder than I had at any time in my life"; he "deliberately refused to take time off for relaxation or 'a break.' "[10] He states that as the time to broadcast the famous "Checkers speech" came near, "I drove myself harder and harder."[11] By this speech, in which he responded brilliantly to charges of his having a secret campaign fund, he saved himself from being dropped as Dwight D. Eisenhower's running mate in the 1952 election. His preparation for the speech parallels what he came to consider the norm in political decision making. The over-intense desire to achieve success is apparent by its symptoms.

In such periods of intense preparation for battle, most individuals experience all the physical symptoms of tension—they become edgy and short-tempered, some can't eat, others can't sleep. I had experienced all those symptoms in the days since our train left Pomona. I had had a similar experience during the Hiss case. But what I had learned was that feeling this way before a battle was not something to worry about—on the contrary, failing to feel this way would mean that I was not adequately keyed up, mentally and emotionally, for the conflict ahead. . . . Two of the most important lessons I have learned from going through the fire of decision are that one must know himself, be able to recognize his physical reactions under stress for what they are, and that he must never worry about the necessary and even healthy symptoms incident to creative activity.[12]

[9] Ibid., p. 105.
[10] Ibid., p. 40.
[11] Ibid., p. 108.
[12] Ibid., pp. 108–9.

Politics, then, became the avenue through which Nixon could work out the need for achievement by getting "keyed up" in "intense preparation for battle" where he would have to undergo the "stress of crisis" and the "fire of decision." The symptoms of overstress and anxiety were, to him, healthy signs of creativity.

As noted earlier, in the active–negative syndrome, the need for self-esteem occurs in conjunction with strong belief in external control.[13] Thus, the active–negative lacks faith in himself and relies heavily on others for judgments concerning the success or failure of his actions. When this external reinforcement is absent the active–negative tends to suffer from bouts of extreme pessimism and self-doubt. Yet this very dependence on others is frustrating to the active–negative because it is a sign of his own internal weakness and a further source of low self-regard. Thus, a strong dependence upon people is frequently accompanied by an equally strong tendency to denigrate them.

In keeping with his character, Nixon worked himself into an emotional and physical frenzy prior to the Checkers speech. When left alone in the last minutes before the speech he had doubts about himself. He looked to his wife for support. He writes:

I turned to Pat [Nixon] and said, "I just don't think I can go through with this one."

"Of course you can," she said, with the firmness and confidence in her voice that I so desperately needed.[14]

Politically his performance was superlative. However, he got so involved in the speech that he lost track of the time. He requested that viewers send letters and telegrams to the Republican National Committee indicating whether he should remain on the ticket, but he was cut off before he could give the address. Although this was a small matter, Nixon had no external cues immediately following the broadcast by which to evaluate the situation. He was left to judge his own performance. Gary Wills describes how Nixon evaluated the situation.

---

[13] Strictly speaking, this is a theoretical—albeit testable—rather than empirical statement. It appears to follow from the theories presented in this book and the case material in this chapter, but a great deal more empirical research is necessary before we can say that this relationship is firmly established. Because the field of political psychology is relatively new, this also holds true for many of the other relationships that explain political behavior.

[14] Nixon, *Six Crises,* p. 113.

> *He threw his [note] cards to the floor in a spasm, told Pat he had*
> *failed; when Chotiner [a member of Nixon's staff] came into the*
> *studio, elated by the skilled performance, Nixon just shook his*
> *head and claimed, "I was an utter flop." Outside the theater,*
> *as his car pulled away, an Irish setter friskily rocked alongside*
> *barking: Nixon turned, Bill Rogers would remember, and twisted*
> *out a bitter, "At least I won the dog vote tonight."* [15]

He went into a state of depression and dictated a letter of resignation
to his secretary. But by this time his staff was familiar with his behavior
during such periods and the letter was never sent. It is significant that
Nixon was afraid of this kind of situation, which he calls "the period
immediately after the battle is over." He attributes his greatest errors
of judgment to these periods, which are simply times when he has to
rely upon himself rather than his staff, party leaders, public opinion,
or other external guides. The absence of self-esteem and self-trust is
evident in the following statement:

> *The point of greatest danger for an individual confronted with*
> *a crisis is not during the period of preparation for battle [when*
> *one is constrained by the situation], nor fighting the battle itself*
> *[also a situation of constraint], but in the period immediately after*
> *the battle is over [that is, when the pressure is off]. Then, completely*
> *exhausted and drained emotionally, he must watch his decisions*
> *most carefully. Then there is an increased possibility of error*
> *because he may lack the necessary cushion of emotional and mental*
> *reserve which is essential for good judgment.*[16]

It cannot be said that this increased possibility of error stems from
the lack of emotional and mental reserve, for Nixon repeatedly tells
us that he is at his best when he is pushed to the limit. Rather, the
danger to him of the "aftermath of crisis" lies in the absence of external
cues. When these are removed, he is left with himself. The Nixon
traits—lack of spontaneity, planning for effect rather than substance
("How will it play in Peoria?"), and the mania for advance work
designed to foresee and prepare for every eventuality (hence extensive
surveillance of alleged enemies)—are all manifestations of his high reliance on external control and his low degree of self-esteem.

[15] Gary Wills, *Nixon Agonistes*, p. 110. Copyright © 1969, 1970 by Gary Wills.
Reprinted by permission of Houghton Mifflin Company, and by permission of the
author and his agents, Scott Meredith Literary Agency, Inc., 845 Third Avenue,
New York, New York 10022.

[16] Nixon, *Six Crises*, pp. 120–21.

Nixon's dependence upon others coexists with a rather dim view of human nature. In *Six Crises* he notes that opinion favorable to Hiss began to change as the accusations against him began to hit home. This was expected in Nixon's cosmology. "Hiss was learning what many people in politics had learned before him: those he thought were his best friends turned out to be the heaviest cross he had to bear." [17] The distrust of human nature and the closed-minded, "tough world" theme emerge in his discussion of the presidential election of 1960, which he lost to John F. Kennedy.

> *Some of my younger and less experienced staff members were bitterly disillusioned by the sudden desertion of some of those we had thought were close and loyal friends, even as the unfavorable returns started coming in. What I tried to tell them was that they, in fact, were the exceptions. Their loyalty through good times and bad was the rarity. Those who reach the top, particularly in the political world, have to develop a certain tough realism as far as friendships and loyalties are concerned.*[18]

Finally, the theme of cognitive closure and a low tolerance of ambiguity emerge at many points in his writing. One especially poignant passage concerns his philosophy regarding crises.

> *In meeting any crisis in life, one must either fight or run away. But one must do something. Not knowing how to act or not being able to act is what tears your insides out.*[19]

Ambiguity and indecisiveness are extremely hard for him to tolerate. As he puts it:

> *There is nothing more wearing than to suppress the natural impulse to meet a crisis head-on, using every possible resource to achieve victory.*[20]

Few persons today dispute the notion that family background and the early home environment significantly influence one's outlook on

17 Ibid., p. 45.
18 Ibid., p. 394.
19 Ibid., p. 143.
20 Ibid., p. 271.

life, and it is here that we may begin to look for clues for some of the processes that work toward the creation of active–negative character types. In the authoritarian personality study discussed earlier, interviews of individuals scoring high on the F scale tended to indicate that dogmatic, closed-minded people were likely to develop in a particular kind of family environment. Their parents were likely to be concerned about the family's social standing in the community. This status anxiety was transmitted to the child, who was forced to conform to current definitions of good behavior or suffer punishment. Punishment for bad behavior would be rendered not because the behavior was harmful to the healthy development of the child, but because it did not accord with the parents' conventional perceptions of what was proper.[21]

This kind of environment sets the stage for an individual high in external control and low in self-esteem. The great emphasis upon acting in line with the wishes and the rules that others lay down leaves little room to engage in behavior designed to fulfill one's own needs. The child's chances of fulfilling the self-esteem need and developing a healthy, positive identity are reduced. However, if the environment is not overly restrictive and authoritarian, the individual may be able to fulfill his needs within the context of the socially acceptable, in which case the extent of the postulated relationship between family background and character type is greatly reduced. Perhaps active–negatives are most likely to emerge in environments that are extremely authoritarian, restrictive, and status or rule conscious.

Nixon appears to have come from this kind of family. His mother's religion and his father's authoritarianism combined to create an environment in which achievement, cognitive inflexibility, and adherence to external standards were emphasized. His mother, Hannah Milhous, was a devout Quaker who saw to it that the family attended church services and religious functions not only three or more times on Sunday but several times during the week as well.[22] Hannah was the dominating force in the family. She represented "hard work and persistence," and the stringent control over emotion and behavior that inhered in her brand of Quaker fundamentalism. The emphasis upon strenuous effort and a firm, actually rigid adherence to the rules was reinforced by Nixon's father Frank, who espoused what has been called " 'Bible-pounding' Methodism."

---

[21] See T. W. Adorno et al., *The Authoritarian Personality* (New York: John Wiley & Sons, 1964) (2 vols.), especially chapter 10, pp. 337–89.

[22] Earl Mazo and Stephen Hess, *Nixon: A Political Portrait* (New York: Harper & Row, 1967), cited in Bruce Mazlish, *In Search of Nixon* (Baltimore: Penguin Books, 1973), p. 32.

*Don [Donald Nixon] remembers that "Mr. Herbert, a contractor,
said that father was the best carpenter in the area. He would
set a tough pace for others, and keep them at it. He worked us
kids to death." One of his endearing habits was to quote, constantly,
the Bible verse about man having to earn his bread in the sweat
of his brow.*[23]

Regarding his father, Nixon recalls that "Dad was very strict and
expected to be obeyed under all circumstances. . . . I learned early
that the only way to deal with him was to abide by the rules he laid
down." Not to do so meant "the touch of a ruler or the strap." [24]

The high need for achievement and the rigid, closed-minded conception of the universe characteristic of the active–negative appear to
be closely related, in Nixon's case, to the brand of Protestantism that
permeated the home. Max Weber captured the essence of this view of
life when he noted an apparent correspondence between certain Protestant minority religious sects, among them Calvinists and Quakers, and
what he called the "spirit of capitalism." This spirit was embodied in
the "Protestant ethic," which stressed "the earning of more and more
money, combined with the strict avoidance of all spontaneous enjoyment of life." [25] The end was not money itself, but a maximum exertion
directed toward succeeding in one's given line of work, one's "calling,"
as Martin Luther put it. For the fundamentalist Protestant,

> *. . . the valuation of the fulfillment of duty in wordly affairs . . .
> [was] the highest form which the moral activity of the individual
> could assume. This it was which inevitably gave every-day worldly
> activity a religious significance, and which first created the
> conception of a calling in this sense. . . . The only way of living
> acceptably to God was not to surpass worldly morality in monastic
> asceticism, but solely through the fulfillment of the obligations
> imposed upon the individual by his position in the world. That
> was his calling.*[26]

However, the basic motivation in the Protestant eschatology as represented by Luther and particularly Calvin was not positive. Luther

[23] Gary Wills, *Nixon Agonistes*, p. 170.

[24] Ibid.

[25] Max Weber, *The Protestant Ethic and the Spirit of Capitalism*, trans. Talcott
Parsons (New York: Scribner's, 1958), p. 53. (First published in 1904.) The Quakers
and Calvinists are mentioned on p. 44.

[26] Ibid., p. 80.

preached that one could not earn his way to heaven by good works, and Calvin's belief in predestination meant that God's decisions concerning who would be saved and who would be damned could not be altered by anything the individual did in his life on earth. All of this led to what Weber called a "disillusioned and pessimistically inclined individualism." [27] It also led to the kind of closed-minded, negatively evaluated activity characteristic of the active–negative. David McClelland, in *The Achieving Society,* sums it up well:

> *As Weber points out, this still left the practical problem for the*
> *ordinary believer of discovering whether he was one of the "elect"*
> *or not. Only by trying in every particular to be like someone*
> *in the Bible who was obviously one of the elect could he hope to get*
> *rid of the fear that he was damned forever. Thus the average*
> *Protestant had to behave well in every respect, not, as Weber points*
> *out, as a "technical means of purchasing salvation, but of getting*
> *rid of the fear of damnation . . . in practice this means that*
> *God helps those who help themselves. [The result is an individual*
> *who possesses] a systematic self-control which at every moment*
> *stands before the inexorable alternative, chosen or damned." Such*
> *a rigid rationalization of all of conduct when combined with*
> *the emphasis on doing one's duty in one's station in life destroyed*
> *the leisureliness, in Weber's mind, with which capitalistic enterprise*
> *had been pursued up to this time. The entrepreneur worked harder*
> *—in fact he could not relax for a moment. The Protestant labor*
> *force he recruited worked harder, and none of them could enjoy*
> *the increased fruit of their labors for fear of losing the conviction*
> *that they were saved.*[28]

McClelland contends that the worldly economic success of members of certain fundamentalist Protestant sects, particularly Calvinists and Quakers, stems not from the Protestant ethic per se, but from the motivation to achievement that it arouses in the individual. By insightful use of empirical data he shows that the rise of ancient as well as modern societies is significantly associated with the presence of a high degree of achievement motivation in the population, while their decline appears to follow from its scarcity.

One might ask why the kind of achievement motivation aroused by the Protestant ethic manifested itself initially in economic rather than

[27] Ibid., p. 105.
[28] David C. McClelland, *The Achieving Society* (New York: Free Press, 1967), p. 48.

other kinds of behavior. Or, to put it another way, does a high degree of achievement motivation lead inexorably to an emphasis upon economic rather than, say, political pursuits? While we cannot give a definitive answer to this question at the present time, some conjectures can be advanced. First, it would appear that economic behavior, particularly behavior of a capitalistic entrepreneurial sort, would be particularly pleasing to a closed mind highly intolerant of ambiguity and concerned with salvation. In this mode of activity one's degree of success from day to day can be directly measured in terms of profits. Second, at the time the fundamentalist Protestant sects emerged it is quite likely that the avenues of political advancement were closed off by the Catholic Church or members of more orthodox Protestant denominations. These groups were able to monopolize positions of social and political power at a time when public opinion favored religious contemplation and selfless good deeds as a path to salvation and looked with disdain upon the pursuit of monetary gain for what appeared to be selfish ends.[29]

When such avenues are not closed off, politics can be an equally rewarding pursuit for the young in a Calvinist or a Quaker family, with an equally measurable yardstick of success. Once in the political arena, one is faced with an ascending hierarchy of positions. In the United States, for example, each house of Congress contains an elaborate set of positions to which particular amounts of power, status, and publicity accrue. In addition, one can move up another ranking hierarchy from, say, governor of a state to a member of the House, then the Senate, and then—for the highly motivated—the presidency. Moreover, political campaigns in a nation without proportional representation can exert a particular appeal for a closed-minded individual high in achievement motivation. One can "gamble all" in a campaign where the outcome is particularly clear-cut. A candidate either wins or loses, and the dichotomy lends itself well to those who see life as a battle between good and evil. Once in politics, Richard Nixon "found his calling."

Nixon never rebelled against a home environment that others might have found unbearably stifling. He either did not seek or was not given an opportunity to define himself apart from his situation and the people who impinged so directly upon his life. His father ranted and raved about corrupt politicians: Richard decided to go into politics to clear it up. His mother preached pacifism: Richard sought to use politics as a means of bringing about world peace. His conception of self remained undefined and his need for self-esteem was never really met. However,

---

[29] Weber makes a similar point in *The Protestant Ethic*. See in particular pp. 56, 65–74.

by continually striving upward and losing himself in the effort to
achieve, he could avoid having to turn inward and face what must have
been an inner emptiness. Nixon's philosophy of life, as reflected in the
pages of *Six Crises,* reveals a number of important personal characteristics, particularly his tendency toward cognitive closure, a high need
for achievement, and a strong desire to avoid having to come face to
face with his lack of a coherent identity and need for self-esteem. He
writes:

> *One man may have opportunities that others do not. But what*
> *counts is whether the individual used what chances he had. Did he*
> *risk all when the stakes were such that he might win or lose all?*
> *Did he affirmatively seek the opportunities to use his talents*
> *to the utmost in causes that went beyond personal and family*
> *considerations?*
>
> *A man who has never lost himself in a cause bigger than himself*
> *has missed one of life's mountaintop experiences. Only in losing*
> *himself does he find himself.*[30]

All of these factors appear to have combined to produce an individual who was concerned primarily with the *process* of politics rather
than the *substance,* with the striving to win rather than the hard choices
involved in making and implementing policy. Nixon's high degree of
external control and desire to avoid having personally to make the
hard choices were manifested in the bureaucratic wall that he erected
around himself once in the White House. The emphasis upon process
appeared in his incessant traveling from one "White House" to another
—Washington, D.C., San Clemente, Camp David, Key Biscayne. Wills
captures the spirit of this emphasis upon process combined with inner
emptiness when he writes of the young Nixon in Whittier and his
fascination with the trains that passed the family's small grocery store:

> *He had no goal he stretched toward, down the track, since there*
> *was nothing in Whittier he rejected. He was not a rebel, against*
> *parents or school or religion. He transcended Whittier by an*
> *act of super-Whittierism. The flame of ambition burned absolutely*
> *pure in him. He had no bright alternative norms, real or*
> *delusionary, against which Whittier was tried and found wanting.*

30 Nixon, *Six Crises,* p. xvi.

His hero was the engineer, throwing a switch that set things in motion—the process, not the destination. . . .

When he yearned away, when his mind churned, . . . when the trains chugged, it was not the magic of a destination that moved him. . . . It was the sheer energy of the effort—the train panting, heaving tons of weight forward; men working all night to fill its capacious maw, their dim light hitting the snorts of steam, puffs of the white whale; then, with grind and pulsation, all the "physical symptoms of tension," the engine picked up labors of a whole neighborhood to run nimbly down its preordained track; not choosing, just pulsing on, making time, racing itself, improving its past mark.[31]

It would be an obvious exaggeration to say that, given Nixon's motivations and perspective, Watergate was inevitable. It would appear, however, that the narrow-minded pursuit of success at all costs led to something that could be called a "Watergate mentality." Once the deed was done, cognitive closure and the ingrained tendency to search outside himself for the causes of his plight kept Nixon from perceiving either the seriousness of the offense or his complicity in the coverup.

Woodrow Wilson

The case of Woodrow Wilson is in many ways similar to Richard Nixon's. Perhaps this is one reason why Nixon viewed Wilson in such a positive and affectionate light.[32] Wilson was the son of a Presbyterian minister who preached a brand of Calvinism similar to that described by Weber in his analysis of the Protestant ethic. The atmosphere of religion and disciplined study permeated his home. Wilson came to accept the metaphysics and moral precepts of Calvinism without question. One's future was predestined; the individual was an "agent in the hands of the Almighty." Therefore, Wilson believed that when one acted in accord with the proper moral principles he "had nothing to fear from kings, governments, even the hand of fate." [33] Calvinistic religious tenets formed the bedrock of Wilson's belief system. As he

---

[31] Wills, *Nixon Agonistes,* pp. 167–68.

[32] Ibid., p. 395.

[33] Ray Stannard Baker, *Woodrow Wilson: Life and Letters, Volume I: Youth 1856–1890* (Garden City, N.Y.: Doubeday, Page, 1927), p. 70.

once put it, "as far as religion is concerned, argument is adjourned." [34] In situations where Wilson believed that religion and moral principles were at stake, he would tolerate no compromise.

Wilson's father, Dr. Joseph R. Wilson, was a commanding figure—large, strong, and in full control of his intellect and wit. Ray Stannard Baker, Wilson's official biographer, writes that the man "had an indescribable quality of presence." Wilson once said that "if I had my father's face and figure it wouldn't make any difference what I said." [35] Wilson's mother, deeply religious and somewhat reserved, was devoted to the family.

Dr. Wilson was not only a strong personality, he was a perfectionist as well, and he took it upon himself to educate his son. He was a stickler for the clear expression of ideas and the proper use of English. "He never permitted the use of an incorrect word or sentence. If there was any doubt, the boy was sent flying for the dictionary." [36] Dr. Wilson would ask his son, who was called Tommy at home, if he understood something. If the answer was affirmative he would ask Wilson to write it out and bring it to him. He would then go over it meticulously. "If the Doctor came upon anything that seemed in the slightest degree ambiguous, he would demand what exactly was meant. Tommy would explain. 'Well, you did not say it,' Dr. Wilson would snap, 'so suppose you try again and see if you can say what you mean this time.'" Sometimes Wilson would have four or five tries before his father was satisfied. The father's philosophy was that "if a lad was of fine tempered steel, the more he was beaten the better he was"; his admonitions were frequently accompanied by a biting and sometimes sarcastic wit.[37]

In their psychological study of Wilson, the Georges conclude that the overall result of this relationship was an individual with a damaged sense of self-esteem and much unconscious resentment of an all-powerful father. This is quite plausible, recognizing of course the difficulty of interpreting what lies below consciousness. One thing is sure. Wilson was not able to seek self-esteem through rebellion against his father, because of the high degree of love, respect, and genuine devotion the two felt towards each other. A flavor of their relationship is conveyed

---

[34] Ibid., p. 68. Also see Alexander L. George and Juliette L. George, *Woodrow Wilson and Colonel House: A Personality Study* (New York: John Day, 1956), p. 5. The Georges' study of Wilson is an excellent example of a political biography with a psychological perspective. Many of the conclusions regarding the causes of Wilson's behavior discussed in this chapter are contained in their study.

[35] Baker, *Wilson: Life and Letters, Vol. I*, p. 31.

[36] Ibid., pp. 37–38.

[37] George and George, *Woodrow Wilson and Colonel House*, pp. 7–8; Baker, *Wilson: Life and Letters, Vol. I*, pp. 37–39.

by their terms of address: "My precious son," "Darling boy," "My beloved father." [38] From Woodrow Wilson's perspective, however, the relationship was not an equal one. He always felt inferior when in the presence of "my incomparable father." According to Baker, Wilson did not make an important decision without consulting his father until he was 40 years old.[39]

Throughout his life Wilson was dependent on the outpourings of sympathy and ego-bolstering from friends who he felt were in total agreement with him. He needed this support to keep going. The Georges contend that Wilson associated friendship or love with identity of opinion because as a boy "Wilson had learned that if he did not earn his father's approval by instantly accepting his every opinion and behaving accordingly, he stood in danger of forfeiting his father's love." [40] This seems logical, although not empirically provable. It appears certain, however, that as an adult Wilson needed a continuous flow of reassurance from people who expressed complete agreement with him on any issue of importance. He would tolerate no ambivalence and would break completely with anyone who was not in agreement, regardless of how long or intense the friendship had been.[41] Colonel House, a close friend and trusted advisor during most of Wilson's years in the White House, knew this and at one point confided to his diary that when Wilson asked for advice or suggestions, "I nearly always praise at first in order to strengthen the President's confidence in himself, which is strangely lacking." [42]

Like Nixon, Wilson appeared to be high on external control. His early reliance upon his father and his later heavy reliance upon friends for psychological support are indicative of this. So too was his fear of introspection. He sought to keep tight control over his thoughts. The Georges write, "All his life long, he shrank from reflecting upon his inner motivation. . . . He once wrote in a letter that he had always had an all but unconquerable distaste for discussing the deep things that underlie motives and behavior." If in fact he harbored a great deal of unconscious or semi-conscious resentment against his father, he had to keep a firm lid on things. "He once remarked that he never dared let himself go because he did not know where he would stop." [43]

38 Baker, *Wilson: Life and Letters, Vol. I*, p. 34.

39 Ibid., p. 30; George and George, *Woodrow Wilson and Colonel House*, p. 9.

40 George and George, *Woodrow Wilson and Colonel House*, p. 31.

41 Ibid., p. 30.

42 Ibid., p. 113.

43 Ibid., p. 11. Also see pp. 130, 164–65.

The upbringing that led to low self-esteem and cognitive closure in matters of religion and moral issues also inculcated a strong need for achievement. For the young Wilson achievement imagery had at least three sources: the perfectionistic demands of his father, Calvinistic religion, and the example set by members of his family. Wilson's forebears on both sides of the family were solid, illustrious individuals. Wilson's maternal grandfather was a well-known Presbyterian pastor. His paternal grandfather had been an editor, a state legislator, a bank director, and a judge. He was "a man of extraordinarily strong convictions and utter fearlessness in the expression of them." [44] Wilson's father, himself, as we said, a Presbyterian minister of considerable renown, had graduated at the head of his college class and was also a college professor. A greatly admired uncle received the doctorate with highest honors from Heidelberg and became a professor and a college president. He, too, expressed the strength of his convictions. When the Church objected to his teaching Darwin's theory of evolution, he chose to give up his position at Columbia Theological Seminary rather than compromise over the issue.[45] All of this combined to make Wilson an ambitious and determined person at an early age. "Papa," he once proclaimed as a child at the dinner table, "when I get to be a man, I'm going to have a lofty position." [46]

Wilson's early training, his home environment, and the examples set for him by his forebears tended to point him toward political rather than economic routes to success and a "lofty position." Although not wealthy, the Wilsons were comfortable, and issues of social, moral, and political import took precedence over any desire to advance the family's economic status.

Wilson departs from the general pattern of the active–negative discussed earlier in that he did not gravitate toward politics by chance or accident. Rather, he expressed a keen interest in government and the techniques of leadership at a relatively early age. He had a fascination for constitutions and debate. At approximately the age of nine he organized the Lightfoot Club, a group composed of his boyhood friends with Wilson as the president. The Lightfoots played baseball and held meetings in his father's barn. Wilson wrote a constitution for the club and saw to it that debates were conducted according to Robert's Rules of Order. "It was as natural for the boy Tommy Wilson to be interested in such an organization as this, and to be its leader, as it was to draw his breath." Where did Wilson get this interest? "His

---

[44] Baker, *Wilson: Life and Letters, Vol. I,* p. 9.
[45] Ibid., pp. 6–23.
[46] George and George, *Woodrow Wilson and Colonel House,* p. 8.

father was not his teacher in this, nor Professor Derry [head of a boy's school Wilson was attending at the time]; it did not even come out of his early reading: it was the essence of the boy's gift." [47]

This "gift" may have reflected a desire, perhaps even a compulsion, to achieve power to dominate others and thereby to compensate for the extent to which he submitted to his father's will. "Not only did Wilson grow up with a taste for achievement and power: he must exercise power *alone*. He could brook no interference. . . . Throughout his life his relationships with others seemed shaped by an inner command never again to bend his will to another man's." [48] The Georges argue persuasively that Wilson was not able to see this inner command for what it was—a desire for control over others, for power. If individuals with a tendency toward cognitive closure are intolerant of ambiguity, then a conscious confrontation between Wilson's religious beliefs and his pursuit of power for personal reasons would place him in a catastrophic psychological dilemma. His solution, the Georges contend, was to keep the conflict below the level of consciousness by masking the drive for personal power behind a pursuit of great moral principles. The result was a classic case of the active–negative behavioral syndrome. Wilson could be charming, convincing, compromising, and very open-minded when engaging in the *pursuit* of power. But once power was attained and his position on an issue he felt important was *challenged,* he would shift the basis of the argument from politics to ethics and morality. He would then view himself as a representative of the highest moral principles and his opponents as the personification of evil. Now he could become intractable, irascible, and completely closed, allowing no compromise whatsoever and breaking irrevocably with anyone who deviated in the slightest degree from his position.

Wilson's latent interest in politics became manifest at Princeton. As an undergraduate he was fascinated with politics and the lives of great political leaders. He was puzzled as to why England had so many great men and America so few. His answer was that in the American political system decisions were made in secret by committees through a process of compromise and bargaining that did not place any premium on one's ability to sway a large audience with a cogent argument and the power of the spoken word. This kind of decision making did not interest him. He was fascinated with England's parliamentary form of government. Here issues were debated in the House of Commons, and the success of the government depended upon the powers of persuasion and oratory expressed by the party leaders. This was much more to his liking than

[47] Baker, *Wilson: Life and Letters, Vol. I,* p. 45.
[48] George and George, *Woodrow Wilson and Colonel House,* p. 11.

what he perceived the U.S. form to be. Wilson loved debate and was fascinated by oratory. He would go out into the woods at Princeton and practice the speeches of Gladstone, Daniel Webster, Patrick Henry, and others.[49] He also practiced public speaking in his father's church when it was empty. This is where he "found himself," this is where he was at home—at the podium, before a large audience that he could sway with the sincerity of his convictions, the power of his argument, and the eloquence of his speech. And why this fascination? He tells us in an article on oratory that he wrote for the *Princetonian*. "What is the object of oratory? Its object is persuasion and conviction—the control of other minds by a strange personal influence and power." [50]

Upon graduation Wilson went to law school thinking that the legal profession would advance him toward a political career. He quickly became dissatisfied with what he felt were the mundane things that lawyers had to concern themselves with. He longed for the podium and a chance to lead large numbers of people. He went into college teaching, achieved a national academic reputation, and became president of Princeton University. Despite his outstanding success and the power and prestige of his position, he remained dissatisfied. He felt that politicians looked down on academics; that they may be consulted but were not in the thick of things. "I am so tired of merely talking profession!" he once said at one point. "I want to *do* something!" He longed for the political arena and the direct employment of his powers of oratory and persuasion over the masses. He was "a leader in search of a cause," a man with "a nebulous desire to lead" rather than a specific program or set of goals that could be implemented through the exercise of political power. Like Nixon and other active–negatives, he was captivated by the process of leading rather than the ends to which it was directed.[51]

In the first decade of this century the Democratic party was rent by dissension. The populists or progressives were the major faction. They were led by William Jennings Bryan, the party's unsuccessful presidential candidate in the elections of 1896, 1900, and 1908. The main planks in the progressive program called for an increased money supply to relieve indebted farmers; more stringent government control over railroads, utilities, and other large corporations and trusts; direct election of senators and a return to popular government in cities then being run by corrupt political machines. Well-heeled, nonagrarian Democrats who didn't want the boat rocked too much thought that Bryan was an

49 Baker, *Wilson: Life and Letters, Vol. I*, pp. 90–92.
50 Ibid., p. 92; George and George, *Woodrow Wilson and Colonel House*, p. 15.
51 George and George, *Woodrow Wilson and Colonel House*, p. 29.

irresponsible radical, and they looked for a leader of stature and more conservative views who could lure the rank and file away from him.

Wilson looked like a good prospect. He was eloquent, was known in the intellectual world, and appeared to possess conservative economic views. As early as 1902 he had come to the attention of George Harvey, editor of *Harper's Weekly* and a man with good connections in conservative Democratic circles. Wilson was known to be critical of Bryan. In a New York speech of 1904 he said that the country "will tolerate no party of discontent or radical experiment." He felt that Bryan had "no brains" and "no mental rudder." Bryan's faction should "be utterly and once for all thrust out of Democratic counsels." In 1906 Harvey began to promote Wilson's candidacy for president.[52]

Despite Wilson's desire to enter politics, he did not immediately seize this opportunity. Once on the approaches to political power he moved with great care. He was eager, but "it was an eagerness tempered by caution, lest he be led unwisely into situations which might reduce his ultimate political potentialities. After all, he was over fifty years of age, too old to take frivolous chances." [53] At first he sought to put an end to Harvey's efforts for fear that the time was not ripe. Editorial response to Harvey's ideas was favorable, but Wilson was completely outside the Democratic party apparatus. He had never held elective office.

Wilson began to speak out more frequently on political matters. Harvey continued to round up conservative support. Wilson made his job easier by coming out against organized labor and government regulation of business. He increased the tempo of his activities with an eye toward nomination as the Democratic presidential candidate in 1908, although he realized that his chances were slim. He campaigned on a platform that Link describes as "reactionary." Bryan was nominated once again.[54]

If Wilson were truly an idealist, a man primarily concerned with holding true to his philosophy, then he would find it extremely difficult to change his political beliefs to increase his chances for election to high political office. If he were primarily after power, however, such changes would not be so difficult. However, by 1910 he was speaking as sincerely and as vehemently in favor of progressivism as he had earlier on behalf of conservative, *laissez-faire* capitalism.[55]

In 1910, after fifteen years as the minority party in the state, New Jersey Democrats were looking for a gubernatorial candidate who could

---

[52] Arthur S. Link, *Wilson: The Road to the White House* (Princeton, N.J.: Princeton University Press, 1947), pp. 96–100.

[53] George and George, *Woodrow Wilson and Colonel House*, p. 47.

[54] Link, *Wilson: The Road to the White House*, p. 122.

[55] See ibid., pp. 122–32.

defeat the opposition and sweep a majority of Democrats into the legislature on his coattails. Harvey approached Boss Smith, head of the Essex County Democratic machine, and suggested Wilson. Smith wanted a seat in the U.S. Senate and needed a Democratic majority in the legislature to obtain it. Wilson looked like he might be able to swing the state back to the Democrats. Never having held elective office, he was not tainted by association with corrupt machine politics. He was a respected figure who could effectively be presented as a progressive, thus reducing opposition to the machine. Despite Wilson's reputation for independence, if the machine put him up, he would be obligated to it. Smith also liked the idea of being a kingmaker. He queried national party leaders about Wilson's chances for the presidential nomination in the election of 1912 and was pleased by the response. Rewards were bound to follow if he had a direct hand in helping a future president. Wilson said that he would accept the nomination if it was handed to him with no strings attached. Smith agreed after being assured that, if elected, Wilson would not attempt to destroy the machine.

The machine got Wilson nominated as the Democratic candidate, much to the chagrin of some of the party progressives, who well knew that he was the candidate of the bosses and the financial interests. He immediately surprised the opposition by boldly expressing his independence. "I did not seek this nomination. It has come to me absolutely unsolicited. With the consequence that I shall enter upon the duties of the office of Governor, if elected, with absolutely no pledge of any kind to prevent me from serving the people of the state with singleness of purpose." [56] This, the machine leaders must have felt, was grand rhetoric, and they must have been gratified by the support it brought their candidate from the progressive Democrats. What he had said was not completely true, however, for Wilson had assured Smith and his forces that he would not attempt to destroy them. But once on the stump it became apparent that victory could not be achieved without bringing the independent Republicans over to his side. To do this he would have to capitulate entirely to the progressive forces and repudiate, perhaps even promise to dismantle, the Democratic machine. And this he did. A victory at the polls would signify that he was head of the party, he said in a speech delivered, at the end of the campaign, in Smith's own territory. This showed a blatant disregard for Smith's power over party machinery in Essex County and Boss Robert Davis's control over the apparatus in Hudson County. If elected, Wilson continued,

[56] Ibid., p. 167.

he would use his position to regenerate the party.[57] His behavior could be interpreted to mean that promises meant little to Wilson when he was engaged in a battle for political power.

The events in New Jersey were of national significance. The Democratic party was searching for a leader who could breathe new life into it and take votes away from the Republicans in the presidential election of 1912. Wilson won a smashing victory in the gubernatorial race, and control over the state legislature passed to the Democrats. Congratulatory messages poured in from outside the state, including one from William Jennings Bryan. The governor-elect of New Jersey was now a national political figure.

Although a novice in politics, Wilson proved adept at political maneuvering. Soon after his election he was placed in the middle of a struggle between the machine and the progressives. James E. Martine, a colorless progressive Democrat, won a majority of votes in a preferential primary for the U.S. Senate, and while the election did not bind the state legislators, the outcome could not be ignored without reneging on a major plank in the progressive program, the direct election of U.S. senators. Boss Smith, who had not run in the primary, wanted the seat and sought to enlist Wilson's aid in rounding up enough votes in the legislature. If Wilson expected to pass the kind of eye-catching legislation that would solidly cement him with a national progressive constituency, he could not afford to alienate progressive New Jersey legislators. He would have to oppose Smith, even though he apparently felt that Smith was the better candidate.[58]

Wilson's response to this situation is interesting in view of his later behavior as president. First, it showed that he could be extremely adept and open-minded when he was unsure of the extent of his own power. He could listen to advice and heed it, and he could work with all of the factions arrayed around an issue. Second, it illustrated his penchant for cloaking a battle for political power as a struggle for great moral principles. Finally, it indicated that once he entered into a battle for power he was inclined to accept nothing short of total victory for himself and total defeat of the opposition. The implications of this first major political battle were that Wilson could compromise in the effort to attain high position, but he would become rigid and inflexible once his power was challenged.

Wilson initially sought in a dispassionate and open-minded manner to dissuade Boss Smith from running. He was unsuccessful. He wrote

[57] Ibid., p. 198.
[58] Ibid., p. 214.

that he "had learned to have a very high opinion" of Smith, that it was "grossly unjust" for the progressives of both parties to view Smith "as the impersonation of all that they hate and fear; but they do, and there is an end to the matter." [59] Wilson waged a tough campaign. He ignored the party organization and spoke personally with nearly all the Democratic legislators. He made ringing speeches in which he declared that the fight was part of "the agelong struggle for human liberty." [60] At the onset of the battle he confided in a letter that "Smith has at last come openly out and defied me to defeat him: and defeated he must be if it takes every ounce of strength out of me." He would have to "do some rather heartless things" that were "against all the instincts of kindliness in me. But you cannot fight the unscrupulous without using very brutal weapons." [61]

Wilson's fiery oratory captivated the progressives and their representatives in the press. The machine politicians were not used to Wilson's straightforward frontal assault. He promised morality and good government rather than patronage, but perhaps most persuasive of all was his popularity with the voters. Old-line politicians could not fail to take note of this chink in the armor of the organization. They began to vacillate. Martine was elected, and Wilson immediately set out to capitalize on his second stunning success.

As noted earlier, Wilson assumed that as governor he would be head of the state party. Once in office he used this view of his position to push actively for progressive legislation. He could argue forcefully for his position; he could cajole when necessary; and he could threaten. Recalcitrant legislators were often brought into line by Wilson's threat to go over their heads and take an issue directly to the people. He was the popular leader of a party swept to victory on a sea of votes from progressive Republicans. Few wanted to see him undermine their chances for reelection. Through the efforts of Wilson and progressives of both parties, a number of significant reform bills were passed.

The next legislative session was another matter. The Smith machine was disgruntled by the treatment it had received and refused to work actively for Democratic candidates. Republican voters were less inclined to cross party lines, for it looked like another victory for the Democrats would again give them the lion's share of the credit for reform legislation. This could only increase their chances of winning the forthcoming presidential election. A Republican majority was returned to the legislature.

[59] Ibid., pp. 213–14; and Ray Stannard Baker, *Woodrow Wilson: Life and Letters, Volume III: Governor 1910–1913* (London: Heinemann, 1932), p. 112.

[60] Link, *Wilson: The Road to the White House*, p. 232.

[61] Ibid., p. 223; and Baker, *Wilson: Life and Letters, Vol. III*, pp. 120–21.

Wilson did not play an active role in this session. He found it very difficult to cooperate with people who were not in total agreement with him—or totally under his thumb. Also, his efforts to get the Democratic presidential nomination took him away from the statehouse. The legislative session of 1912 is noteworthy primarily for the number of times Wilson vetoed legislation. In the national political picture this mattered little, for by now his reputation was already made.

As this brief political history indicates, on the eve of Wilson's nomination and subsequent election to the presidency he was a man with limited experience in the give-and-take of democratic politics. His rise from president of Princeton to president of the United States was truly unique. He had advanced far and fast because he was able to use the advantages of the active–negative character to achieve unusual successes at Princeton as well as in the governorship. He could concentrate his energies, he could work indefatigably toward accomplishing a single goal, he could argue his case with great sincerity and intensity. At times it appeared that he was able to break the back of his opposition through sheer strength of will and power of persuasion. At each critical juncture in the path to the White House he was able to escape the disadvantages of the active–negative character. The governorship came to him at a time when he was under increasing fire at Princeton for his inability to compromise with the opponents of some of his policies, and he went on to the presidency at a time when the situation in New Jersey had changed to such an extent that his brand of leadership could no longer bring political success. Had he not been distracted, it is possible that he would have become involved in a politically debilitating feud with the New Jersey legislature. In one letter he referred to the legislators as "small men" who "have ignorantly striven to put *me* in a hole by discrediting themselves!" He considered the Senate majority leader, also a university professor, to be a man with "plenty of brains, of a kind, but without a single moral principle to his name! I have never despised any other man quite so heartily. . . ." [62] The Georges write:

One suspects that only the lure of achieving higher office enabled him to contain his rage. The situation had that explosive ingredient— what he perceived as a challenge to his authority in his sphere of competence—which never failed to rouse in him an all but ungovernable need to make his will prevail.[63]

[62] George and George, *Woodrow Wilson and Colonel House,* p. 103.
[63] Ibid.

As it happened it was only in the White House, when America's entry into the League of Nations was at stake, that the denouement occurred.

Wilson's case illustrates the need for caution in applying social-psychological theories to specific cases. For example, Wilson was not simply a closed-minded individual. When it appeared expedient, he was ready to compromise his political and economic beliefs, or revise long-held opinions of people. He did an about-face regarding Bryan, whom he wound up actively courting to get the presidential nomination. On subjects about which he knew little he was open to advice. Much of his legislative program of 1911 resulted from consultation with progressive Republicans, who sometimes drafted bills for him. Even his final obsession, the League of Nations, did not spring originally from him. Wilson, little interested in foreign affairs, relied on Colonel House, a close friend and trusted advisor, to keep him abreast of such matters. It was the efforts of House that suggested to him the worthiness of the idea of an international organization designed to ensure world peace.[64]

Wilson, however, seemed to assume a closed perspective on subjects in which he felt competent. As he put it at age thirty, "in matters in which I have qualified myself to speak I could never be any man's follower." [65] He also became closed when he believed that his power was being challenged. In this situation he would become exceedingly dogmatic and would simply refuse to compromise, preferring to lose everything in battle rather than to compromise. One of his first tasks as president was to guide a tariff-reform bill through Congress. When newspapers reported that he was considering some form of compromise in order to get the bill through the Senate he was piqued: "I am not the kind that considers compromises when I once take my position." [66] Rather than being an isolated instance, this was characteristic of Wilson once he had taken a stand. In such cases he would view his opponents as personal enemies rather than as fellow politicians with constituencies to represent and elections to face.

Although he fought desperately to command the heights, he could not seem to give himself credit for victory. This, we have hypothesized, stemmed from a strong sense of external control and low self-esteem. "I am so constituted that, for some reason or other, I never have a sense of triumph . . ." he wrote in response to a note from a friend congratulating him for getting the tariff-reform bill through Congress—something that his two predecessors, Theodore Roosevelt and William

64 Ibid., p. 189.
65 Ibid., p. 117.
66 Ibid., p. 135.

Howard Taft, had not been able to do.[67] His response to a challenge to his views on anything falling within his area of expertise, and his inability to find ego reinforcement in success, suggest that psychological motives and characteristics were more important than political principles as guides to his behavior.[68]

Once this kind of individual is in the presidency he is easily susceptible to viewing every challenge to his program as a supreme test of his ability and mettle. It is usually only a matter of time before a situation arises in which victory cannot be won without compromise. Instead of opting for a compromise solution to the issue, the active–negative turns it into a holy war. He proceeds to divide his supporters, and often the country, into "for" and "against" factions. The nuances are overlooked, points of agreement between factions are forgotten, and the political atmosphere fills with rancor. Perhaps the major political significance of this type of person is that his behavior is so predictable—at least in hindsight. Having gone this far, however, we cannot take the next step and say that this type is necessarily better or worse than any other type. An active–negative president may be perfectly suitable when the country faces crisis; Congress is bottling up needed legislation because it is hopelessly entangled in political disputes; and people are losing confidence in the government. In his first term, Wilson whipped Congress into action and because of his persevering and dogmatic leadership it passed a spate of progressive legislation that might have been years in coming without him. The main problem with the active–negative seems to be that once he has taken a stand on an issue that is important to the fulfillment of his psychological needs, he is no longer able to discriminate between situations that call for compromise and those that do not. This is of little import in respect to minor, transient issues, but of extreme significance in respect to major issues of war or peace, prosperity or depression, democracy or dictatorship.

Wilson's unsuccessful battle with the Senate over ratification of the Treaty of Versailles was what sealed his fate and lent, perhaps unfairly, a tinge of failure to the image of his presidency. The treaty contained a provision establishing a League of Nations, which many hoped would mark the beginnings of a successful effort to avert another great international conflict. On the eve of World War I the major contending nations had been among the most powerful in the world. At the end of the war, both victor and vanquished were exhausted, spiritually as well as financially. Because the United States was now the strongest nation in the world, proponents of the League felt that if the

---

[67] Ibid., p. 137.

[68] The Georges reach a similar conclusion, ibid., pp. 115–16.

United States did not join and fill the power vacuum it would be only a matter of time before the hatreds inflamed by the war would unite with deep-seated feelings of nationalism and again plunge Europe into armed conflict.

It is not illogical that Wilson came to see himself as a great peacemaker, and the League of Nations as a truly great contribution that he could make to the world. His religion taught that the believer must do good works. He was the leader of a nation that was not bound by secret treaties or secret agreements to extract territory and concessions from defeated nations. He believed that he could inspire the peoples of the world and their leaders to adopt a more idealistic form of international relations. All his life long he had been fascinated with constitutions. Now "he saw an opportunity to write nothing less than a constitution for the whole world." [69] The League concept, clothed in the proper moral garb, fully aroused Wilson's idealism. This was precisely the kind of situation that inflamed his passion for hard work and sacrifice, and for the acceptance of his views without modification. He adopted the idea as his own and refused to share the credit for any part of it with either his close advisors or the Republicans, whose feelings were particularly important because the United States would not be bound to the League unless the treaty which contained it was ratified by a two-thirds majority in the Senate.[70]

In his first term as president, Wilson was able to get his program through because the Democrats controlled both houses of Congress and he used party loyalty and patronage to good advantage. In the first half of his second term he was able to use the nonpartisan atmosphere fostered by America's involvement with the war in Europe to keep Congress in line. Just before the congressional election of 1918 he asked the voters to register their acceptance of his leadership by voting for Democratic congressional candidates. This was a mistake, for the presidential party usually loses seats in off-year elections. As it was, the Republicans gained control of both houses of Congress. Since Wilson himself had made the connection between the election and approval of his leadership, he might have been expected to view the outcome as a sign that he should share more of the decision-making power with the opposition, especially with regard to the nature and form of the proposed League of Nations. The need for cooperation was even more compelling because a long-time critic, Henry Cabot Lodge, was now Republican floor leader and chairman of the Senate Foreign Relations Committee. If the treaty and therefore the League were to have any

69 Ibid., p. 198. Also see pp. 197–99.
70 Ibid., p. 208.

chance of ratification, Republican views would have to be solicited and given some consideration.

Wilson was blind to the need for compromise. It appeared to many at the time, and many more in retrospect, that he did everything possible to alienate the Republicans. He refused to see the recent election as a victory for the opposition, but instead took it as a victory for himself. He chose to believe that the people had voted against those Democratic candidates who were "luke-warm" in their attitudes toward him.[71] He decided to represent the United States personally at the Paris peace conference despite his recent repudiation at the polls. The delegation he chose to attend with him contained individuals favorable to his views—"yes men" as they were widely described at the time. No senators were invited in either official or unofficial capacities. Information about the proceedings was withheld from Congress "so that, as he publicly proclaimed, the Senate would find it difficult to make alterations." [72]

Despite Wilson's heavy-handed behavior, senatorial opinion toward the League was generally favorable, and the consensus was that the treaty would get through the Senate over the opposition of Lodge if only some modifications could be made in the League covenant. The Senate was restive after years of Wilson's browbeating; now that the war was over and the urgency of recent events was past, many senators felt that some recognition of the legislative role should be forthcoming from the executive. A few changes, more symbolic than substantive, would be sufficient. Further, the elections of 1920 were on the minds of many Republicans, and it would not do to let Wilson take all of the credit for something that had such widespread public support. Lodge and Wilson, bitter enemies, had locked horns many times before. Lodge was dead set against the League, but could not get enough votes in the senate to defeat it. His strategy was to append reservations to the League. The reservations would be mild enough to gain the support of pro-League senators, so the treaty would probably pass with the necessary two-thirds majority. The following passage summarizes Lodge's perception of the situation:

On one occasion, Senator Watson said to him, "Senator, suppose that the President accepts the Treaty with your reservations. Then we are in the League, and once in, our reservations become purely fiction."

[71] Ibid., p. 238.
[72] Ibid., pp. 205–8.

Lodge smiled. "But, my dear James, you do not take into consideration the hatred that Woodrow Wilson has for me personally. Never under any circumstances in this world could he be induced to accept a treaty with Lodge reservations appended to it."

"But that seems to me to be a rather slender thread on which to hang so great a cause," Watson replied.

"A slender thread!" exclaimed Lodge. "Why, it is as strong as any cable with its strands wired and twisted together." [73]

Wilson steadfastly refused to accept the reservations even though this was the only way in which the treaty could pass the Senate. Moderates in both parties made a number of attempts to get him to change his mind. He would not budge. "The Senate must take its medicine," he said at one point.[74] He demanded that Senate Democrats vote against the treaty with reservations attached. Enough followed him to ensure that it came up short of a two-thirds majority in the final vote.

To the question whether active–negatives are more likely to come from mass or elite backgrounds there is not yet a definitive answer. However, some inferences can be made, subject to further, much-needed research. To avoid the deficiency motivation characteristic of the active–negative—that is, to reach the level of self-actualization at which challenges are enjoyed and issues are sought out that demand creative solutions—a person must have adequately fulfilled the lower needs. But the masses, and particularly members of the blue-collar and lower-middle classes who are upwardly mobile and therefore much in need of achievement, would appear to be less able to attain such a self-actualization level because they are more vulnerable to economic dislocation than are those of higher status with equally high needs for achievement.

Maslow contends that at each step toward self-actualization the individual is presented with a choice between staying with what is safe, secure, and familiar, and advancing into something that is unfamiliar and perhaps a bit frightening. "Apparently growth forward customarily takes place in little steps, and each step forward is made possible by the feeling of being safe, of operating out into the unknown from a safe home port, of daring because retreat is possible." [75] A testable hypothesis would be that the greater a person's degree of economic insecurity, the less likely is he to venture toward self-actualization and the more likely is he to cling tenaciously to what little he has.

[73] James E. Watson, *As I Knew Them* (Indianapolis: Bobbs-Merrill, 1936), p. 213, as cited in ibid., pp. 279–80.

[74] Ibid., p. 311.

[75] Abraham H. Maslow, *Toward a Psychology of Being*, 2nd ed. (New York: Van Nostrand, 1968), p. 32.

If circumstances preclude a "safe home port," the person must expend most of his energy, perhaps even most of his life, trying to build and protect it. This emphasis upon protection of material and social position is likely to extend to protection of self, and to produce an individual more inclined toward defending self-esteem from threat than toward growth. We might recall the correlation between stable democracies and high levels of economic development, and some of the reasons for it. Where most of the population is living in poverty, people are too busy trying to eke out a bare living to pay any attention to politics, and government is run by elites alone. Where most of the population is above the poverty mark but too economically insecure to achieve an adequate sense of self-esteem, democracy is still not feasible because the population lacks the confidence necessary to inform itself about issues and act on their information. Further, where people are primarily concerned with ego-defense, authoritarian leaders who engage in displays of raw power and blame foreign and domestic enemies for everyone's problems will be more consonant with the needs of the population than moderate, open-minded democratic types.

This is not to say that active–negatives cannot emerge out of the elite. Wilson's family enjoyed economic security and was part of the intellectual elite of the day. But the combination of religious fundamentalism, an extremely dominating father, and a high need for achievement, we hypothesized, made him deficiency motivated. His psychological uncertainty did not evolve out of the insecurity that is part and parcel of a marginal economic existence. The other three presidents that Barber labels active–negative—Herbert Hoover, Lyndon Johnson, and Richard Nixon—came from distinctly marginal surroundings. Hoover was the son of a blacksmith who died just as his business began to yield returns; his devout Quaker mother took in sewing to make ends meet. After her death, when he was eight, he was passed from one relative to another. Nixon's family lived from hand to mouth, barely making it on the income from their grocery store. Johnson grew up in conditions of rural poverty.[76]

THE ACTIVE–POSITIVE PRESIDENTIAL PERSONALITY: TWO CASE STUDIES

The active–positive president is, as might be expected, markedly different from the active–negative. He is not burdened with deep-seated feelings of inadequacy. While he may admit to some weaknesses, he feels confident that he can measure up to the demands of the presidency.

[76] See Barber, *The Presidential Character*, pp. 120–21, 130–32, 396–99.

He is not obsessed with the job. He can step back, laugh at himself, admit mistakes and learn from them. He exhibits the characteristics of the self-actualizer. Power is not used to seek fulfillment of the lower, egocentric needs like self-esteem. It is put in service of the higher self-actualization needs—"the pleasure of production, creation and growth of insight." [77]

The self-actualizer in politics is motivated more by a desire to achieve personal growth and improve the lot of people in general than by a desire to enhance his reputation and advance his political career. He can be more spontaneous, more detached, more autonomous, and more open to experience than the active–negative, who tends to spend his effort defending his ego rather than opening it up to new paths of development. The self-actualizer is likely to possess a "superior perception of reality," to use Maslow's phrase, for he is free of the ego-defensive person's high personal involvement in important issues. He can take a more objective look at an issue and weigh the relative merits of arguments on all sides. Two presidents who embody the active–positive personality are Franklin D. Roosevelt and John F. Kennedy.

Franklin D. Roosevelt

Franklin Delano Roosevelt was born into an environment that was quite different from those of the young Herbert Hoover, Richard Nixon, and Lyndon Johnson. Roosevelt's mother Sara Delano and his father James came from old, well-established families of considerable wealth. James Roosevelt, a patrician gentleman, investor, businessman, and country squire, preferred life in the country to activity in the world of finance, and so he endeavored to spend as much time as he could overseeing things at his 900-acre Hyde Park, New York, estate with its commanding view of the Hudson River. Franklin was an only child and his world was secure. Whatever problems his father may have encountered in his business dealings were rarely brought home to Hyde Park, perhaps because he was rarely bothered by them. He had enough wealth and enough contacts in financial circles to weather any economic crisis or depression that was likely to come along.[78] His mother had been raised in an environment where "the older members of the family carefully kept away from the children all traces of sadness or trouble or the news of anything alarming." Her early life was "tranquil and

---

[77] Ibid., pp. 210–11.

[78] See Kenneth S. Davis, *FDR: The Beckoning of Destiny, 1882–1928* (New York: Putnam's, 1971), p. 29; and Frank Freidel, *Franklin D. Roosevelt: The Apprenticeship* (Boston: Little, Brown, 1952), pp. 12–13.

unmarked by adult emotions." She brought her son up in the same tradition.[79]

Although Roosevelt was an only child in a wealthy family conscious of its social position and proud of its ancestry, he was neither overly spoiled nor unduly pressured to succeed. His parents practiced aristocratic moderation and reserve. Their home was spacious and comfortable but not lavish. They believed in *noblesse oblige*, but not in overdoing it. They were not "comers." Having no sense of social inferiority, they did not need to push their son to success:

> *They enjoyed a security so fundamental, so stable, so permanent*
> *that they need feel no envy over the meteoric rise of the*
> *multimillionaires. Likewise, they could feel little anxiety over*
> *the misery of the jobless and hungry, save to do their Christian*
> *duty towards assisting these unfortunates.*[80]

They kept their contacts limited to members of their own class. Before Franklin was a year old his parents saw to it that his name was entered on the list of students who would be allowed to enter Groton, an exclusive boys' prep school.

Roosevelt's parents were firm but not strict: Sara said, "We never subjected the boy to a lot of unnecessary don'ts, and while certain rules established for his well being had to be rigidly observed, we never were strict merely for the sake of being strict." [81] Nor were rules absolute. If the boy was in doubt about a rule he could try doing without it, as in the case of following the daily routine that his parents had established for him. At one point he expressed the opinion that this routine was infringing upon his freedom. Other than returning for meals at the proper time, he was allowed to do as he pleased. One day of this seemed sufficient, for the next morning he voluntarily returned to the regular pattern.

Franklin was sheltered but not so much so that he developed a totally unrealistic view of the world. On occasion his parents would leave him with relatives or his nurse while they went on trips (when he was four, they were away for three months). While his parents were certainly important forces in his life, they were not overly domineering, and they did not quash any emerging sense of self-esteem by forcing him to conform to a mold of their making. His father "believed in keeping Frank-

---

[79] Davis, *FDR,* p. 40.
[80] Freidel, *Franklin D. Roosevelt,* p. 14.
[81] Cited in ibid, p. 23; and Barber, *The Presidential Character,* p. 214.

lin's mind on nice things, on a high level; yet he did it in such a way that Franklin never realized that he was following any bent but his own." [82] James made plenty of time available for his son. The two could frequently be seen riding on inspection tours of the estate. In the winter they went tobogganing, sledding, and ice-boating together; in the summer they fished and sailed. "The learning the boy experienced was full of action and specifics—how to deal with fog, trees, ice, postage stamps, fish. There was not much theory in it and not much room for standing by and watching." [83]

Roosevelt's family provided him with the safe, secure port from which he could launch wholeheartedly into the search for self-esteem and then self-actualization. His quest for self-esteem appears to have been successful, and we can infer that he was able to generalize from love of self and family to love of others, to the human species in general. He enjoyed people, and displayed good humor and self-confidence. Will Rogers describes a visit to the White House shortly after Roosevelt's inauguration to the presidency. At this time the nation was in the grip of the worst depression in its history; factories were closed, millions were unemployed, people were in despair. "Where is the president?" Rogers asked Eleanor Roosevelt. "Wherever you hear the laugh," she replied. Rogers described the president's mood.

> *I don't mean that he is unmindful of all those out of work. But,*
> *by golly, he is not sitting down moping over it. He has a grin on*
> *his face. This man absolutely believes that he is going to help*
> *those people. It is not conceit, it is absolute confidence. . . .*
> *He knows things are going to be all right.*[84]

Roosevelt had a way with people. Even his arch-enemies found it hard to resist his charm.

> *Huey Long of Louisiana, the "Kingfish," described the problem*
> *in ornithological terms. According to him, Roosevelt was a scrootch*
> *owl—unlike Herbert Hoover, who was a hoot owl. A hoot owl*
> *would knock a hen off the roost and seize her as she toppled down.*

---

[82] Freidel, *Franklin D. Roosevelt*, p. 23; also cited in Barber, *The Presidential Character*, p. 214.

[83] Freidel, *Franklin D. Roosevelt*.

[84] M. S. Venkataramani, ed., *The Sunny Side of FDR* (Athens, O.: Ohio University Press, 1973), p. 4.

"But a scrootch owl slips into the roost and scrootches up to the hen and talks softly to her. And the hen falls in love with him, and the first thing you know, there ain't no hen." [85]

The Roosevelt family was religious, but not compulsively so. In his youth Franklin could find all sorts of reasons for avoiding church on Sunday. He was influenced strongly by the atmosphere of Christian humanism that permeated Groton School under Headmaster Endicott Peabody, an Episcopal clergyman. Peabody felt that the manor-born had an obligation to serve those less fortunate than they, and he tried to develop a social conscience in his students. He expressed the hope that some of his charges would go into politics. The emphasis was on improving the human condition, not on a fight between good and evil, or the saved versus the damned. Franklin could hardly help being receptive to Peabody's call, for it augmented his great admiration for his politically minded cousin Theodore, who had set quite an example —first as governor of New York, then as president of the United States.

After Harvard Franklin went to law school but, bored with academic studies, did not finish. He missed the excitement of student elections and the many extracurricular activities that had earlier occupied most of his time in college and brought him into almost continuous contact with people. What could he do in life that would allow him to realize the ambitions and hopes of the parents who provided so well for him? What could he do that would conform to the standards of service to others that Peabody so fervently espoused at Groton? And what could he do that would satisfy his desire to be in the thick of the action, where important decisions were being made and where something was always going on?

He lacked neither money nor social success and prestige, especially after he married President Theodore Roosevelt's niece. More of the same could hardly satisfy his ambitions. Further, he "had come of age in an era when neither business nor social triumphs any longer carried . . . acclaim. The new age acclaimed success in building overseas empire, or in achieving humanitarian or political reform, and Roosevelt was swept along by the age." [86] He had money, he had a relative who was president, and he liked people.

Roosevelt's pleasure in dealing with people was indicative of his self-actualizing personality. Although he was born at the top, he did not let his circumscribed social orbit narrow his perspective. In his first

[85] Ibid.
[86] Freidel, *Franklin D. Roosevelt*, p. 85.

real job, as a clerk in charge of municipal cases for a New York firm, he met the masses face to face. "For the first time Roosevelt came into continual direct contact with those who were neither of his own class nor servants of his class. And he liked it." [87] Politics was a natural for him, and he began dreaming about the presidency while still a law clerk. Asked by representatives of the Democratic party to run for the state Senate, he accepted even though it appeared that he stood little chance of success.

Like Wilson, he announced his independence of machine politicians. By dint of hard campaigning and the disarray in Republican ranks, he managed to get elected on his first try, in the Democratic landside of 1910. He went into public life as a 28-year-old amateur.

He lacked the power, national reputation, and rhetorical skill that enabled Wilson to begin forcing his opponents into line as soon as he entered the political arena. And he did not step into anything like the power vacuum that gave Wilson such an opportunity to shape things according to his will. He began, however, like Wilson, with a zealous attempt to block the election of a machine candidate to the U.S. Senate; Roosevelt's quarry was William F. Sheehan. After much ado and publicity, Roosevelt and his group of insurgents were outmaneuvered and outgunned. They succeeded in getting Sheehan's name dropped, but the wily Tammany politicians forced them into a situation in which they had no choice but to vote for James O'Gorman, another, albeit less offensive, member of the Tammany organization.

Had Roosevelt been a closed-minded person he would probably have quickly met defeat. Roosevelt soon discovered that the political situation in Albany, the state capital, was not amenable to a basic restructuring along the lines of good versus evil: The Tammany organization contained good as well as bad politicians, the former including Alfred E. Smith and Robert F. Wagner, Sr.; and it spoke for the urban masses, a significant but often overlooked portion of the New York electorate. Besides, the organization was powerful enough to end his career if he let idealism and strongly held preconceptions about policy matters blind him to political reality. Whether he liked it or not, he always had to remain ready to compromise his princples in the face of superior opposition forces in his party. "Backed by reformers, Roosevelt late in 1911 attacked a charter for New York City that was sponsored by Tammany. Senate lines were closely drawn and Roosevelt was in a position to kill the charter, but Tammany . . . threatened to reshuffle congressional districts and put . . . [him] into a hopelessly Republican

[87] Ibid., p. 83.

area." [88] He voted for the charter, and then went back to criticizing it. Under these conditions it was hard for him to avoid an open-minded approach that looked at more than one side of a political issue. Roosevelt learned from his first experience in politics.

Above all, he learned the lesson that democratic politicians must learn: that the political battle is not a simple, two-sided contest between opposing parties, or between right and wrong, or between regulars and irregulars, but, as in the Sheehan episode, a many-sided struggle that moved over broad sectors that touched many interests. [89]

Such lessons are not always easy to learn. A closed-minded individual using politics as a vehicle for overcoming low estimates of self would have withered under the heat of forced compromise and the need to adopt a piecemeal, never-all-or-nothing approach to policy-making. Roosevelt learned to get along with the Tammany leaders, even though they successfully engineered his defeat in a senatorial primary election in 1914. His sense of self-esteem appeared to be strong enough for him to view his opposition as nonthreatening. They were fellow politicians, not implacable foes. He did not engage in a personal vendetta against them or react in an intense, emotional fashion in an effort to prove his superiority despite the costs to government and party. This sense of accommodation helped get him the Democratic vice-presidential nomination in 1920.[90]

He remained active in party affairs despite the defeat of the Democratic party's presidential ticket throughout the 1920s, and despite a serious bout with polio that left him permanently crippled. In 1928 he was the party choice in the New York gubernatorial election, which he won by a narrow margin. He increased his margin of victory in 1930, partly through skillful campaigning and partly because of a deepening economic depression that worked against the incumbent Republicans. As the popular governor of the most populous state in the Union—a state with a set of problems nearly as great as those faced by the nation at large— he was able to obtain the Democratic presidential nomination in 1932.

It may be argued that Roosevelt's political success on the eve of his

[88] James MacGregor Burns, *Roosevelt: The Lion and the Fox* (New York: Harcourt Brace Jovanovich, 1956), p. 43.

[89] Ibid.

[90] See ibid. for a statement on what is in effect Roosevelt's healthy sense of self and identity.

election to the presidency in 1932 was due to several characteristics of his personality. His ability to get along with people kept him from so alienating powerful figures that they became implacable enemies who torpedoed his plans at the crucial moment (as Lodge did to Wilson) or worked so strenuously and with such vehemence that they were able to sabotage his political career. His willingness to compromise and to seek a middle road when faced with entrenched opposition spared him from ever staking his whole career and reputation on any single issue, let alone on an issue on which his position was bound to fail. His outlook, his experience in the deadlocked New York legislature, his tolerance of ambiguity and his desire to experience life—to grow by acting in it rather than defending himself by reacting to it—made him more prag-matic than idealistic, more practical than philosophical.

> *Roosevelt loved to juggle ideas, he hated to antagonize people,*
> *he was looking for proposals that would appeal to a wide variety*
> *of groups, whatever the lack of internal consistency. . . . Roosevelt*
> *had no program to offer, only a collection of proposals, some*
> *well thought out . . . others vague to the point of meaninglessness.*
> *On the whole he was remarkably temperate; there was little passion*
> *or pugnacity [in his campaign speeches].*[91]

Roosevelt entered the White House with more spirit than philosophy. Perhaps more than anything else, the nation needed reassurance in its time of troubles. He provided it. In his inaugural speech he confidently told the nation that "the only thing we have to fear is fear itself." His confidence was not like that of the true believer, however. It did not stem from belief in a political ideology, "an oversimple, holistic ex-planation for what is wrong, who and what are responsible for what is wrong, and what must be done to set things right." [92] A deeply held ideology leads its holder to believe that he has a monopoly on the truth, that there is but one correct answer to every question, one "right way" to look at everything. Roosevelt's confidence came from a belief in his talents and abilities, not from a carefully developed ideology. Those imprisoned by a rigid ideology surround themselves with people who agree with them and filter out information that does not fit with their view of the world. Roosevelt did the opposite. Without an articulate ideology to guide him, he looked to others. Tolerant of contradiction

[91] Ibid., pp. 142–43.

[92] James C. Davies, *Ideology: Its Causes and a Partial Cure,* University Programs Modular Studies (Morristown, N.J.: General Learning Press, 1974), p. 2.

and anomaly, he sought information from a diverse group of individuals.

Open- and closed-minded political leaders differ mainly in their attitudes toward power and the use and treatment of information. Nixon and Wilson sought to set themselves up as powerful, distant figures who were above the day-to-day hurly-burly of politics. They were inclined to use power to *dominate*—to get others to do their own bidding—either through exhortation and appeal to the president's high principles or, if that failed, by threats to destroy a politician's power base. Nixon tried to streamline the executive office bureaucracy and centralize the process of decision making. He sought to simplify the administrative structure and eliminate duplication. Both Nixon and Wilson were uncomfortable with information that contradicted their strongly held views. Nixon, who isolated himself behind a wall of White House staff that filtered out dissonant information, stands in marked contrast to Roosevelt. With regard to the use of power, Roosevelt sought to *manipulate* rather than overtly dominate. "The Roosevelt tactic, instant and instinctive, was to kill by kindness." At one point when a group of dissatisfied veterans arrived in Washington to demonstrate, Roosevelt met with the leaders, saw to it that their followers had an adequate place to encamp, provided food and medical attention, and sent Mrs. Roosevelt down to talk with the men and lead a few singing sessions. " '[Former President] Hoover sent the Army,' said one veteran; 'Roosevelt sent his wife.' " [93]

Another tactic was to set up competing organizations headed by administrators with widely diverging personalities. This "kept his administrators unsure, off balance, confused, and even exasperated. With ambition pitted against ambition, the power of decision remained more securely in his own hands." [94] Roosevelt's New Deal came to life in a plethora of acronymic administrative units designed to deal with the depression. Many of them had overlapping jurisdictions. For relief and public works, for example, there were FERA, NRA, CWA, PWA, and WPA. Harold Ickes and Harry Hopkins were the chief administrators, and although their jurisdictions overlapped, their personalities did not. Hopkins was an intense man who sought with missionary zeal to get as much to as many as possible—with little regard for the cost or the coherence of the organizations involved. Roosevelt could ask him "to invent jobs for four million men and women in thirty days" and expect to get it done, one way or another. Ickes, on the other hand, "was a very careful, deliberate administrator, who took pains to examine personally every

---

[93] Arthur M. Schlesinger, Jr., *The Coming of the New Deal* (Boston: Houghton Mifflin, 1959), p. 15.

[94] Louis W. Koenig, *The Chief Executive*, rev. ed. (New York: Harcourt Brace Jovanovich, 1968), p. 164.

detail of every project and the disposition of every nickel that it cost." [95] One agency would offset the other, and each administrator would provide a different view of the situation. Roosevelt could divide and rule, and keep the communications channels open at the same time. He ruled as a broker rather than a dictator. The result was something akin to organized chaos. Nevertheless it appeared to the nation that something was being done to fight the depression—something short of either revolution or a return to unbridled laissez-faire capitalism.

The overall effects of Roosevelt's administration are difficult to assess, even in retrospect. The biggest problem with what may be called his open-minded leadership is a certain lack of overall vision that allows government to intervene where necessary in as efficient and unobtrusive a manner as possible. At it was, under Roosevelt's leadership the federal government extended its influence—perhaps unnecessarily—into many sectors of the nation, and he became the father of a large and expensive government bureaucracy and a strong executive branch of government. Despite this, economic troubles continued to plague the nation until World War II set the factories and farms in full motion. If these are considered negative aspects of his administration, they should be weighed against the fact that democracy remained a stable, viable form of government in the United States during a time when many in Europe, and even in the United States, began to see dictatorship as the only way out of social and economic crisis.

John F. Kennedy

Like FDR, John Fitzgerald Kennedy was born into an affluent family that had political connections. His maternal grandfather was the mayor of Boston. At the time of John's birth his father Joseph was the assistant manager of a shipyard—a position that brought him into contact with Franklin D. Roosevelt, then Assistant Secretary of the Navy.[96]

Joseph Kennedy's grandfather was one of countless Irish immigrants who came to the United States during the potato famine. His father, an upwardly mobile saloonkeeper who rose to moderate political and economic prominence in the rough-and-tumble world of the Boston Irish, wanted his son to "make it" in the outside world. Joe took the first step by going to Harvard, which "could be a hard experience. There would be no crude discrimination of the bullying sort, but a subtle, cruel exclusion, to remind one that he was an intruder in a

95 Robert E. Sherwood, *Roosevelt and Hopkins* (New York: Grosset & Dunlap, 1950), pp. 52–53.

96 Barber, *The Presidential Character*, p. 295.

place to which others were born." [97] At Harvard Joe was "doubly an outsider." He was marginal because he was a Catholic and of Irish descent in a Protestant environment where there were no Irish among the socially prominent; and he was marginal because he was leaving the Irish-Catholic community.[98] Only a powerful ambition to succeed and gain recognition could keep one going in these circumstances, and whatever slights Joe suffered only fanned the flames of his desire to get ahead.

Joe's intense ambition could have been transmitted to the children in an ego-deflating, mind-closing manner had he not been away on business so much—and had he not been so successful. If, like Frank Nixon, he had encountered a series of failures in his endeavors to get ahead, the children might have been targets of his frustration, and their self-esteem would have suffered. As it was, "Joseph devoted sixteen hours a day to business; before long he was traveling extensively, piling up the fortune that would make him a millionaire well before he was 35." [99] Rose Kennedy took over most of the tasks involved with raising and caring for the children. "She wanted her children to be 'stimulated by their parents to see, and touch, know, and understand, and appreciate'; so stimulated, they should find their way." [100] She would take a firm stand on the rules necessary for getting along in the family, but was careful to explain the reasons for the rules rather than demanding authoritarian submission to them.

To be sure, there was an emphasis on achievement. JFK said at one point, "I can feel Pappy's eyes on the back of my neck." Rose Kennedy supported this and Joseph pushed it when he was home. He "pressed his children hard to compete, never to be satisfied with anything but first place. The point was not just to try; the point was to win." [101] In theory, at least, there was enough achievement motivation in Joseph Kennedy to drive any child to distraction. But the children were frequently left on their own with the servants and, as noted above, Joseph was away much of the time. In addition there were nine children in all. Although Joseph favored his eldest son Joseph, Jr., and set him up as an example to the others, Rose appeared more objective and equitable, even a little distant in focusing her attention. All of these circumstances moderated the intensity of the parental desire for achievement that was transmitted to any one child. The result was a level of achievement high

[97] Richard J. Whalen, *The Founding Father: The Story of Joseph P. Kennedy* (New York: New American Library, 1964), p. 25.

[98] Ibid.

[99] Barber, *The Presidential Character*, p. 295.

[100] Ibid., p. 296.

[101] Ibid., pp. 297–98.

enough to allow one to complete his education and get started on a successful career without being so great that the individual was driven to compulsive behavior. Had John Kennedy been an only child, the story might have been different.

The Kennedy family was close, warm, and supporting. Joe's financial success shielded his children from the quiet desperation, the life and death struggle that cannot help but have a strong impact on the offspring of parents with high aspirations for them but without the economic ability to give them a reasonable chance to fulfill them. The active competition between John and his older brother, Joseph, Jr., ensured that the former would not come out with an either/or, all-or-nothing view of reality. John often came out second best. This taught him how to settle for less than everything he hoped for. In the process he discovered that life was more than a continuous struggle between absolute victory and total defeat.

As ideal types, it may be argued that Roosevelt was the better example of an open-minded political leader with a strong sense of self-esteem. The Kennedys were socially marginal. Roosevelt's father "never had to leave one city and move to another because he felt there was too little social acceptance of his children, but Joseph Kennedy had moved from Boston to Bronxville for precisely that reason when his sons were teenagers." [102] As late as 1960 the marginality still rankled. It was manifested in what David Halberstam called a certain "hunger" or "edge," a "totality of desire for the office" that was part of John's motivation.[103] Roosevelt did not have an older brother. John's self-esteem was on occasion dealt some heavy blows by Joe, Jr., who was in many ways superior to him, particularly in physical prowess and, as their competition for dates in college would attest, in good looks.[104] Even his political career was something of a hand-me-down from big brother. Joseph Senior expected his eldest son to go into politics. When a Senate seat was vacated in 1946, John stepped in because Joe, Jr., had been killed in World War II.[105] And finally his election to the presidency in 1960 turned out to be something less than a clear victory. His margin, in total votes, was the slimmest ever recorded in a presidential race.[106] This pelted his self-esteem a bit, but did not permanently damage it. It also tended to open his mind. He entered the White House with a little

---

[102] David Halberstam, *The Best and the Brightest* (Greenwich, Conn.: Fawcett Publications, 1973), p. 123.

[103] Ibid., pp. 122–23, also p. 16.

[104] Barber, *The Presidential Character*, p. 301; and Hank Searls, *The Lost Prince: Young Joe, The Forgotten Kennedy* (New York: World, 1969), p. 99.

[105] Barber, *The Presidential Character*, pp. 309–10.

[106] Ibid., p. 293.

less confidence and more caution than had Franklin D. Roosevelt. But he was looking forward to the job.[107]

> *"Sure," he said, "It's a big job. But I don't know anybody who can do it any better than I can. I'm going to be in it for four years. . . . It isn't going to be so bad. You've got time to think. You don't have all those people bothering you that you had in the Senate—besides, the pay is pretty good."* [108]

When John Kennedy came to the presidency there was no domestic crisis equal to that encountered by Roosevelt. He faced a Congress resistant to sweeping domestic change, but he had much more freedom of action in foreign affairs; it is in this arena that we will look for examples of his behavior as president.

By 1961 the cold war was heating up. The United States was engaged in an arms race with the Soviet Union; the Russians were creating problems in Berlin; and insurgent movements were becoming increasingly active in Southeast Asia. Kennedy began by gathering a formidable group of advisors. Some, like McGeorge Bundy and Robert McNamara, epitomized what could be called an intellectual, hard-nosed approach to politics. Like Kennedy, they were "dispassionate and skeptical." [109] They believed "that sheer intelligence and rationality could answer and solve anything." [110] Other advisors, in less favor and often possessing less glamour, questioned the lack of passion, philosophy, or emotional depth in this amoral approach. One presidential advisor, Arthur Schlesinger, Jr., noted that it was difficult to refute the arguments in favor of the abortive Bay of Pigs clandestine invasion of Cuba, because the military and CIA proponents of the operation would talk only of tangibles—men, invasion craft, air power. Other factors, such as the morality of a U.S. supported attempt to overthrow the Castro government, the effect of the operation on world opinion, its legality in terms of existing treaties, and the like, were intangibles. They did not lend themselves to direct measurement and portrayal in logistical diagrams. To advocate scrapping the plan on the basis of such issues made one look like a "soft-headed idealist" in an administration that prided

---

[107] For a statement on Kennedy's confidence in himself as compared to Lyndon Johnson's and Richard Nixon's, see Halberstam, *The Best and the Brightest*, p. 123.

[108] Hugh Sidey, *John F. Kennedy, President* (New York: Atheneum, 1963), p. 11.

[109] Arthur M. Schlesinger, Jr., *A Thousand Days: John F. Kennedy in the White House* (Boston: Houghton Mifflin, 1965), p. 259.

[110] Halberstam, *The Best and the Brightest*, p. 57; see also p. 125.

itself on realism.[111] Chester Bowles, then Undersecretary of State, summed up one of the problems with this kind of detached, open-minded approach:

> *The question which concerns me most about this new administration is whether it lacks a genuine sense of conviction about what is right and what is wrong. . . .*
>
> *Anyone in public life who has strong convictions about the rights and wrongs of public morality, both domestic and international, has a very great advantage in times of strain, since his instincts on what to do are clear and immediate. . . .*
>
> *. . . The Cuban fiasco demonstrates how far astray a man as brilliant and well intentioned as Kennedy can go who lacks a basic moral reference point.[112]*

Kennedy was badly burned by the Bay of Pigs episode, but he neither reacted vindictively nor sought to place the blame on anyone else. In the future he would place less credence in the advice of narrow-minded "experts." He was growing in the job. This was particularly evident in the period between his visit with Khrushchev in June 1961 and the Cuban missile crisis of October 1962. Kennedy wanted to talk personally with Khrushchev, in hopes of easing world tensions. Arrangements were made for a meeting in Vienna. The president expected to engage in a frank, reasonable discussion about the respective responsibility of the two world leaders, the prospects for peace, and the problems they faced. Instead he got a tirade against the United States and some veiled threats. He finally responded in kind, and when the meetings broke up neither side had given in. Tensions were high, and there was fear of a nuclear war over Berlin, partially because the Berlin Wall symbolized the intransigence of communist regimes.[113] One reporter thought that the President was "shaken" by the experience.[114] Kennedy seemed to believe that his youth (he was 45, young for leadership of a world power) and inexperience, particularly as they were manifested in the Bay of Pigs fiasco, were being interpreted as a sign of weakness, that Khrushchev felt that the president "had no guts. So he just beat hell out of me." [115] Others thought differently—it was just Khrushchev being himself.

[111] Schlesinger, Jr., *A Thousand Days,* p. 256.

[112] Cited in Halberstam, *The Best and the Brightest,* p. 88.

[113] See Theodore C. Sorensen, *Kennedy* (New York: Harper & Row, 1965), pp. 543–50.

[114] Halberstam, *The Best and the Brightest,* p. 96.

[115] Ibid., p. 97.

It would appear that at this point Kennedy lacked a certain degree of confidence in himself, that he was touchy about his comparative youthfulness—it had come up in the conversations—and was still smarting from his obvious miscalculation over the Cuba operation. Despite these feelings he did not impetuously lash out at the Soviet leader. He said that the meetings were "somber" but "useful." [116] He stepped up the pace of military preparedness, but it was not done carelessly or as if for revenge.

The Cuban missile crisis provided the greatest test of Kennedy's mettle. At Vienna the president had been able to take the measure of his opponent. He had learned from his mistakes and grown in depth and self-assurance. Despite the browbeating he received from Khrushchev, he exhibited a keen ability to perceive the world through the eyes of his opponent. This would play an important part in the crisis, which cast the shadow of a possible nuclear holocaust.

In October 1962 American intelligence discovered that the Soviets were installing medium-range missiles in Cuba with the capability of hitting targets up and down the Eastern U.S. seaboard. This was something Khrushchev assured the president was not happening. Kennedy's response to discovery of the missiles was neither passive nor precipitous. He ordered that more evidence be gathered, and he formed a committee of military and civilian authorities to discuss the options. He probed the committee members and, in contrast to the Bay of Pigs operation, refused to take anything for granted.

He kept his composure. While Soviet Foreign Minister Gromyko assured him in conference that Cuba would remain free of offensive weapons, Kennedy did not indicate that he had contradictory information. However, U.S. forces were mobilized around the world, and a blockade of Cuba was decided upon. Some congressional leaders angrily protested that such action was far too little, favoring instead an invasion of Cuba. Kennedy held firm to his position, realizing the difficulties that his opponent Khrushchev was in. Like the open mind, Kennedy sought to know as much about the situation of those he opposed as he did about the situation he faced himself. "The theme of the third [and final] act," writes Barber, "would have to be Khrushchev, and Kennedy's careful determination to help him out of the box *he* [Khrushchev] was in." [117] The blockade alternative gave Khrushchev more time to think, to find a moderate way out, and to deal with the militant wing of his own party. Kennedy ordered restraint and sought to ensure that there would be no accidental, precipitous moves even though provocations for such action, such as the shooting down of a U.S. spy plane, had

[116] Schlesinger, Jr., *A Thousand Days,* p. 377.
[117] Barber, *The Presidential Character,* p. 335. Emphasis in original.

occurred. After some tense and trying moments, an agreement was reached with the Soviets: the United States was to agree not to invade Cuba and to lift the blockade; the Soviets would agree to remove the missiles. It was a deal. Kennedy, obviously elated with the outcome, did not let himself show his feelings. He would allow nothing to take place that would humiliate the Soviets. The Russians could not be made to think that they had suffered a defeat.[118] Therein lies one of the keys to the course of events: a clear, open-minded appreciation of the situation faced by the enemy.

The desire to seek information from a number of diverse sources, to evaluate that information in an objective light, and to arrive at a course of action that is decisive enough to get the point across without at the same time painting oneself—or one's opponent—into a corner are characteristic responses of the open mind in politics. In the case of John Kennedy, this kind of thought process and approach to life helped avert what could have been a nuclear war or a military confrontation with the Soviet Union in the American backyard.

SUMMARY AND CRITIQUE

In this chapter we discussed two kinds of president: the closed-minded, deficiency-motivated type, and his opposite, the open-minded, growth-motivated one. The reader may have noted that each has his peculiar deficiencies. The first type is often rigid and willing to reduce politics to the level of a personal vendetta. He is inclined to stick with a potentially disastrous course of action, despite advice to the contrary. Nixon refused to deal with the realities of Watergate, and Wilson would not compromise on the League of Nations. The second type of president is inclined to lack an overall philosophy and a clear moral perspective. He tends to take things as they come, often with inadequate consideration of the long-term effects of a given decision. Roosevelt, for example, did not worry about the implications for the future that inhered in a polyglot bureaucracy that involved itself with many heretofore private sectors of American life, and Kennedy did not foresee the future effects of active U.S. intervention in the political affairs of Southeast Asia. Which type is to be preferred?

Neither Wilson nor Kennedy fit perfectly the mold of the ideal active–negative or active–positive character type as outlined in this chapter. This should indicate that while our interpretation can provide some guidelines to the behavior one might expect from a particular

---

[118] Ibid., p. 337.

type of political leader, there is plenty of room for improvement in the conception and application of the model. Although there are other types of presidential character, the two discussed in this chapter were chosen for their dramatic contrasts. In addition to the types above, Barber discusses passive–positive and passive–negative types and various other aspects of political behavior that were not covered here.

Once again we should note that any classification scheme does a certain injustice to the subject matter. The oversimplification can be defended, however, for the purpose of such schemes is not to include and explain everything, but to outline only those aspects of a power-holder's perceptions and personality that are linked to behavior that is likely to seriously effect large numbers of people, for good or ill.

The job of constructing valid models of presidential character is difficult because few followers are capable of objectively perceiving their leaders. Moreover, most powerful political leaders, such as U.S. presidents, are in a position to manipulate their image and control both the amount and kind of information available about them. This means that even greater interpretive caution must be imposed upon what is already, given the current state of the art, a highly speculative enterprise.

Other relationships adumbrated in this chapter deserve further scrutiny and criticism. The inferred links among social class, religion, and presidential character deserve particular mention. Truman came from a family that was not much better off than the Nixons, but most observers would call him an active–positive, and there is certainly no direct, inflexible relationship between religion and character type. Rather, these factors provide clues to important environments and relationships. Class status is not a *cause* of defense motivation; rather, it is a surrogate, an indicator of the possible degree of insecurity and pressure that one could infer *might* have been characteristic of the family environment in which a person spent a lot of time during the most formative years of life. Obviously, not everyone who was raised in a strong fundamentalist religious environment comes out with a weak ego and a closed mind. At the same time the researcher would be remiss if these possible indicators of important processes were overlooked. For while they may not in themselves be direct causes of behavior, they can be important clues to the unique underlying dynamics of the individual's personality and character. Often, however, some rather long inferential leaps have to be made. The longer the leap, the more room there is for debate and reinterpretation—and possible error.

In discussing U.S. presidents we have in effect been considering the minds of the elite. Very few indeed seriously strive to be elected president, and fewer still of course succeed in the endeavor. In the next chapter we will give some thought to the minds of the masses—those who are not active politically and who have no ambition to hold public office. This group of individuals is amorphous and varied; it is also the repository of power awesome enough to command the attention of any astute politically minded elite.

Selected Bibliography

BARBER, JAMES DAVID, *The Presidential Character.* Englewood Cliffs, N.J.: Prentice-Hall, 1972.

BURNS, JAMES MACGREGOR, *Roosevelt: The Lion and the Fox.* New York: Harcourt Brace Jovanovich, 1956.

GEORGE, ALEXANDER L., and JULIETTE L. GEORGE, *Woodrow Wilson and Colonel House: A Personality Study.* New York: John Day, 1956.

HALBERSTAM, DAVID, *The Best and the Brightest.* Greenwich, Conn.: Fawcett Publications, 1973.

McCLELLAND, DAVID C., *The Achieving Society.* New York: Collier-Macmillan, 1967.

NIXON, RICHARD M., *Six Crises.* Garden City, N.Y.: Doubleday, 1962.

WEBER, MAX, *The Protestant Ethic and the Spirit of Capitalism,* trans. Talcott Parsons. New York: Scribner's, 1958.

WOODWARD, BOB, and CARL BERNSTEIN, *The Final Days.* New York: Simon & Schuster, 1976.

5

Popular images of politics

We saw in the last chapter that members of the elite, in this case presidents of the United States, differ in their views of reality; degrees of motivation; types of personality; and ways of perceiving, ingesting, and evaluating information. Can such variation be found among the masses as well?

Although it is always difficult to generalize to broad sectors of the population, evidence from research surveys and intensive studies of individuals yields a number of findings concerning the large majority of people. From such data, the picture that emerges may not fit any single individual perfectly, but is nevertheless quite accurate for a number of people.

The majority of the population—the working classes and many portions of the middle class—is concerned with a narrow time perspective: the immediate, the here and now.

*The . . . psychological world in which the average person lives—
the world he is concerned with—the world important to him—his
reality world—has very narrow boundaries in both space and time;
it does not extend very far into the future. His world is likely
to be a highly restricted microcosm made up of immediate problems
vital to him. Hence he wants help immediately.*[1]

In Europe, as in the United States, the concrete predominates over the abstract for such persons. In one study of workers in France and Italy it was found that the concept of "the working class" was not salient. Seventy-two percent of the French and 69 percent of the Italian respondents were "not at all" interested in workers' movements in other countries.[2] Action undertaken in unison with other workers was directed

[1] Hadley Cantril, *The Politics of Despair* (New York: Collier Books, 1962), p. 84.
[2] Ibid., p. 121.

toward immediate rather than long-range ends—the worker being "willing to sacrifice himself or go on strike *only* if he is quite certain there will be some immediate and concrete advantage to him." [3]

In Robert Lane's intensive study of fifteen members of the upper working class in "Eastport," a large American city, the immediate and concrete emerge strongly in responses to questions on basic elements of the American political creed. About the concept of freedom, for example, a packinghouse checker sums up the feelings expressed by most of the group:

> *"My God, I work where I want to work, I spend my money where I want to spend it. I buy what I want to buy. I go where I want to go. I read what I want to read. My kids go to the school that they want to go to, or where I want to send them. We bring them up in the religion that we want to bring them up in. What else—what else could you have?"* [4]

The right to criticize the government, to allow competing ideas to contest each other, and to question the fundamental "truths" of the political system did not occur. In other contexts many criticized individuals in the government, but such criticism was not related to the abstract concept of freedom to criticize, and all criticism was well within the confines of generally accepted values. No questions concerning the basic structure of the political system were raised, and throughout, the immediate, personal, economic situation superseded any more abstract political discussion. "The lives of men of Eastport, like most Americans' lives, are much more concerned with the business of buying and selling, earning and disposing of things, than they are with the 'idle' talk of politics." [5]

Politics is certainly not one of the most concrete of subjects, especially on the basic issues of the human condition. How, for example, is the political system to be so structured as to reconcile the competing demands posed by the belief in human equality and the belief in the desirability of maximum individual freedom? When, in a democracy, does the need to preserve order take precedence over the rights of the individual, and what sort of balance should be struck between the two? Is there but a single set of "correct political behaviors and government

---

[3] Ibid.

[4] Robert E. Lane, *Political Ideology: Why the American Common Man Believes What He Does* (New York: Free Press, 1962), p. 24.

[5] Ibid., p. 25.

structures"—for example, those specified in the U.S. Constitution and the amendments attached thereto—or are other forms of government equally correct in their underlying assumptions, say, a nation basing its government upon a belief in human inequality? Should we send foreign aid to a repressive dictatorship that supports our foreign policy goals, or should we allow it to fall to a popular movement that expresses strong anti-U.S. sentiments but will make the government more representative?

For most of the men Lane interviewed, these questions are simply irrelevant. There are no individual conflicts, obligations, or group attachments that bring such abstract political issues down to the level of the concrete. As a result, politics possessed low salience. When asked what effect the government has on their lives, "they respond with trivial answers ('It cleans the streets') or perhaps deny that it affects their lives at all ('The government doesn't bother me any')." [6] In his study of European workers Cantril finds that many who vote for the Communist party do not share its ideology, a precise, coherent, interrelated set of beliefs that provides adherents a sophisticated view of historical causality and directs them toward active engagement in politics.[7] Rather, the Communist vote is viewed as a form of protest against the immediate, often precarious, economic situation. As the secretary of a French labor union put it, "I tell you that the workers are distrustful of Communism. They support it in votes because they would have nothing else to fight the *patrons* [the boss, the factory owner, the capitalist] with if they didn't." [8]

Again, the concrete, short-range issues predominate. In a study of human concerns and aspirations in fourteen nations, it is in the category "least educated" that the lowest percentages are found under the relatively abstract categories of international and political aspirations,[9] as indicated in table 1.

Although a majority in each educational category expressed aspirations regarding immediate economic concerns (employment, social security, standard of living, etc.), the highest percentage of such concerns falls in the least educated category.

---

[6] Ibid, p. 33. On the role of group loyalties among Americans, see ibid., p. 32.

[7] See Willard A. Mullins, "On the Concept of Ideology in Political Science," *American Political Science Review*, 66, no. 2 (June 1972), 498–510.

[8] Cited in Cantril, *The Politics of Despair*, p. 119.

[9] Hadley Cantril, *The Pattern of Human Concerns* (New Brunswick, N.J.: Rutgers University Press, 1965), pp. 249–50. International aspirations involved peace, disarmament, better relations with the communist bloc, and the like. Political aspirations involved honest, efficient, balanced or representative government, freedom, political stability, etc.

Table 1   *Education by Type of Aspirations*

	International	Political	Economic
Best educated *	29%	41%	66%
Middle educated	36	35	66
Least educated	14	29	71

Source: Adapted from Hadley Cantril, *The Pattern of Human Concerns* (New Brunswick, N.J.: Rutgers University Press, 1965), pp. 249–50. Multiple responses possible.
* Best educated had at least some university education; middle educated at minimum attended some high school; least educated did not.

This lack of interest in politics leads to cognitive compartmentalization—the ability to adhere to contradictory positions; for example, the expressed belief in a general postulate such as "equality" can be contradicted by its application to a concrete situation: "I don't want any racial minorities in the neighborhood."

This characteristic is noted by Philip Converse in his discussion of belief systems in mass publics.[10] Converse analyzes belief systems in terms of two "levels of information." The first level is simply a knowledge of the linkage or correlation between a set of concepts without any idea of the reason why the two are connected. "Communists are atheists" is one such linkage and may be made for no other reason than the individual's belief that "those Communists are for everything wicked." This reflects an existential rather than causal mode of thinking; that is, the individual thinks only "That's the way it is" rather than asking "Why?"

The second level requires "constraints"—forces that tie two or more idea elements together. The more abstract and complex an individual's belief system, the more likely are various idea elements to be linked by a causal view, and hence constrained. The individual possessing a complex, constrained belief system has a better grasp of events and can explain a much wider variety of phenomena than an individual whose belief system is not so complex or constrained. On the other hand, explanations resulting from a sophisticated causal analysis will be much less amenable to diffusion throughout the society than will the more simplistic "existential" explanation. "Facts alone" do not constitute a causal explanation. For example, the news item "The president vetoed a bill increasing veterans' benefits" is easily grasped and transmitted. However, that the increase in the purchasing power of such a measurable segment of the population, with definable tastes and buying

[10] Philip E. Converse, "The Nature of Belief Systems in Mass Publics," in David E. Apter, ed., *Ideology and Discontent* (New York: Free Press, 1964), p. 214.

habits, would contribute to inflation in an "overheated" economy may not be equally evident. That the president chose to veto the bill, thereby penalizing the veteran (or the consumer) rather than some other segment of the economy, in an attempt to fight inflation is one explanation that is likely to go unnoticed by those acting on the first level of information. Another less-than-obvious explanation might be that the president felt that many veterans were quite likely to vote against him regardless of his actions, whereas if he instead approved a bill to increase social security payments, many living largely on fixed incomes would remain loyal to him despite an inflation that was turning them into prime targets for the campaign rhetoric of the opposition. Perceiving the linkage between the signing of the social security bill and the vetoing of the veterans' bill requires a conception of political causation that might well be lacking in the poorly constrained belief systems of great numbers of the voting public. For them, no relation is seen; one bill passes, another fails. The two are never causally connected.

As the ladder of income and education is descended, the constraint —the "contextual grasp" of political situations, the level of knowledge and ability to process information regarding things political—declines rapidly. Response becomes increasingly simplistic, narrow, and compartmentalized. The central elements in the belief system also undergo a corresponding change. "These objects shift from the remote, generic, and abstract to the increasingly simple, concrete, or 'close to home.' " [11] At the lower reaches, the result is a perceptual world strikingly similar to that of the closed mind; " 'limited horizons,' 'foreshortened time perspectives,' and 'concrete thinking' " predominate.[12]

To learn of the types of political thinking extant in the population, Converse analyzed responses to an open-ended question asking the individual for his own evaluation of the current political situation.[13] The researchers looked for evidence of the respondent's means of organizing his thinking about political matters. Five levels of conceptualization emerged.

1. The top level included respondents who used "a relatively abstract and far-reaching conceptual dimension as a yardstick against which political objects and their shifting policy significance over time were evaluated." [14] This dimension, or major organizing and constraining

11 Ibid., p. 213.
12 Ibid.
13 Ibid., p. 216.
14 Data were taken from surveys covering the 1956 presidential election.

factor, was usually the liberal–conservative continuum. Individuals evaluating the political situation on the basis of this (or another) purely cognitive or intellectual dimension were called "ideologues."

2. The second group, the "near ideologue," used such a dimension but with less consistency.

3. On the third level were persons who based their analysis upon group preferences. They evaluated candidates and events in reference to the advancement of their group goals: Was a candidate for the working man or big business? for the farmers or the urban interests? and so on.

4. The fourth level included a general "nature of the times" response, revealing a lack of particularized political information but indicating a general feeling for how things were faring for the nation as a whole.

5. The final category involved responses that indicated a high degree of political ignorance: support for a party out of habit, personal qualities of the candidate involved without regard to political stance and issue orientation, or a confession of ignorance on the issues and candidates.[15]

Converse's findings demonstrated that a majority of the electorate was below the level of conceptualization at which perceptions of political issues, candidates, and government structure are integrated into a logically coherent whole. Converse was able to classify only 3.5 percent of all voters as "ideologues" (the most conceptually sophisticated group); and of the total sample—combining both voters and nonvoters —only 2.5 percent were similarly classified. Of the five levels of conceptualization, the third level, at which individuals evaluate candidates and events largely on the basis of group interest, contained the largest proportion of respondents (42 percent). The two lowest levels of conceptualization— "nature of the times" and "nonpolitical"—contained over four times as many respondents as did the two most sophisticated levels of conceptualization. In sum, Converse demonstrated that only a small proportion of the American electorate had a moderately or highly sophisticated conceptualization of political life.

However, the 1956 election, upon which Converse based his conclusions, featured the bland, "above-politics" image of Eisenhower and the low-keyed opposition of Adlai Stevenson. A more recent analysis of American political conceptualizations yielded two important supports for Converse's findings while casting them in a historical perspective. Analyzing survey data gathered between 1952 and 1972, Norman Nie, Sidney Verba, and John Petrocik found that the 1956 election represented "the low point in level of conceptualization" over this 20-year

---

[15] Ibid., pp. 215–17.

period.[16] Nevertheless, they found that the proportion of the electorate that could be classified as "ideologues" according to Converse's criteria had risen from 3 percent in 1956 to only 6 percent by 1968; moreover, the proportion falling in the two lowest levels of conceptualization did not change between 1956 and 1968.[17] Thus, while the level of conceptualization may have been atypically low during the 1956 election, later data generally support Converse's overall conclusions.

During the 1950s other research in addition to Converse's assessed mass conceptual sophistication by measuring the ability to link a specific case to a general principle. Herbert McClosky, for example, found that consensus existed for the general principles of democracy among both elites and masses; over 88 percent of both his elite and mass samples agreed with the statement: "I believe in free speech for all no matter what their views might be." [18] Yet, responses to more specific items suggested that a large proportion of the masses refused to support general principles of democracy when they were put to test in specific situations; only 48 percent of McClosky's mass sample agreed that "people ought to be allowed to vote even if they don't do so intelligently." In other words, a large proportion (roughly half, in the above case) expressed support for a general principle of democracy while failing to apply that principle to a specific situation.

Later researchers, however, reassessed McClosky's and others' findings and demonstrated that, at least in some areas, the mass public's ability to link the general and the specific had increased. David Lawrence, for example, examining 1971 data, concluded that "large majorities of respondents with tolerant general norms apply them consistently in specific situations." Also, this consistency generally increased as education increased.[19] Still, he found some specific issues on which general principles were not applied; for example, 52.7 percent would refuse to allow a demonstration to legalize marijuana.[20] Thus, although the mass public's ability to apply abstract democratic principles to specific situations appears greater in the 1970s than in earlier periods, inconsistency remains for some specific situations.

Not only has mass ability to link specifics to general democratic principles appeared to increase since the 1950s but, according to other

[16] Norman H. Nie, Sidney Verba, and John Petrocik, *The Changing American Voter* (Cambridge, Mass.: Harvard University Press, 1976), p. 122.

[17] Ibid., p. 117.

[18] Herbert McClosky, "Consensus and Ideology in American Politics," *The American Political Science Review*, 58 (June 1964), 376.

[19] David G. Lawrence, "Procedural Norms and Tolerance: A Reassessment," *The American Political Science Review*, 70 (March 1976), 99.

[20] Ibid.

research, coherence of attitudes *over* issue areas has also increased.[21] Specifically, survey research demonstrates that larger proportions of the electorate today tend to be more consistently liberal or conservative over a wide variety of issue areas than was true in the past (that is, a person taking a liberal stand on one issue—for example, welfare—would tend to be similarly liberal over a variety of other issues—integration, foreign affairs, etc.). The trend toward greater consistency across issues first appeared in the early 1960s: From 1956 (the first year in which measurement was made) through 1960, few Americans tended to be consistently liberal or conservative across issues, but by 1964 the proportion increased rapidly and remained at this higher level through 1973.[22] Many political scientists attribute the increase to the political nature of the times. In the 1950s, when issue consistency was low, politics was bland and the major issues were largely ones of foreign policy, which had little impact on the daily lives of most Americans. In the 1960s and 1970s, the civil rights movement, Vietnam, crime, drugs, and the economy all impinged on the daily lives of many Americans. Thus, millions of Americans were personally affected by the political issues of the 1960s and 1970s, while few Americans were affected by the remote political issues of the 1950s. Furthermore, the presidential elections of 1964 through 1972 all had ideological candidates who emphasized issues —Goldwater in 1964, Wallace in 1968, and McGovern in 1972; such emphasis on issues in these campaigns probably accounts for some of this increase in issue consistency.

Not surprisingly, as issue consistency increased during the 1964, 1968, and 1972 elections, so did issue *voting;* at the same time, party voting declined. (Issue voting means voting for the candidate closest to the voter's issue preference; party voting means voting on the basis of political party identification.) During the 1972 election, issue voting was at a fairly high level. Arthur Miller et al. found "a substantial relationship between the issues and vote. [This suggests] that a broad segment of the population in 1972 was reacting to politics in a rather sophisticated manner." [23]

The increase in issue voting can be explained largely by three factors. First, issue voting tends to increase when the candidates offer a *choice* on the issues. If both major-party candidates either take the same issue

21 Nie, Verba, and Petrocik, *The Changing American Voter,* chapters 8 and 9.

22 Ibid., p. 129. The discussion which follows draws on pp. 96–109.

23 Arthur H. Miller, Warren E. Miller, Alden S. Raine, and Thad A. Brown, "A Majority Party in Disarray: Policy Polarization in the 1972 Election," paper presented at the 1973 Annual Meeting of the American Political Science Association, New Orleans, pp. 29–31.

position or decline to take any, issue voting is impossible. As mentioned above, in the 1964, 1968, and 1972 presidential elections at least one of the major candidates took consistently liberal or conservative issue stands.

A second explanation for some of the rise in issue voting is the steady erosion in public support for the two parties. As Paul Abrahamson has noted, whereas prior to 1964 roughly 75 percent of the American electorate identified with one of the two major political parties, by 1974 the proportion of party identifiers had declined to 60 percent.[24] The decline in party voting is summarized in Table 2. From 1952 to 1960 party voting increased steadily (the higher the correlation, the greater the tendency to vote for the candidates from the voter's own party), while from 1964 it steadily declined. More significantly, squaring the correlation coefficients will tell us the amount of variation in the vote that can be explained by party identification: In 1960, 49 percent of the variation in the vote could be explained by party identification; by 1972, only 26.1 percent.

The third and final explanation for the increased sophistication of the mass public and the rise in issue voting is the changing educational level of the mass public; a greater proportion of highly educated young people is entering the electorate, replacing their less-educated elders. In 1952, only 15 percent of the electorate had some college education, while 61 percent had less than a high school degree; by 1972, 29 percent of the electorate had some college training, while only 38 percent had less than a high school degree.[25] Thus, over a 20-year period, the proportion of college-educated persons in the electorate had almost doubled while the proportion of the electorate without high school diplomas had declined by over one-third.

Moreover, while persons of all educational levels have demonstrated

Table 2 *Correlations between Party Identification and the Presidential Vote, 1952–1972*

1952	1956	1960	1964	1968	1972
.65	.68	.70	.62	.50	.51

Source: Arthur H. Miller and Warren E. Miller, "Issues, Candidates and Partisan Divisions in the 1972 American Presidential Election," *British Journal of Political Science*, 5 (October 1975), 422.

[24] Paul R. Abrahamson, "Generational Change and the Decline of Party Identification in America," *The American Political Science Review*, 70 (June 1976), 469–78.

[25] Nie, Verba, and Petrocik, *The Changing American Voter*, p. 120.

increased sophistication in conceptualizing politics, those with some college demonstrated the largest absolute gain in attitude consistency. On foreign and domestic issues over the last 16 years, the average gain in attitude consistency correlations was .27 for the college educated; their consistency correlation was .47 in 1972. For those lacking a high school degree, the gain was .24; their consistency correlation was .34 in 1972. Thus, the rising educational level of the American electorate accounts for at least part of the increased levels of issue voting, attitude consistency, and conceptual sophistication.

POLITICAL PARTICIPATION AND CITIZEN ATTITUDES

Within any mass public, levels of political participation tend to vary from person to person; some tend to be highly participative in political life, while others are largely nonparticipative. Some vote and engage in no other political acts, while others never vote and yet engage in a wide variety of other political activities. Recent studies of political participation in America, Japan, Austria, India, and Nigeria reveal interesting differences in levels and types of political participation, and yet when political participation is viewed from a cross-national perspective common patterns emerge.

The largest single study of political participation to date focused on political participation in America.[26] Basing their research on a national sample of the American electorate, Sidney Verba and Norman Nie explored four "modes" of participation: voting, campaign activity, community activity (through informal groups and formal organizations), and citizen-initiated contacting of public officials. The first two modes concern electoral activity, while the latter two relate to nonelectoral acts. Verba and Nie viewed these four modes of activity as conceptually distinct from one another, and the results of their data analysis suggested that the four modes were also *empirically* distinct.

Verba and Nie's research revealed six types of participants, shown in table 3. The Inactives, composing slightly over a fifth of the electorate, took virtually no part in any political activity. The Voting Specialists, also about one-fifth of the population, overwhelmingly engaged in only one of the four modes of participation—they voted in national and most local elections. The Parochial Participants were the smallest segment of the sample; they voted with average frequency, but more nearly uniquely they all reported engaging in one of the nonelectoral modes of participa-

26 Sidney Verba and Norman H. Nie, *Participation in America: Political Democracy and Social Equality* (New York: Harper & Row, 1972).

Table 3 *The Six Types of Political Participants*

Inactive	22%
Voting Specialists	21
Parochial Participants	4
Communalists	20
Campaigners	15
Complete Activists	11
Unclassifiable	7
	100%

Source: Adapted from Sidney Verba and Norman Nie, *Participation in America:* *Political Democracy and Social Equality* (New York: Harper & Row, 1972), pp. 79–80.

tion—particularized contacting. They became highly active and participative in political life when their personal interests were affected. Although the Communalists, like the Parochial Participants and the Voting Specialists, tended to vote frequently, they differed from these other types by tending to engage in community affairs while shunning campaign activity. On the other hand, the Campaigners tended to be active in political campaigns and yet inactive in other community affairs. Finally, the Complete Activists were those individuals who tended to engage in all four modes of participation at relatively high levels.[27]

Verba and Nie's research demonstrated that for a large segment of the American electorate (about 60 percent), political participation comprised only one or two modes of activity; persons who engaged in campaign activity tended not to overlap with either those who engaged in communal activity or those who engaged in particularized contacting. Similarly, Communalists tended to be a unique stratum, as did Parochial Participants. Yet, all but the Inactives tended to vote with regularity. Thus, the research suggested that political participation in America tends to three or four unique dimensions.

Research on the structure and content of political participation in Japan, Austria, India, and Nigeria yields a somewhat similar pattern of four modes of participation—voting, campaign activity, communal activity, and contacting.[28] Finding such similarities in countries as diverse as the United States, Japan, India, Austria, and Nigeria strongly suggests that certain patterns or structures of political participation are common to all democratic nations.

[27] Ibid., pp. 79–81.

[28] Sidney Verba, Norman H. Nie, and Jae-on Kim, *The Modes of Democratic Participation: A Cross-National Comparison* (Beverly Hills, Ca.: Sage Publications, 1971).

Moreover, across national boundaries a common *process* of political participation appears to account for some of these variations in political participation, and to explain "why different groups participate at different rates." [29] This process or model is most commonly known as the "standard socioeconomic model of political participation," presented below: [30]

Socioeconomic Status ⟶ Civic Orientations ⟶ Participation

It is a common finding in the literature of research in political participation that persons of higher socioeconomic status (or social class) tend to participate at greater levels than persons of lower socioeconomic status. This is true not only for democratic countries, but also for communist nations on which data are available.[31] The explanation for the relationship between socioeconomic status and participation is that increased levels of the components of socioeconomic status—education, income, and higher status occupation—are generally accompanied by more positive attitudes toward political life; one's level of interest in politics and one's sense of both political efficacy (influence over the political process) and the duties of citizenship all tend to increase with socioeconomic status. Moreover, these positive orientations tend the individual to higher levels of political participation. This is not to say, however, that other factors such as political party affiliation, affiliation with a voluntary association, race, or community size are unimportant; rather, we are saying that the standard socioeconomic model is able to account for much of the variation in political participation.[32] Additionally, this model aids us in explaining the variation in participation across nations. However, although the socioeconomic model explains quite well the variance in both campaign activity and communal activity across nations, the model does not explain the variance in voting and particularized contacting.[33]

While the participation studies neglect other modes of participation

29 Ibid., p. 55.

30 This model appears in Verba and Nie, *Participation in America,* chapter 8; Verba, Nie, and Kim, *The Modes of Democratic Participation,* p. 55; and Norman Nie, G. Bingham Powell, and Kenneth Prewitt, "Social Structure and Political Participation," *The American Political Science Review,* 63 (June and September, 1969), 361–78 and 808–32.

31 In Yugoslavia, for example, participation in workers' councils is strongly related to socioeconomic status. See Sidney Verba and Goldie Shabad, "Workers' Councils and Political Stratification: The Yugoslav Experience," paper presented at the 1975 Annual Meeting of the American Political Science Association, San Francisco.

32 Verba and Nie explained up to 25 percent of the variance in the four modes of participation using this model. See Verba and Nie, *Participation in America,* p. 135.

33 Verba, Nie, and Kim, *The Modes of Democratic Participation,* pp. 56–64.

prevalent in some democratic polities [34]—specifically, protest and interest-group activity—the modes examined and the model of participation developed in these studies give us a general understanding of the participation process. Furthermore, the standard socioeconomic model suggests some important *consequences* of participation in democratic polities.

As we have seen, the standard socioeconomic model predicts that persons of high socioeconomic status will participate disproportionately in the political affairs of the polity, while persons of lower socioeconomic status will be disproportionately inactive. What consequences does such a lopsided distribution of political participants have on policy outcomes? The evidence indicates that the policy preferences of upper-class participants differ from those of the population as a whole but coincide with those of the elected political elites. This issue congruency between upper-class participants and political elites is due largely to greater participation rates of the upper-class, rather than the common background of elites and upper-class participants.[35] Yet, no research has demonstrated a linkage between upper-class participants' attitudes and actual policy outcomes.

SELF-ESTEEM, APATHY, AND ALIENATION
AS RELATED TO ELITES AND MASSES

Research results are mixed. Low self-esteem seems to correlate with apathy about political affairs when it is too low for politics to be a vehicle for compensation (the kind of vehicle it was for Woodrow Wilson and Lyndon Johnson). Research conducted by Morris Rosenberg on high school students indicates a correlation between low estimates of self and political apathy. Thirty-one percent of the individuals scoring at the top of a self-esteem scale had a "great deal" of interest in national and international affairs; none of those scoring at the bottom of the scale had this degree of interest.[36] While 53 percent of the group highest in self-esteem discussed political affairs with a great deal of intensity, only 14 percent of the low scorers did. And while 14 percent of the group high in self-esteem were "less likely than others to be asked about their political views by others," almost half of those lowest on the self-esteem scale (45 percent) were in this position.[37]

The study also indicated that individuals low in self-esteem were

---

[34] See, for example, Jerrold G. Rusk, "Political Participation in America: A Review Essay," *The American Political Science Review,* 70 (June 1976), 583–91.

[35] See Verba and Nie, *Participation in America,* chapters 16–20.

[36] Percentages taken from Table 1 of Morris Rosenberg, "Self Esteem and Concern with Public Affairs," *Public Opinion Quarterly,* 26 (1962), p. 203.

[37] Ibid., p. 204.

afraid to discuss public affairs because they might embarrass themselves.[38] The conformist moral outlook (Kohlberg's stage 3) is amply evident, as is a fixated existence on the self-esteem level of the Maslow hierarchy. People afraid to express their opinions about politics can do little else but follow those who are not so restrained. At this level an individual's entire mood may be determined by his interpretation of what other people think of him.

We may take it as a guiding principle that people afflicted with a fundamental feeling of worthlessness do not accept this state with equanimity; on the contrary, a gnawing, anxiety-provoking feeling of inadequacy may be one of the most distressing and depressing of human emotions. It is thus understandable that the individual who lacks respect for himself should be inordinately concerned with the impression he makes upon others. If he gains their favor, approval, or affection, then the devastating conviction of his own insignificance and worthlessness is alleviated. If, on the other hand, he arouses their scorn, contempt, or censure, then he is confirmed in his fears of his worthlessness and tends to be consumed with feelings of anxiety and depression.[39]

On the individual level, Rosenberg indicates, feelings of inadequacy, and perhaps even "self-hatred," create a "tragedy of no mean proportions, compounded of depression, tension, and anxiety." For the society the tragedy may be equally great—at least for one that professes to be democratic: "For if democracy provides a mechanism by which citizens can have their wills translated into political policy, then it becomes farcical to speak of democracy if it is broadly based upon an ignorant, uninterested, and uninfluential electorate." A population with a high degree of self-esteem is, indeed, one of the "personality prerequisites of a democratic society." [40]

Survey research evidence indicates significant numbers of people in the United States (and probably greater proportions in societies with lower mean educational levels) who are low in self-esteem. Research also indicates that those low in self-esteem tend to come from the lower socioeconomic strata of the population. They also tend to possess associated beliefs about the nature of man and society, and are inclined to suffer from anomie. Anomie is a state of relative normlessness. It im-

[38] Ibid., p. 206.
[39] Ibid.
[40] Ibid., p. 211. Cf. Lane, *Political Ideology*, p. 54.

plies a lack of direction and of commitment to social objects (one's fellow human) and social structures (government).

In a national sample of the general population and a sample of politically interested leaders (delegates to the Democratic and Republican national conventions held in 1956), important differences were found in the level of self-esteem, anomie, and perception of the world as a cruel place. As table 4 indicates, half of the sample of the general population falls into the low-self-esteem category, twice the percentage of the convention delegate sample. A third of the delegates are high on the self-esteem scale, compared to approximately one-sixth of those in the general population sample.[41]

Another set of items tapped the *anomie* dimension, which Herbert McClosky and John Schaar define as:

> *a state of mind . . . a feeling that the world and oneself are adrift, wandering, lacking in clear rules and stable moorings. The anomic feels literally* de-*moralized; for him the norms governing behavior are weak, ambiguous, and remote. . . . The core of the concept is the feeling of moral emptiness.*[42]

Feelings of anomie can open up a Pandora's box, for they reduce the effect of externally imposed standards normally internalized (incorporated into the individual's mind) through socialization (the social-learning process). Once social standards are internalized as personal norms, they act to synchronize the fulfillment of personality needs with acceptable channels of endeavor, expression, and social interaction.

Table 4 *Political Leaders and the General Population by Self-Esteem*

	Self-Esteem		
	Low	*Medium*	*High*
Political leaders (campaign delegates)	24%	42%	34%
General population	50	35	15

Source: Computed from Table III in Paul M. Sniderman and Jack Citrin, "Psychological Sources of Political Belief: Self-Esteem and Isolationist Attitudes," *American Political Science Review*, 65, no. 2 (June 1971), 408.

41 See Paul M. Sniderman and Jack Citrin, "Psychological Sources of Political Belief: Self-Esteem and Isolationist Attitudes," *American Political Science Review*, 65, no. 2 (June 1971), 401–17.

42 Herbert McClosky and John H. Schaar, "Psychological Dimensions of Anomie," *American Sociological Review*, 30, no. 1 (February 1965), 19.

Where anomie exists these standards either were not developed or have broken down under conditions of stress and social conflict. Like increasing power or freedom to act and influence others, increasing degrees of anomie successively free the individual from the social limitations on behavior; with each degree of increase in anomie the individual's personality and cognitive (belief system) characteristics hold greater sway as determinants of behavior.

A change in the degree of anomie in the population is likely to change the basis of political appeals. Where anomie is minimal or confined to inactive segments of the population, political appeals will be made at an intellectual level. The pros and cons of issues and government policies will be discussed in a logical, "rational" manner. The relative power of contending groups will be assessed and a number of competing viewpoints aired. As the number of anomic individuals ready to participate (at least to vote) in politics increases, so do political appeals based upon emotion, ego defense (attempt to build up self-esteem and ego strength), and stereotypes. With an anomic political audience, the politics of frustration and prejudice carry the day.

As table 5 indicates, the most anomic individuals are found in the mass of the population, particularly among those low on the educational and occupational scales. Here are people who

are outside the articulate, prosperous, and successful sectors of the population. Anomic feelings appear most frequently and most strongly among those who, for whatever reason, are stranded in the backwaters of the symbolic and material mainstream, those whose lives are circumscribed by isolation, deprivation, and ignorance. . . .[43]

Table 5 *Political Leaders and the General Population by Anomie*

	Anomie		
	Low	*Medium*	*High*
Political leaders (campaign delegates)	60%	32%	8%
General population	26	39	35

Source: Computed from Table III in Paul M. Sniderman and Jack Citrin, "Psychological Sources of Political Belief: Self-Esteem and Isolationist Attitudes," *American Political Science Review*, 65, no. 2 (June 1971), 408.

[43] Ibid.

Beliefs about the world as an unpleasant, threatening place are often found in company with low self-esteem, feelings of alienation, and anomie. In the Cruel World Index, a variable designed to tap this dimension of what we have seen is a characteristic outlook of the closed mind, we again find greater percentages of the mass public in the medium and high categories (table 6), indicating that they believe the world to be an "unhappy, threatening place in which true values cannot be preserved." [44]

Low self-esteem, a belief that the world is a threatening place, anomie, alienation—all tend to reflect a low degree of faith in people and a tendency to view the state as a necessary instrument of suppression and control. Individuals with this "misanthropic" outlook, researchers have found, are more willing than others less pessimistic to advocate the suppression of individual liberties. The "misanthrope" is also prone to be suspicious of others and to explain events occurring around him by means of dark conspiracies. Given his poorly developed cognitive equipment, his narrow horizons, and his negative view of mankind, his conspiratorial view of history provides a satisfactory explanation and is harmonious with his closed-minded belief system.[45]

Such individuals provide a reservoir of political negativism. Seldom if ever do they vote *for* anything. On the contrary, they are usually mobilized politically when an "enemy," a "wrongdoer," or a "conspiracy" appears on the scene against which they can vent their animosity to humankind, society, politics—even self. The result is a burst of emotional outpouring aimed at whatever hapless scapegoat is chosen for the target.

Table 6 *Political Leaders and the General Population by Cruel World Index*

| | Cruel World Index | | |
	Low	*Medium*	*High*
Political leaders (campaign delegates)	53%	37%	9%
General population	35	42	23

Source: Computed from Table III in Paul M. Sniderman and Jack Citrin, "Psychological Sources of Political Belief: Self-Esteem and Isolationist Attitudes," *American Political Science Review*, 65, no. 2 (June 1971), 408.

[44] Sniderman and Citrin, "Psychological Sources of Political Belief," p. 407.

[45] For an analysis of the relationship between views of human nature and political beliefs, see Morris Rosenberg, "Misanthropy and Political Ideology," *American Sociological Review*, 21 (1956), 690–95.

Unaware of political norms and usually apathetic, the masses are likely to enter politics when it serves as a vehicle for the "projection of their personal fears and discontents." [46] Feeling powerless in politics and the community, viewing the world as a threatening place, and being prone to believe in the conspiratorial view of social events, the masses are often mobilizable when confronted with a situation in which they have a chance to vote down something desired by the "power elite." In a study of defeated referendums in two American cities where the mass vote was mobilized, researchers noted that the campaign moved from a consideration of specific issues to an attack upon the

> *experts and local leaders; this atmosphere [of controversy] was*
> *provoked and perpetuated by the attacks of self-appointed*
> *opposition leaders—perhaps local counterparts of the demagogic*
> *leaders of mass movements—who in their opposition. . . . professed*
> *representing the interests of "the people."* [47]

Other studies of voting turnout have indicated a similar phenomenon. Defeat of the measure on the ballot results from "a consistent pattern of negative voting among the socially and economically deprived segments of the population, segments which usually contribute disproportionately to the nonvoters." [48] The general conclusion is that people who feel powerless, who see themselves as buffeted by forces beyond their control, who believe that the world is a threatening place, and who are consequently suspicious of others are the ones who vote "no" on the issue regardless of the particular merits of the case.[49]

RAPUANO: A MASS MAN

There is, of course, no perfect "mass man," but there are people who exhibit many of the characteristics discussed above. Describing them can help put flesh on the bare bones of political theory and empirical data. Rapuano was one of the men interviewed intensively by Robert Lane, as described in *Political Ideology.*

[46] John E. Horton and Wayne E. Thompson, "Powerlessness and Political Negativism: A Study of Defeated Local Referendums," *American Journal of Sociology,* 67, no. 5 (March 1962), 486.

[47] Ibid., p. 488.

[48] Ibid.

[49] See also William A. Gamson, "The Fluoridation Dialogue: Is It an Ideological Conflict?" *Public Opinion Quarterly,* 27, no. 4 (Winter 1961), 526–37.

Rapuano was one of seven children of an illiterate immigrant. Rapuano worked himself up to the position of checker in a meat and provision company. He makes a bit more than his neighbors; his wife does not have to work, and he can send his children to a private school. He "keeps out of trouble with the law; he has never been on relief; he is a veteran and a patriot; indeed, no one could be more patriotic than Rapuano." [50] Rapuano is conscientious; he worries about his work and perhaps for this reason has developed ulcers. He believes strongly that we have as much freedom in the United States as we could possibly use. In fact, he is one of the men in Lane's sample who is afraid of more freedom—a reflection of his view of human nature. " 'I mean, if there's any more freedom to be had,' he says, 'what else could there be, except going around killing people?' " [51]

This view is not surprising in light of the problems Rapuano has in controlling his own behavior. As Lane puts it, he has a certain "volatility of emotion." At one point (at age 40) he had some difficulty with his helper in the meat packing plant. The helper objected to Rapuano's manner of speaking to him and threatened to "knock him down." Rapuano said:

"Well, if you're going to knock me down, let's go outside and you knock me down," see? And we were outside and I hit him five times, and that was it, see? He doesn't come to me any more and tell me he's going to knock me down anymore, see? And in fact he's doing better since I hit him. I think I ought to hit him often. (pause) Oh, yes, I think I broke a rib on him and loosened a couple of teeth.[52]

Rapuano is also impulsive and quick to anger:

He fights with Communists on street corners; he had a habit of turning over ash cans in Jewish neighborhoods before he reformed (I find no traces of this kind of rabid anti-Semitism now); he fires off a postcard to Khrushchev to "shut your big fat mouth." His fear of freedom . . . is fed by a secret fear of what an angry man might do without the restraints of government and society and convention and family to help him out.[53]

[50] Robert Lane, *Political Ideology* (New York: Free Press, 1967), p. 1.
[51] Ibid., p. 42.
[52] Ibid., p. 49.
[53] Ibid., p. 50.

As an immigrant's son, he was caught in a conflict of cultures. The demands of parents and family frequently conflicted with those of school and peer group. Lane indicates that he shows signs of ambivalent identification or loss of identity.[54] Because he feels insecure in his self-conceptions, is worried about the uncertainties of his job, and has difficulties controlling his emotions, it is not surprising to find that he is somewhat impatient with the process of democratic government. The indecisiveness, ambiguity, and ever present cross-pressures associated with it create anxiety. Democracy "gets in its own way," he says; government should be "streamlined." His desire for strong external controls is mirrored in the belief that "the President should have, if not a strict dictatorship, [then at least] 'some unlimited powers.'" His views of human nature emerge again in his discussion of the electorate. Only those who are "intelligent" should be allowed to have the franchise. "Just because a man is—just because he's a human being, doesn't make him smart enough to vote." [55]

In line with this mode of thought, Rapuano, and others like him, adhere to a *cabalistic,* or conspiratorial, concept of social causation and social control: [56] Two cabals or conspiracies control events by manipulating the levers of power behind the scenes, one for the good of the society, the other, in purpose, for ill. The first consists of "legitimate, high-status" groups, such as businessmen, that provide the individual with a secure, unambiguous reason to believe that although his own world is one of chaos and uncertainty, the political world is run by "the kind of absolute power that is psychologically most needed but is clearly hard to find in Congress or the President." [57] When a person's life is full of anxiety and tension, one tends to look away from the ambiguity and cross-pressures that exist in the political world—especially in that of a democracy. Belief in an all-powerful conspiracy serves to "still the demand for a guiding hand, a conscious intelligence, a dominant force in society. It is a counterweight to the chaotic forces of drift and change welling up in anarchic fashion within the individual." [58]

As noted in an earlier chapter, the closed mind tends to see the world in terms of power and dominance relationships: strong versus

---

[54] Ibid., p. 111.

[55] Ibid., p. 108.

[56] See ibid., p. 114. Eleven of the fifteen men Lane interviewed appeared to be free of this form of thinking. In none of the four, including Rapuano, who were not, Lane indicates, had this mode of thought approached neurotic or paranoid conditions that impaired "normal" functioning. See ibid., pp. 122–23.

[57] Ibid., p. 126.

[58] Ibid.

weak, right versus wrong. No real value or valence (positive or negative effect) is placed upon this situation: Control by the dominant few over the submissive many is not deemed injurious or necessarily bad, nor is it deemed necessarily good. Rather, it is accepted as an inevitable part of the natural order. "It's got to be that way." "This is the nature of things." A person resigns himself to his fate, "more in sorrow than in anger," as Lane puts it, or as in the case of Rapuano, who envies those in power, "more in envy than in anger."

But if a person is powerless in the face of the "in" conspiracy, it would also be intolerable, given such a great deal of concern with hierarchical power relations, to further a low sense of ego strength and self-esteem by admitting that one is "on the bottom." Those with cabalistic views therefore have a second cabal, an evil conspiracy threatening to overturn things. This cabal frequently serves as a projection of the impulses they have such trouble controlling. For Rapuano, the evil conspiracy that must be scourged is the communists.[59] Of the group interviewed by Lane, Rapuano had the strongest anticommunist feelings:

> "I have a very, very strong feeling about Communism. I can't—I—to me, an American Communist is—it's—I can't explain it. It's just— there's not words to describe how I feel about that." [60]

Ethnically marginal and concerned with dominance–submission relationships, Rapuano is afraid that the communists will " 'enslave' him and 'dominate' him." [61] His ethnic marginality helps turn him into a superpatriot, a "one-hundred percent (and therefore nonmarginal) American." He was foursquare in favor of Senator Joseph McCarthy's anticommunism crusade:

> "I thought [Senator McCarthy] was a great man. I've thought that when they censured him in the Senate—I thought that was part of the scheme of the Communist conspiracy to do that, and they succeeded. Now there's a man that fought for—for this

---

[59] Ibid.

[60] Ibid., p. 50.

[61] Ibid. Lane indicates that Rapuano is a low scorer on the F (fascism) scale. He argues that Rapuano is searching for a "we-group," a stable identity, rather than complete submission to authority. Nevertheless, it is clear that he is "led to view the democratic order with skepticism." Ibid., p. 186.

country. He fought for people like me, against Communists,
and yet they tied his hands and censured him. . . . I thought he
was a great man. We should have more people like him." [62]

When asked about his views of the "ideal government," Rapuano
said that it would be a simple one; certainly, he implied, not a government as complex and counterbalanced as the present constitutional one.
Elections would be held infrequently if at all; " 'there wouldn't be any
voting every year or so—that would be out.' " The government could
be run by a council with members elected for life, unless one of their
number turned out to be too radical. Then " 'the first thing you do is
just grab him bodily and just eliminate him.' " [63]

Several themes emerge from this discussion of Rapuano: the need
for direction from above; an orderly rather than an ambiguous, dis-
orderly world; and structure—a hierarchically organized universe where
one's place and identity are known and secure, and where one is not
considered marginal. Such characteristics predispose many among the
masses to accept an elitist political structure. That is, they accept their
station in life and they accept the elites as people who have earned or
in some way deserve their positions of power (provided that they are
not members of the "bad" cabal). Rapuano, for example, believes that
"income is proportionate with ability." He resigns himself to his position
in life.[64]

Nevertheless, a lower-class existence carries a certain amount of tension
in a society that purports to be equalitarian. The working-class men
that Lane interviewed were in some respects getting the best of both
worlds: a world that was in some senses equalitarian, which made them
better than those below them, who had not "worked as hard"; and a
world that was in other ways inequalitarian, which allowed them to
rationalize somewhat their position as members of the working class.
Lane sums up some of the dynamics of the situation in propositional
form:

The greater the strain on a person's self-esteem implied by a
relatively low status in an open [i.e., equalitarian] society, the greater

---

[62] Ibid., p. 120. On ethnic marginality, see ibid., pp. 128–29.

[63] Citations from ibid., p. 175. Lane believes Rapuano is one of two in the sample
of fifteen who show definite symptoms of alienation. The rest, while essentially passive
in orientation, did appear to believe that government in some way or another was representative of "the people"; that is, while expressing a basic subject orientation, they
manifested allegiance to the political system.

[64] Ibid., pp. 66–67.

the necessity to explain this status as "natural" and "proper" in the social order.[65]

Similarly,

The greater the emphasis in a society upon equality of opportunity, the greater the tendency for those of marginal status to denigrate those lower than themselves. This view . . . has a psychological "justification" in that it draws attention to one's own relatively better status and one's own relatively greater initiative and virtue.[66]

None of the individuals in Lane's sample thought that complete equality was desirable. Many felt uneasy about having to mingle with others of higher status who might look down on them. All of the men worked hard at jobs that were not necessarily pleasant; many held more than one job and had little if any leisure. Equality of income and presumably even equality of educational opportunity would be like giving "a block and tackle to Sisyphus after all these years." Many of the men wouldn't like it. Having "rolled the stone to the top of the hill so long, they despise the suggestion that it might have been in vain. Or even worse, that their neighbors at the foot of the hill might have the use of a block and tackle." [67]

Thus, the lower classes appear to need someone below them to reinforce their sense of self-esteem regarding their own situation, and need someone above them to provide the sense of security, guidance, and control necessary for the order and structure that reduces feelings of inadequacy. Equality provides none of these things. It only increases anxiety and tension.

The twin themes of order and fear of equality [68] are not confined to Lane's 1950s sample of fifteen men. These issues have emerged in bold outline in the 1960s and 1970s insofar as one pair of political analysts have combined the two into the major issue of the 1970s as they see it—the issue around which a new electoral majority will be built. Richard Scammon and Ben J. Wattenberg call this "the social issue."

Americans, they say, are "beginning to orient themselves politically along the axes of . . . social situations . . . described variously as law

[65] Ibid., p. 79.
[66] Ibid.
[67] Ibid., p. 78.
[68] See ibid., chapter 4, "The Fear of Equality."

and order, backlash, antiyouth, malaise, change, or alienation." [69] The majority of voters, these authors hasten to point out, are "unyoung, unpoor, and unblack." They are, instead, "middle-aged, middle-class, middle-minded." [70]

Their concern over law and order is understandable, especially when the need for structure is high, as it is in the Rapuano-style personality. In addition, increasing rates of technological and social change, competing life styles, and a so-called "new morality" add greatly to the cacophonous stimuli that impinge upon them and cannot be ignored. When one's own ego, self-esteem, and hard-earned position in society are threatened by changing times and changing standards of evaluation, the "threat of abandonment," the threat of meaninglessness, indeed loom large. The masses cannot be expected to give up their bare foothold on the lower levels of the status hierarchy without a struggle, some reaction to what they perceive as a challenge. Rapuano responded to the threat of communists by physically assaulting them. Should a figure appear in politics promising to do the same thing—at least symbolically—we would expect Rapuano and others like him to take note. George Wallace was such a man, and he mobilized their fears and discontents about "the social issue." "Send them a message," he told them. Let the Washington politicians know your feelings about integration, law and order, government "give-away programs" and the counterculture. Bring government back to the people!

The Wallace phenomenon reflected the awakening of a mass electorate to the political situation because of the threat of change that was engulfing it. What President Nixon called his "silent majority" would in all probability have continued to remain silent and passive had it not appeared to them that they were being drowned out by the more vocal groups composed of students against the Vietnam war and members of minority groups intent upon putting into practice equalitarian portions of the American ideology.

The nature of Wallace support and the issue orientation of those voting clearly indicate both the mass nature of his constituency and the source of his appeal—his followers' orientation toward the "social issue."

As indicated in table 7, the majority of Wallace voters identified with the working class. Of greater significance is the large percentage who came from working-class families—individuals who, like Rapuano, have attempted to strive upward, have in part succeeded, and now seek to retain their foothold. Such individuals are sometimes prone to feel-

---

[69] Richard M. Scammon and Ben J. Wattenberg, *The Real Majority* (New York: Coward, McCann & Geoghegan, 1970), p. 20.

[70] Ibid., p. 21.

Table 7 *Socioeconomic Background of Humphrey, Nixon, and Wallace Vo*
1968 Election

	Wallace Voters	Humphrey Voters	Nixon Voters
Identify with working class	64%	55%	44%
Family was working-class	80	68	57
Manual occupation	40	36	28

Source: Computed from Richard M. Scammon and Ben J. Wattenberg, *The Real Majority* (New York: Coward, McCann & Geoghegan, 1970), p. 195.

ings of marginality and have had difficulty establishing a stable identity. Problems of insecurity and emotional control lead them to seek ties with traditional morality (the Protestant ethic, hard work, the assumption of scarcity) and to favor the maintenance of an orderly, stable environment that will counteract the gnawing uncertainty that plagues them (remember Rapuano's ulcers). At the same time, the existence of an enemy or a cabal provides an opportunity for projecting their negative feelings onto another group. For the white working- and lower-middle-classes in the United States, the civil rights and student antiwar movements of the 1960s provided an ideal scapegoat. This is reflected in the attitudes of Wallace voters (table 8).

In 1972 Wallace pitched his appeal directly to the common person. His enemies were the rich who "go without paying taxes," the government officials and bureaucrats who appear removed from the people and uninterested in their plight ("I bet if you opened half of their brief-

Table 8 *Differences in Attitudes toward Civil Rights and Urban Unrest*
of Humphrey, Nixon, and Wallace Voters (1968 Election)

	Wallace Voters	Nixon Voters	Humphrey Voters
Disapprove of permitting protest marches	65%	49%	42%
Against federal push to school integration	75	48	28
Civil rights people pushing too fast	87	66	49
Black actions seen as mostly violent	83	72	58

Source: Richard M. Scammon and Ben J. Wattenberg, *The Real Majority* (New York: Coward, McCann & Geoghegan, 1970), p. 196.

cases, all you'd find would be a peanut butter sandwich"), and the intellectuals. The masses have always appeared to manifest nascent anti-intellectualism. The educated individual, usually more open-minded cognitively, as discussed in Chapter 3, is not characterized by over-simplistic explanations or policy recommendations. Yet oversimplification is the hallmark of those who build a successful mass movement. (*Newsweek* magazine called the Wallace campaign in the 1972 Florida primary, which he won, "devastating in its simplicity.") [71] The intellectual is also less prone to adopt an emotional rather than a logical, systematically reasoned position. An intellectual explanation will seldom be understood by those operating with thought processes that are "simple and straightforward." [72] This lack of understanding will, in time, make it appear that the government, and especially the advisors and proponents of various aspects of government policy, with their academic degrees and all, have "lost touch with the people." In addition, a reaction against those with more education and positions of high status, power, and prestige is a way to strengthen a weakened sense of self-esteem, reduce one's sense of powerlessness, and reaffirm an unstable identity, as the Jules Feiffer cartoon indicates. George Wallace was a master at tapping these sensitive areas of the mass mind:

We're here tonight because the average citizen in this country—the man who pays his taxes and works for a living and holds this country together—the average citizen is fed up with much of this liberalism and this kowtowing to the exotic few [Wallace speaking at a rally].

We're sick and tired of the average citizen being taxed to death while these multibillionaires like the Rockefellers and the Fords and the Mellons and Carnegies go without paying taxes. . . . We've got to close up these loopholes on those who've escaped paying their fair share so we can lower taxes for the average citizen— the little businessman, the farmer, the elderly, the middle class.

Few can resist the call for reduced taxes, especially those caught in a day-to-day struggle to make ends meet in a period of inflation. Shifting to the government and the intellectuals, Wallace said:

This is a people's awakening. These pluperfect hypocrites in Washington don't know what's coming over you. Well, if they'd

[71] *Newsweek,* 27 March 1972, p. 23.
[72] Converse, "The Nature of Belief Systems," p. 212.

I WALK
ON THE
STREET,
I FEEL
UNSAFE.

I GET ON
A BUS,
I FEEL
UNDESIRABLE.

I GO TO THE
OFFICE. I FEEL
UNNECESSARY.

I GO HOME,
I FEEL
UNRECOGNIZED.

I TURN ON TV,
I FEEL 'GOOD'
ALL OVER.

WATERGATE.

© 1973 Jules Feiffer

Dist. Publishers-Hall Syndicate

gone out and asked a taxi driver, a little businessman, or a beautician or a barber or a farmer they'd have found out. But no, they don't ask these folks when they make their decisions. They ask some pointy-headed pseudo-intellectual who can't even park his bicycle straight when he gets to the campus, that's who they ask. But they're not ignoring you now. You're tops. You're the people.

Wallace was well on the way to becoming a strong force at the Democratic presidential convention of 1972 when an assassination attempt stopped him short.

The apparently rapid mobilization of a usually apathetic portion of the electorate has led to a "rediscovery of the working [class] American." [73] As noted in an article in the *Washington Post*, "Truck drivers, dock workers, factory hands and shoe clerks are being rediscovered as an enormous political force that may be bent on counter-revolution." [74]

The explosively sudden electoral participation of previously uninterested portions of the public has given rise to the phenomenon of the "flash party," a movement that represents "spasms of political excitement in unusually hard times on the part of citizens whose year-in, year-out involvement in political affairs is abnormally weak." [75] The flash party is characterized by a rapid rise and sudden fall, as the emotions of the masses cannot be kept for long at a fever pitch. The Wallace phenomenon in the United States was one example. The Poujadist movement in France was another. Pierre Poujade was a charismatic man of the masses. In 1956 he mobilized a discontented, alienated part of the French population against the taxation policies of the government. His strength came largely from the lower middle classes, "particularly small provincial shopkeepers economically on the decline who were in revolt against modern trends that threatened them with extinction." [76]

Where frustrations are great, and where anomie, alienation, and subsequent lack of electoral participation have kept political experience mimimal, radical action and often violence are just around the corner. The Poujadists organized violent protests against tax inspectors and kept them from entering the offices of the small artisan and businessman. Policy statements and a coherent program were noticeable by their

[73] Paraphrase of a front page headline appearing in a September 1969 *Washington Post*, cited in Scammon and Wattenberg, *The Real Majority*, p. 223.

[74] Cited in ibid.

[75] Philip E. Converse and Georges Dupeux, "Politicization of the Electorate in France and the United States," in *Elections and the Political Order*, Angus Campbell, et al., eds. (New York: John Wiley, 1966), p. 270.

[76] Maurice Duverger, *The French Political System*, trans. Barbara North and Robert North (Chicago: University of Chicago Press, 1958), p. 97.

absence. Political negativism and simplicity of expression, on the other hand, were hallmarks of campaign rhetoric. The major plank in the political platform was the slogan, "Get rid of them!"—a slogan aimed at non-Poujadist deputies seeking reelection.[77]

The similarities between the Poujadist war cry and Wallace's "Send them a message" are striking. In each case the demand and the dynamic were the same: The demand was a halt to forces of change and consequent uncertainty and threat; the dynamic was the opening up of an opportunity to express pent up frustration and assuage the hurt to self-esteem done by long-standing feelings of political powerlessness. The result was an orgy of political negativism and the creation, almost overnight, of a mass party. "It was predicted that the Poujadists would win 5 to 10 seats; instead, they won 52 and polled 2,500,000 votes—almost 10 percent of the electorate.[78] Scarcely a year later the party went into a precipitous decline from which it never recovered. The emotions of the masses are indeed transient and short-lived. By 1976, Wallace's appeal was ended. In both cases, the attraction to a charismatic, but institutionally weak, individual leader was temporary.

SUMMARY AND CRITIQUE

The political perspective of the masses is generally limited. They frequently act as a negative force in politics, voting against rather than for an issue or candidate. In a crisis the masses are likely to look for a leader to show them the way out, because they lack strong feelings of political efficacy and, often, self-esteem. But they also constitute a powerful, sometimes volatile force in politics. At one moment the masses may be quiescent, at another they may be actively aligned behind a charismatic leader.

Among several criticisms that may be leveled against the arguments presented in this chapter, one is that they are elitist: The people—in theory the "backbone of democracy"—are tainted by authoritarianism, and when they become actively involved in politics strong antidemocratic urges are expressed. The implication, of course, is that the educated must lead because others are incapable—an "elitist" conclusion.

The true elitist, however, would argue that no change in the differentiating characteristics of elites and masses, or in the relations between them, is possible or desirable. However, in the view here presented, "the masses" are potential threats to democracy only when they are on

---

[77] Ibid., p. 96.
[78] Ibid.

the lower rungs of the Maslow hierarchy—when they are deficiency motivated. If a large enough proportion of the American electorate func-
tioned on the level of growth motivation, then the distinction between
elites and masses would be reduced.

Such individual changes are not easily induced. Yet, if economic
conditions remain stable and great numbers of people do not find their
livelihoods and self-esteem threatened, and if equal opportunities for
meaningful higher education are provided, then over time growth rather
than deficiency motivation would come to characterize the majority of
citizens. At this point the distinctions drawn in this chapter would be
less operative.

In politics and the political system elites and masses, responsibility
and power come together. Power and the political system are the subjects of the next chapter.

Selected Bibliography

ALMOND, GABRIEL, and SIDNEY VERBA, *The Civic Culture.* Boston, Mass.: Little,
Brown, 1963.

CONVERSE, PHILIP E., "The Nature of Belief Systems in Mass Publics," in *Ideology and Discontent,* David E. Apter, ed. New York: Free Press, 1964.

DYE, THOMAS R., and L. HARMON ZEIGLER, *The Irony of Democracy.* Belmont,
Ca.: Wadsworth, 1970.

EDELMAN, MURRAY, *The Symbolic Uses of Politics.* Urbana: University of Illinois
Press, 1967.

LANE, ROBERT E., *Political Ideology.* New York: Free Press, 1962.

LIPSET, SEYMOUR MARTIN, *Political Man.* Garden City, N.Y.: Doubleday, 1960.

MICHELS, ROBERT, *Political Parties,* trans. Eden Paul and Cedar Paul. New York:
Dover Publications, 1959.

MILLS, C. WRIGHT, *The Power Elite.* New York: Oxford University Press, 1959.

MOSCA, GAETANO, *The Ruling Class,* trans. Hannah D. Kahn, ed. and rev. Arthur
Livingston. New York: McGraw-Hill, 1939.

6

Power and the political system: an overview

Politics can be understood in general terms as the means by which authoritative allocations of values are agreed upon and distributed to the society. Values are the scarce goods, both symbolic and material, by which people's various needs are satisfied. Government is involved in both the production of these goods (by taxation) and their distribution through government policies. In addition, governments "regulate conflict within society . . . [and] organize society to carry on conflict with other societies. . . ." [1]

The action government takes in fulfilling these functions is *authoritative* because it is supported by both *power* and *legitimacy*.[2] Government has the power to take its "just due" because it has a monopoly on the legitimate means of coercion, that is, the police and the armed forces. Hence it can apply negative sanctions to force recalcitrant citizens to comply with its laws and decrees.

Legitimacy means that the government structure, characteristics, and mode of operation are considered correct and proper by the majority of citizens. Thus, normally the majority will voluntarily comply with the decrees of government. The legitimate government is one that reaches and carries out its decisions in a fashion that is consonant with the attitudes, values, and beliefs of the citizenry. Where legitimacy is lacking, where the form and actions of government do not accord with the basic beliefs of the population, political instability usually results, and coercion must be used to control the population.[3] Because its

[1] Thomas R. Dye, *Understanding Public Policy* (Englewood Cliffs, N.J.: Prentice-Hall, 1972), p. 2.

[2] Ibid.

[3] Cf. Edward N. Muller, "Correlates and Consequences of Beliefs in the Legitimacy of Regime Structures," *Midwest Journal of Political Science,* 14 (1970), 392–412, and the sources cited therein. See also David Easton, *A Systems Analysis of Political Life* (New York: John Wiley & Sons, 1965), chapter 19; and Dorwin Cartwright, "Influence, Leadership, Control," in *Handbook of Organizations,* James G. March, ed. (Chicago: Rand McNally, 1965), pp. 1–47.

energy is diverted from the attempt to solve social problems, government based upon force alone is usually transitory.

THE POLITICAL SYSTEM: AN ANALYTICAL PERSPECTIVE

The political system is the mechanism whereby binding decisions are made for society as a whole. As David Easton has written, "Even in the smallest and simplest society someone must intervene in the name of society, with its authority behind him, to decide how differences over valued things are to be resolved." [4] No society contains a perfectly satisfied population, nor is any society without conflict between groups pursuing contradictory interests. No society is therefore without a political system. The term *system* has proved useful to political scientists because of the ability of systems theory to simplify the components of government and to place them in a perspective that is both analytical and dynamic: *analytical* because it separates government into the component parts and relationships that are found in every political system; *dynamic* because it gives the researcher a guide to the forces that lead to change as well as those that make for stability.

The political system may be defined as a set of individuals and institutions that act together in a regularized and recurring manner to find solutions for problems that cannot be solved within the non-government segments of society. [5] The political system is analytically differentiated from the environment: the former includes "all those actions more or less directly related to the making of binding decisions for a society," [6] and the latter includes all of those segments of society not so involved.

The political system can be viewed as part of an exchange process. Citizens transmit *demands* to political authorities; they ask the government to do certain things. These demands are communicated through channels to the decision makers who devise a policy that is then ad-

---

[4] David Easton, *The Political System* (New York: Alfred A. Knopf, 1953), pp. 136–37, as cited in Milton C. Cummings, Jr., and David Wise, *Democracy Under Pressure* (New York: Harcourt Brace Jovanovich, 1971), p. 19.

[5] This definition and the following discussion draw upon the following sources: Morton A. Kaplan, "Systems Theory," in *Contemporary Political Analysis*, James C. Charlesworth, ed. (New York: Free Press, 1967), pp. 150–63; Easton, *A Systems Analysis*; Robert C. Bone, *Action and Organization* (New York: Harper & Row, 1972), pp. 46–47; and Dye, *Understanding Public Policy*, pp. 18–20.

[6] David Easton, "An Approach to the Analysis of Political Systems," *World Politics*, 9 (April 1957), 87, as cited in Bone, *Action and Organization*, p. 46.

ministered by the government bureaucracy, reaching the citizen as an authoritative decision that is binding on all parties involved. The citizen, in turn, accords *support* to the political system both before and after the decision. The greater the correlation between demands and policy outcomes, the greater the support for the government, and the more legitimate the political system. Notice, however, that demands must be articulated and communicated to the input channels of the political system before they can be considered. Needless to say, the educated, active portion of the community is likely to be primarily involved in this process. Figure 1 presents a schematic diagram of a systems-theory approach to the political system.

The political system is responsible for maintaining a basic degree of order and regularity in human relationships such that the population will be able to satisfy its needs. Its monopoly over the means of legitimate compulsion is what chiefly distinguishes the political from other aspects of society.

Legitimate force is the thread that runs through the inputs and outputs of the political system, giving it its special quality and salience and its coherence as a system. The inputs into the political system are all in some way related to claims for the employment of legitimate compulsion, whether these are demands for war or for recreational facilities. The outputs of the political system are also all in some way related to legitimate physical compulsion, however remote the relationship may be. Thus, public recreational

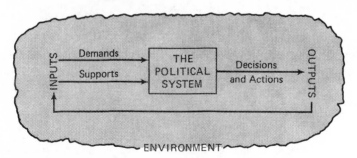

Source: David Easton, A Systems Analysis of Political Life *(New York: John Wiley & Sons, 1965), p. 32.*

Figure 1   A Systems Model of the Polity

facilities are usually supported by taxation, and any violation of the regulations governing their use is a legal offense.[7]

Invested with legitimate force, individuals acting on behalf of the political system carry out the number of activities needed to fulfill its order-maintaining and problem-solving functions. They act to determine the major goals of the society; they formulate policy designed to achieve these goals; and they adopt rules through which these policies can be implemented. These activities may lead to the maintenance of the existing order or to its alteration in response to problems arising from inside and outside the society.

Policy decisions are implemented through administration. Since the government that is based upon consensus and voluntary acquiescence is the most effective one, politicians may endeavor to mobilize support for government policy and its implementation among important segments of society. Finally, government engages in the solving of disputes that arise between contending parties when its rules are applied to actual situations. This is the juridical function.[8]

POWER

Rarely does a binding decision satisfy everyone or are all possible effects of a decision clearly seen beforehand. Hence, nearly every definition of politics and every discussion of "things political" involves the probability that politicians will require someone to do something that he might not otherwise have done. *Power* has therefore been considered by many to lie at the heart of politics.

Power may be defined in general terms as "the capacity of an individual, or group of individuals, to modify the conduct of other individuals or groups in the manner in which he [the powerholder] desires." [9] The exercise of the powerholder's will leads to compliance

---

[7] Gabriel A. Almond and James S. Coleman, eds., *The Politics of the Developing Areas* (Princeton, N.J.: Princeton University Press, 1960), p. 7. See also Oran R. Young, *Systems of Political Science* (Englewood Cliffs, N.J.: Prentice-Hall, 1968), p. 2; Max Weber, as cited in Robert A. Dahl, *Modern Political Analysis* (Englewood Cliffs, N.J.: Prentice-Hall, 1970), p. 5; and S. N. Eisenstadt, *The Political Systems of Empires* (New York: Free Press, 1963), p. 5.

[8] This discussion of political functions relies upon Eisenstadt, *The Political Systems of Empires*, p. 6. In chapter 7, a more extensive discussion of political functions will be presented.

[9] R. H. Tawney, *Equality* (New York: Harcourt Brace Jovanovich, 1931), p. 230, as cited in Harold D. Lasswell and Abraham Kaplan, *Power and Society* (New Haven, Conn.: Yale University Press, 1950), p. 75.

of those to whom the power is directed. The exercise of power can thus meet a leader's need for self-esteem and self-actualization. Because power can thus be a desirable personal commodity, a political career can be more attractive than others for people who have a high need for deference. Occasionally a politician reveals by his actions or his words that he enjoys the sheer power of office and expects to receive the proper amount of deference from those with whom he deals. For example, *Newsweek* reports that Richard Nixon was angered by the price he received for Florida real estate holdings he sold to a land trust shortly after his election in 1968. The largest shareholder in the trust attempted to give an explanation. "He got as far as 'But Dick . . .' when Mr. Nixon exploded: 'Don't you dare call me Dick. I am the President of the United States. When you speak to me, you call me Mr. President.' " [10]

While power may be viewed as a commodity, as a set of rewards and punishments that the powerholder has at his disposal and uses to gain the compliance of others, it may also be considered as constituent to a relationship between two or more individuals; there is no leader if there are no followers who are willing or at least able to do as he wishes. As Carl Friedrich writes, "Power is . . . that relation among men which manifests itself in the behavior of following." [11] The concept of power implies that the actions taken by followers in response to the desires of the powerholder are *not* those they would take if left to their own devices. Indeed, complete consensus on the ends (and means) of society would obviate the need for powerholders (for leaders and followers); should such a consensus ever exist the state would "wither away" as envisioned in the communist utopia of Karl Marx. No man would will that another act in any fashion contrary to his own desires. That this condition nowhere exists is evident in the universality of political systems.

The extensive use of power in the form of physical compulsion indicates that the basic consensus upon which the polity rests has been shaken, perhaps irreparably. Should politicians expend most of their energies in the exercise of this form of power, the outcome may go quite against their wishes or expectations. Power, as a relationship, may in the end depend just as much upon the follower as it does on the leader. Recently, the lone man with a gun succeeded in assassinating two Kennedys, one a president, the other a presidential candidate. Presidents Johnson, Nixon, and Ford had to seek refuge from the lone unconsenting citizen behind elaborate security precautions ever since,

[10] *Newsweek*, 20 August 1973, p. 31.

[11] Carl J. Friedrich, "Political Leadership and the Problem of Charismatic Power," *Journal of Politics*, 23 (February 1961), 5.

though even such elaborate precautions have not always proved effective, as in the case of George Wallace. Should the governed ever decide en masse to withdraw their consent, the governors would be faced with a crisis grave enough to shake the political system to its foundations.[12] As the sixteenth-century French writer Etienne de La Boétie said of the power of a tyrant: "He who abuses you so has only two eyes, has but two hands, one body and has naught but what has the least man of the great and infinite number [of people in] . . . your cities, except for the advantage you give him to destroy you." [13] It is no wonder that politicians look with some awe, perhaps even fear, at the great, acquiescent "silent majority." A majority that did not remain silent and quiescent might indeed present a problem.

Physical compulsion indicates an absolute unwillingness of followers to comply with the wishes of those in positions of authority. Therefore, most discussions of politics move quickly to an emphasis upon influence, persuasion, and such associated ideas as charisma and leadership ability. For example, the power of the American president to persuade is mentioned much more frequently than the power to coerce. Harry S Truman knew this as well as anyone. Truman, with tongue in cheek, envisioned the newly elected Eisenhower, accustomed to the military chain of command in which sanctions can be directly applied for noncompliance with orders, sitting at the desk in the Oval Office saying, " 'Do this, do that'— and nothing will happen."

AUTHORITY

Authority is closely associated with power; authority is formal or legal as distinguished from personal power. It is power assigned to a position by the popularly accepted ground rules for the operation of the political system.[14] For example, the Constitution assigns certain powers to the president. This gives him the authority, "the right to command and direct, to be heard or obeyed by others," [15] when acting in areas reserved for his office by the Constitution. By the authority that inheres in that

12 See Herbert Simon, "Notes on the Observation of Political Power," in Donald R. Reich and Paul A. Dawson, *Political Images and Realities* (Belmont, Ca.: Duxbury Press, 1972), pp. 278–79.

13 Etienne de la Boétie, "Discours de la Servitude Volontaire," in *Oeuvres Completes d'Etienne de la Boétie* (Paris: J. Rouam & Cie., 1892), p. 12, as cited in Gene Sharp, *The Politics of Nonviolent Action* (Boston: Porter Sargent, 1973), p. 11.

14 Lasswell and Kaplan, *Power and Society*, p. 133.

15 Jacques Maritain, *Man and the State* (Chicago: University of Chicago Press, 1954), p. 126, as cited in Sharp, *The Politics of Nonviolent Action*, p. 11.

office the president's actions are accepted voluntarily by the populace, and his directives are therefore carried out without the employment of force or sanctions.[16]

Note that there are two objects of focus: a position, or role, in an institution, and an individual occupying that position. By *role* we mean the set of patterned expectations about behavior that the members of society attach to a position (here the presidency) in an institution (the executive branch of government). An institution, in turn, is a set of interrelated roles designed to so organize and coordinate behavior as to achieve a goal or perform a function. It is these positions to which authority inheres; though a man may gain power in his own right because of charisma and leadership ability,[17] the man in the position (or the *incumbent*, as he is sometimes called) gains power simply by occupying that position. It was long felt that Richard Nixon, for example, lacked personal appeal and magnetism, as was revealed by his tendency to remove himself from the public eye, to avoid news conferences, and to speak through intermediaries during the Watergate crisis. Yet, while the polls indicated that the president's popularity had declined precipitously and that a majority believed the president had known about an alleged "coverup" of Watergate and had done nothing about it, he continued to command obedience in the areas of his constitutional authority simply because of his position. Despite all the "revelations of misplaced loyalties, of strange measures of the ethical, of unusual doing in high places," and of a feeling that "the very glue of our ship of state seems about to become unstuck," [18]

> . . . *the majority of people still shied away from talk of removing the President from office. "Impeachment is the political equivalent of capital punishment," said a leading Democrat, "and so far the American people don't favor capital punishment for the President." The Boston* Globe *editorialized: "It may be that President Nixon is banking on what social psychologists call the threshold beyond which the body politic cannot go in thinking ill of its leadership or itself. It may be that a 'He's-the-only-President-we've-got' syndrome is beginning to develop."* [19]

16 Sharp, *The Politics of Nonviolent Action,* p. 11.

17 For a discussion of the distinction between the "authority of position" and the "authority of leadership," see Chester I. Barnard, *The Function of the Executive* (Cambridge, Mass.: Harvard University Press, 1938).

18 Supreme Court Justice Harry Blackmun in an August 1973 speech to the American Bar Association meeting in Washington, D.C. Cited in *Time Magazine,* 20 August 1973, p. 9.

19 "Can Public Confidence be Restored?" *Time Magazine,* 20 August 1973, pp. 9–10.

The reluctance of the people to see Nixon impeached was an indication of the power of the *office,* the authority that is attached to this particular political position independent of the qualities and attributes of the incumbent. Indeed, anyone watching the televized Watergate hearings will recall the innumerable times when witnesses—from James McCord, the electronics expert caught in the Watergate, to L. Patrick Gray, former acting director of the FBI who allegedly burned sensitive documents at the behest of presidential advisors—testified that they were somehow acting under orders that had been cleared by the president, the man in *the* office, the man with *the* authority.

Some persons' belief in the authority of the presidency appears to be enough to persuade them to commit—or at least authorize—clearly illegal acts. Perhaps the strongest position on this issue was taken by presidential aide John Ehrlichman. Despite the unwillingness of FBI director J. Edgar Hoover to engage in burglary to obtain files on Daniel Ellsberg, co-defendant in the Pentagon Papers trial, Ehrlichman gave approval "for a 'covert' check of Ellsberg's psychiatric files," which resulted in the break-in of the Los Angeles office of Dr. Lewis Fielding.[20]

The authority of the president is so great in the minds of some that the office is above the law. For Ehrlichman this seems to have been the case. In the course of the Watergate hearings Senator Herman Talmadge asked Ehrlichman about his feelings concerning the rights of the individual versus the power of the executive; specifically, how would he respond to the declamation of the eighteenth-century English statesman, the elder William Pitt, to the effect that:

The poorest man may in his cottage bid defiance to all the force of the crown. It may be frail—its roof may shake—the wind may blow through it—the storm may enter, the rain may enter— but the King of England cannot enter—all his force dare not cross the threshold.

Ehrlichman said, "I am afraid . . . that has been considerably eroded over the years, has it not?"[21] The Watergate break-in and the resulting hearings, trials, and much of the argument revolved around the question of the president's "inherent authority to protect the national security."[22] The question of authority is crucial to the conduct of any political

---

[20] See "Ehrlichman Hangs Tough," *Newsweek,* 6 August 1973, pp. 18–26.
[21] *Time Magazine,* 6 August 1973, p. 12.
[22] Ibid.

office, and its significance increases with the power of the office itself. Few can escape the implications of this question when, again in response to a query from Senator Talmadge, this time as to "whether the President's power to protect national security might extend to other crimes— including murder," Ehrlichman's answer was: "I do not know where the line is, Senator." [23]

PERSUASION

Unlike authority as a means of exercising power, persuasion implies compliance without the explicit threat of sanctions; the individual conforms to the persuader's wishes because of the cogency of his arguments, or the power of his personality, or to gain the benefits that the persuader may be able to provide. The threat of sanctions may be implicit, however. Protection against violence, for example, has been viewed by such philosophers as the seventeenth-century Englishman Thomas Hobbes as the source of governments. To Hobbes man was a grasping, violent creature, and life outside of a society (that is, a political state) "nasty, solitary, poor, brutish and short." It therefore took little effort on the part of a leader to persuade the follower to exchange his individual sovereignty (his freedom to do whatever he wishes) for protection. Power is thus derived from cooperation based upon persuasion and its correlate, leadership. As Friedrich writes:

If a value or purpose to be realized requires the cooperation of a number of human beings, then the power of one or several among them will rest upon his or their capacity to provide the leadership for securing the desired good. They "lead" the way, so to speak, and those who follow recognize their capacity to do so.[24]

Such cooperative arrangements lead to "consensual power," maximum mutual cooperation between leader and follower and minimum coercion. They depend upon a unity of interests and shared or congruent goals toward which the behavior of leader and follower ought to be directed. In this kind of situation persuasion is the dominant form of power.

All forms of influence possess a power base and a motive base. The power base is composed of the leader's resources (money, charisma,

---

[23] Ibid.
[24] Friedrich, "Political Leadership and Charisma," p. 7.

respect, expertise, etc.) that allow him to reinforce the values, strengthen the beliefs, or fulfill the desires of his potential following.[25] The motive base is composed of those of the follower's values, beliefs, or desires that are actuated by the leader's expenditure of resources to modify the follower's behavior. "Every force operative on the powerholder has as its source of energy a motive base with the follower in the form of his needs and values." [26]

Maslow's hierarchy provides us with a concept of human needs, and Kohlberg's stages of moral development outline the cognitive hierarchy that parallels the Maslow hierarchy. It is evident that an individual low in self-esteem with feelings of alienation could be motivated to attach himself to a leader who proved able to build up his sense of self by providing him with a symbolic "place in the sun" and giving him scapegoats on which to release frustration. The defeated referendums noted in chapter 5 are illustrative. Opposition leaders were able to tap a salient mass feeling and capitalize on it.

THE COMPONENTS OF POWER

In their analysis of power, J. R. P. French, Jr., and B. Raven identify five types.[27] Two of these types are familiar: *Coercive power* is based on the follower's belief that the leader has the power to punish him for noncompliance; *legitimate power* is based on the follower's belief that the powerholder has a right to influence him and he has an obligation to follow. Like authority, legitimate power is attached to a position rather than an individual. The three other types of power identified by French and Raven are: *reward power, referent power,* and *expert power.* In the case of reward power, the follower believes that the leader has resources—benefits that will assist the follower in reaching his goals and fulfilling his needs. Political patronage is a common example; once in office, many politicians are able to place their loyal

---

25 See Robert A. Dahl, "The Concept of Power," *Behavioral Science,* 2 (1957), 203. Power base is not synonymous with the actual exercise of power; rather, like Simon's concept of value position, it may be viewed as an indicator of power. Cf. Simon, "Notes," originally published in *The Journal of Politics,* 14 (November 1953), 500–516 and reprinted in Donald R. Reich and Paul A. Dawson, *Political Images and Realities* (Belmont, Ca.: Duxbury Press, 1972), pp. 270–84.

26 Cartwright, "Influence, Leadership, Control," p. 31. This conception is derived from J. R. P. French, Jr., and B. Raven, "The Bases of Social Power," in *Studies in Social Power,* Dorwin Cartwright, ed. (Ann Arbor: University of Michigan, Institute for Social Research, 1959), pp. 150–67.

27 Raven and French, "The Bases of Social Power," p. 29.

supporters in government jobs, steer government contracts their way, and the like. The morass of problems associated with campaign fund raising and spending in the 1972 presidential campaign exemplifies the use of patronage. The followers (campaign contributors) acceded to the leader's demand for money because of the benefits that accrued to them after his election, or because of the potential danger of not contributing.

In the case of referent power, the follower does as the leader bids because he identifies with the leader. This identification is based on affinities of attitude and of opinions concerning the goals pursued by the leader. However, it is also implicit that the leader can fulfill some need, express some ability, or make manifest some characteristic that the follower finds beneficial but could not have accomplished alone.

Leaders sometimes gain a following by lessening inhibitions that prevent followers from engaging in desired or satisfying behavior prohibited by law or custom. In riots, lynchings, and "witch hunts" (or, in European history, pogroms: organized destruction of Jews or other despised minorities), leaders may provide followers with an example of destructive behavior and a rationale for engaging in it. Leader legitimation nullifies the social norms against such behavior. A resonant chord is struck by the leader in his potential following, for aggressive behavior against an agent of frustration or an agent-surrogate (a "scapegoat") is an inherently satisfying response to frustration.[28] Indeed, the most-used tool in the demagogue's bag of tricks is the power of identification gained by exploiting the frustrations and psychological needs of the group he seeks to influence. His tactics work particularly well with those who are approaching cognitive closure, have weak egos, and are in need of self-esteem. The demagogue plays upon the needs and weaknesses of such people. He says that he cares about them, that they possess great potential power, and that while they are truly important to society they are, alas, exploited and forgotten by it. He tells them that their plight is not of their own doing—thereby unburdening them of responsibility for their condition. They are manipulated, he says, by evil forces that he will exorcise. He then mobilizes their fears, hostilities, prejudices, and frustrations, directing them against the hapless scapegoat who, in a great oversimplification, is labeled as the cause of all ills. Because the leader provides his followers a haven where their injured self-esteem can be assuaged, their weak egos strengthened (no matter how low their station in life the leader always finds an enemy that is even

---

[28] See the major statement on the frustration–aggression hypothesis in John Dollard et al., *Frustration and Aggression* (New Haven, Conn.: Yale University Press, 1939). For further analysis and discussion of this hypothesis and research concerning it, see, among others, works by Leonard Berkowitz and Albert Bandura.

lower in the eyes of his following), and their frustrations released, he is able to capitalize upon the resulting power of identification to harness the energies of a following for his own political purposes.

The fifth type of power base, expert, or informational, power, allows a leader to modify the behavior of the follower who believes that the leader possesses superior information and ability. The patient defers to his doctor and carries out his recommendations in the hope of getting well; his health depends upon it. The doctor, in turn, defers to the auto mechanic when his car breaks down. Many people are unwilling to question decisions of politicians in such areas as national defense, because they believe the politicians, and especially the president, are privy to a great deal of secret information and therefore "know what they are doing."

The expert's possession of information and skills that are of immediate value to the follower is one source of his ability to control the behavior relevant to his area of expertise. But he also possesses control over the flow and dissemination of information. The politician, for example, is often able to exert control over the mass media, timing the release of information and governing its emphasis. President Nixon was able to spend considerable amounts of public monies on the bombing of Cambodia by keeping both the action and the expenditures from congressional and public view. The manipulation of information is itself a source of power, as is control over what issues are brought up for debate and public consideration.[29] The destruction of files and memos pertaining to the Watergate case by members of the White House staff and the Committee for the Re-Election of the President represents a recent attempt to control events by controlling the existence and dissemination of information. The old adage, "knowledge is power," and its corollary, "information is power," are as true today as they ever were.

THE LEGITIMATIONS OF POWER

The five types of power discussed above may all be present to some degree in any leader–follower relationship, although more often the types involved will vary according to the personality of the leader, and his following. Generally speaking, these types are reducible to three major classifications, or what Max Weber called three "inner justifications

---

[29] See Peter Bachrach and Morton S. Baratz, "Two Faces of Power," *American Political Science Review*, 56 (December 1962), pp. 947–52.

[or] . . . basic *legitimations* of domination: traditional power, bureaucratic power and charismatic power." [30]

Traditional power, to Weber, signified "the authority of the 'eternal
yesterday,' i.e., the mores sanctified through the unimaginably ancient
recognition and habitual orientation to conform." [31] The strength of
long-established habits and the absence of any contrary notions of
political organization are the foundation of power in traditional king-
doms and empires. Bureaucratic authority, on the other hand, is much
more "conscious" in nature, grounded as it is in the acceptance of
expertise and an impersonal, efficiency-oriented division of labor and
specialization of function. This is "domination by virtue of 'legality,'
by virtue of the belief in the validity of legal statute and functional
'competence' based on rationally created rules" [32] and behavior that, at
least in theory, can be evaluated according to specific, measurable
criteria of effectiveness. Weber describes a kind of power that can exist
in the absence of either tradition or bureaucracy. This is charismatic
power, power stemming from "the extraordinary and personal *gift of
grace* . . . , the absolutely personal devotion and personal confidence
in revelation, heroism, or other qualities of individual leadership." Such
power may be exercised by "the prophet or—in the field of politics—by
the elected war lord, the plebiscitarian ruler, the great demagogue, or
the political party leader." [33]

None of these three kinds of power in absolute form is conducive to
the healthy development of man's potentialities, as the following discussion will indicate. If any one form so predominates that the other
two are only marginally present, the political system based upon it will
militate against the advance of the majority of citizens up the Maslow
hierarchy of needs to self-actualization. For example, in a society based
primarily on traditional power, social status is usually ascriptive; each
person inherits membership in a class or estate at birth. Because social
prerequisites are monopolized by the well-born, those societal decisions
not prescribed by custom will be made by people who are given great
quantities of power without regard to their talent or ability.

As the traditional regime based upon loyalties to family, locality, and,
frequently, a divine-right ruler declined, and the modern state based
upon rational–legal authority evolved, so did the power and the sig-

[30] See H. H. Gerth and C. Wright Mills, *From Max Weber: Essays in Sociology*
(New York: Oxford University Press, 1958), p. 78.

[31] Ibid., pp. 78–79.

[32] Ibid., p. 79.

[33] Ibid., p. 78.

nificance of bureaucracy as a form of social and political organization.[34] Mobility, income, and social position in modern society are generally based on criteria uniformly applicable throughout the society; ability, intelligence, and task performance, as measured by standards that are in theory and intent objective, are more important in a modern society than are ties of family and friendship, and inherited social position, which are of major significance in a traditional society. Rules and standards, not people per se, matter most in modern society.

In traditional society, a locality was relatively independent both politically and economically. This is not the case with modern society. The farms feed the cities—and a blight on crops in Idaho may lead to rising prices in New York, Atlanta, and San Francisco. In a society based on intensive division of labor, specialization of function, and a consequent high degree of interdependence among all parts of the whole, the tasks of integration, interpretation, and regulation loom large. Government becomes increasingly important, and so does bureaucracy.

The change from traditional to modern potentially changes the basic modes of human interaction. Under the traditional system, the "folk" or *Gesellschaft* society,[35] human relationships are governed by ties to locality, the acceptance of custom, and deference to status. In the complex modern society, the multiplicity of necessary functions are divided into minute subdivisions.[36] Each function is fulfilled by a different institution; the behavior of those within the institution is further subdivided, compartmentalized, and rendered subject to "objective" indicators of performance. Human interactions outside of the primary group (for example, the family) tend therefore to be impersonal and mediated by the functions people are engaged in fulfilling: priest–parishioner, service station attendant–customer, doctor–patient, professor–student, and the like. Rarely if ever does one or a few persons perform all of the functions necessary to sustain us. Rarely do we come to personally know many of the people with whom we interact, with a totality that allows us to form a composite picture of the roles they occupy and their "personality," their unique blending of the whole role set.

Communication between people in modern society tends therefore to be quick, to the point, and limited to the respective functions the parties to a transaction fulfill. Our image of the bureaucrat is more

---

[34] For an analysis of the types of political, social, and administrative systems prevalent in ancient societies, see Eisenstadt, *The Politcal Systems of Empires.*

[35] See David Riesman et al., *The Lonely Crowd* (Garden City, N.Y.: Doubleday, 1953), p. 28.

[36] For a conception of the functions ("functional requisites") of society, see Marion J. Levy, Jr., *The Structure of Society* (Princeton, N.J.: Princeton University Press, 1952), pp. 149–97.

than likely confined to a face behind a window and a hand giving us a receipt, a book of stamps, a temporary driver's license.

In Max Weber's definition, bureaucracy was the rational side of the rational–legal foundation of modern societies: "Bureaucratic administration means fundamentally the exercise of control on the basis of knowledge. This is the feature of it which makes it specifically rational." [37] Among the most important of the number of elements that characterize the bureaucratic mode of organization are: centralization of control and supervision (hierarchy); differentiation of function, and hence specialization, the development of expertise, and qualifications for holding a position in the bureaucracy; secrecy or discretion; and precision in task performance and continuity in the organization as a whole. That is, bureaucracy is capable of persisting through time regardless of the fate of the political leaders in titular control.[38]

If technical knowledge is indispensable to a society, so, too, is specialized bureaucracy, the agent through which such knowledge is developed and applied, and which therefore, says Weber, is "as inevitable as the dominance of precision machinery in the mass production of goods." Perhaps just as inevitable is the power that stems from the possession of this knowledge. But while technical knowledge alone is enough to give bureaucracy a "position of extraordinary power," bureaucratic organizations or those who control them

> *have the tendency to increase their power still further by the knowledge growing out of experience. . . . For they acquire through the conduct of office a special knowledge of facts and have available a store of documentary material peculiar to themselves. While not peculiar to bureaucratic organizations, the concept of "official secrets" is certainly typical of them. It stands in relation to technical knowledge in somewhat the same position as commercial secrets do to technological training. It is a product of the striving for power.[39]*

Once set in motion, bureaucracies develop an amazing ability to endure. "The question is always who controls the existing bureaucratic machinery. And such control is possible only in a very limited degree

[37] Max Weber, "The Essentials of Bureaucratic Organization: An Ideal-Type Construction," in *Reader in Bureaucracy*, Robert K. Merton et al., eds. (New York: Free Press, 1952), p. 27.

[38] This list is adapted from Carl J. Friedrich, "Some Observations on Weber's Analysis of Bureaucracy," in *Reader in Bureaucracy*, Merton, et al., eds., p. 29.

[39] Weber, "The Essentials of Bureaucratic Organization," p. 26.

to persons who are not technical specialists." As a result, "the trained permanent official is more likely to get his way in the long run than his nominal superior, the Cabinet minister, who is not a specialist." [40]

Some critics of contemporary society wonder if the purpose for which a bureau or agency was instituted is not lost in the effort to keep it in existence. Charles A. Reich writes that over time the " 'accomplishments' of administration are almost secondary; after a while what it does ceases to have an outside reference; it acquires an autonomous life of its own." [41] Once the process of bureaucratization is started it may be hard to stop. It may be nearly impossible to dismantle an existing bureau that has a strong vested interest in its existence, has clientele groups among the organized portion of the electorate, and has contacts in the higher reaches of government *without building a counterbureaucracy to oppose it!* Weber writes: "When those subject to bureaucratic control seek to escape the influence of the existing bureaucratic apparatus, this is normally possible only by creating an organization of their own which is equally subject to the process of bureaucratization." [42]

One of the basic dangers of bureaucracy discussed by Reich is the relinquishment of decision-making power by the arena of politics and its usurpation by the arena of administration, of "science," so to speak. The people and their chosen representatives lose their power over basic decisions to the specialists and professionals who, at least in theory, being "value-free," are able to make decisions on the basis of objective, amoral judgments rather than subjective, moral judgments. Of course, no one can be truly value-free. The general belief in value-free administration affects the society, however, for those holding the belief accord substantial authority and legitimacy to the decisions and actions of the bureaucracy. In this view, the bureaucracy has the "last word"; it makes "the final decision"; it employs the "most rational decision-making process known to man."

Against specialized knowledge and compartmentalized information, the individual discovers that decision-making power has been removed from his hands and relegated to a massive, faceless organization against which he is powerless. It is no coincidence that Carl Friedrich, writing of Weber's ideal-type conception of bureaucracy as the repository of expertise, objectification, and centralized command, finds that the institutions in modern society coming closest to this portrayal are an army, a totalitarian party with bureaucratic underpinnings, and a large business organization that lacks employee or labor participation. [43]

---

40 Ibid., p. 25.

41 Charles A. Reich, *The Greening of America* (New York: Bantam, 1971), p. 107.

42 Weber, "The Essentials of Bureaucratic Organization," p. 25.

43 Friedrich, "Some Observations on Weber's Analysis," p. 31.

Abuses of bureaucratic power are among the major themes emerging from human experience in modern society. These abuses have been made possible by the organized impersonality of bureaucracies. Graphic portraits of the pitiful figure of the lone individual standing before the massive bureaucratic Juggernaut are provided by the writers Franz Kafka and Arthur Koestler. Frequently, such individuals either have been in the bureaucratic apparatus themselves or had trusted it implicitly and believed in its objectivity, its "zero-defects" mentality.

In his novel *Darkness at Noon*, Arthur Koestler describes the thoughts of Rubashov, a former bureaucrat and Communist party member now being maneuvered, at the time of the infamous Soviet purge trials of the 1930s, into signing a false confession implicating him in a conspiracy against the party leader (Stalin). As Rubashov thinks of his situation and that of Ivanov, his interrogator and a friend of long standing, he sees the "objectivity" and "adherence to rules" that are the bread-and-butter of the bureaucrat coming to the fore:

> *Ivanov had said that their roles could equally well have been reversed; in that he was doubtless right. He himself and Ivanov were twins in their development. . . . [They] were nourished by the same umbilical cord of a common conviction; the intense environment of the party had etched and moulded the character of both during the decisive years of development. They had the same moral standard, the same philosophy, they thought in the same terms. Their position might just as well have been the other way round. Then Rubashov would have sat behind the desk and Ivanov in front of it; and from that position Rubashov would probably have used the same arguments as had Ivanov. The rules of the game were fixed. . . .[44]*

Rubashov had condemned others to death from his position in the bureaucracy. This had been demanded by the "objective" forces of history as interpreted by the party leader and carried out by the party bureaucracy. Now he wondered if Ivanov, his old friend, would do the same.

> *During their discussion, he had repeatedly asked himself whether Ivanov was sincere or hypocritical; whether he was laying traps for him, or really wanted to show him a way of escape. Now, putting*

[44] Arthur Koestler, *Darkness at Noon* (New York: Macmillan, 1966), p. 89. Excerpts from *Darkness at Noon* on this and the following pages reprinted by permission of the Macmillan Company and A. D. Peters & Co., Ltd.

*himself in Ivanov's position, he realized that Ivanov was sincere—
as much so, or as little, as he himself had been toward Richard or
Little Loewy [two of those Rubashov had himself condemned to
death].*[45]

And why should Rubashov think any differently? The demands of
government, the demands of purposes larger than the single individual,
the demands of power and responsibility, the *demands of organization*
militated against the individualistic side of two polar conceptions of
ethics.

*"I don't approve of mixing ideologies," Ivanov continued. "There
are only two conceptions of human ethics, and they are at opposite
poles. One of them is Christian and humane, declares the individual
to be sacrosanct, and asserts that the rules of arithmetic are not
to be applied to human units. The other starts from the basic
principle that a collective aim justifies all means, and not only
allows, but demands, that the individual should in every way be
subordinated and sacrificed to the community. . . . Humbugs and
dilettantes have always tried to mix the two conceptions; in
practice it is impossible. Whoever is burdened with power and
responsibility finds out on the first occasion that he has to choose,
and he is fatally driven to the second alternative. Do you know,
since the establishment of Christianity as a state religion, a single
example of a state which really followed a Christian policy? You
can't point out one. In time of need—and politics are chronically
in a time of need—the rulers were always able to evoke 'exceptional
circumstances,' which demanded exceptional measures of defense.
Since the existence of nations and classes, they live in a permanent
state of mutual self-defense, which forces them to defer to another
time the putting into practice of humanism. . . ."* [46]

But to what end was all of this argument and badgering of Rubashov?
What was the purpose of the fabricated confession that lay at the
conclusion of endless days and nights facing the burning rays of the
lamp focused on him as he was forced to look at his uniformed, leather-
booted inquisitor through watering, squinting eyes? Why must he be
paraded before the masses in a "show trial" where he would freely
admit his guilt? He, Rubashov, a former high official of the party;
Rubashov, a man who spent his total energies furthering the revolution

45 Ibid.
46 Ibid., p. 128.

that, having succeeded, had elevated him to fame: What now could the party demand from him? Why must he be painted in the worst possible light, as a saboteur and an enemy of the people? It was simple. The leader knew, and the bureaucrats were following his orders. The masses were stupid, yet an accusation of ignorance would do little to move them out of their lethargy and into the factories just being built. As Gletkin, his new inquisitor, put it:

> *If one told the people in my village that they were still slow and backward in spite of the Revolution and the factories, it would have no effect on them. If one tells them that they are heroes of work, more efficient than the Americans, and that all evil only comes from devils and saboteurs, it has at least some effect.*

Rubashov and others like him were to be made scapegoats for the problems facing the nation. They were to be used by the party apparatus in its attempt to harness the energy and negativism of the masses in the pursuit of social goals. Rubashov himself had written of the characteristics of the masses and thought he knew them:

> *It is necessary to hammer every sentence into the masses by repetition and simplification. What is presented as right must shine like gold; what is presented as wrong must be black as pitch. For consumption by the masses, the political process must be coloured like gingerbread figures at a fair.*[47]

Now he was to play the devil. "Your testimony at the trial will be the last service you can do the Party," said Gletkin,[48] who continued:

> *Your task is simple . . . to guild the Right, to blacken the Wrong. The policy of the opposition (of which you are a part) is wrong. Your task is therefore to make the opposition contemptible; to make the masses understand that opposition is a crime and that the leaders of the opposition are criminals. That is the simple language which the masses understand. If you begin to talk of your complicated motives, you will only create confusion amongst them. Your task, Citizen Rubashov, is to avoid awakening sympathy*

[47] Ibid., p. 190.
[48] Ibid.

and pity. Sympathy and pity for the opposition are a danger to the country.[49]

The party demanded Rubashov's confession and his life. He did as commanded. After Rubashov had signed his confession and been returned to his cell, the secretary who had been present during the lengthy interrogation congratulated Comrade Gletkin on his success. " 'That,' said Gletkin, glancing at the lamp that had shone so brightly in Rubashov's eyes, 'plus lack of sleep and physical exhaustion. It is all a matter of constitution.' " [50]

Rubashov the educated, intellectual individual was in the end no match for Gletkin, so recently the ignorant peasant, who was now a bureaucrat backed by the overwhelming power of the party apparatus.

A novel of similar scope and power is Franz Kafka's *The Trial.* Kafka portrays the effects of a decision of the judicial bureaucracy upon Joseph K., a high bank official accused of a crime. The charge is not his to know; it is a secret of the court. Joseph K. is led through a labyrinth of stuffy corridors and tawdry offices populated by disdainful petty bureaucrats. He finds himself slowly reduced to helplessness by his interminable search for information about the alleged crime and the progress of his case, information which remains always just slightly beyond reach, lost somewhere in the never-ending levels of administrative hierarchy.

The charge sets Joseph K. apart from his fellow citizens. Everything depends upon the whims of the bureaucracy. He is at their mercy; he is without weapons, lost and alone. A community of the accused, which would give power in numbers and counterorganization, is ruled out by the nature of things. As another member of the accused tells him:

Combined action against the Court is impossible. Each case is judged on its own merits, the Court is very conscientious about that, and so common action is out of the question. An individual here and there may score a point in secret, but no one hears it until afterwards, no one really knows how it has been done. So there's no real community, people come across each other in the lobbies, but there's not much conversation.[51]

[49] Ibid., p. 193.

[50] Ibid., p. 195.

[51] Excerpts on this and the following pages from *The Trial, Definitive Edition, Revised,* by Franz Kafka, translated by Willa and Edwin Muir. Copyright 1937, © 1956 and renewed 1965 by Alfred A. Knopf, Inc. Reprinted by permission of Alfred A. Knopf, Inc.; Schocken Books, Inc.; and Martin Secker & Warburg Limited.

Superstition, fatalism, and immobility in the face of the administrative apparatus he confronts finally predominate in the world of the accused, a world where one is completely preoccupied with the accusation, the progress of one's case, and the blight upon one's record. A similar situation is faced by people who are labeled insane. Society certifies that a given individual possesses the qualifications necessary to occupy an office from which he is allowed to decide when to affix such a label upon those who come before him. Once attached, the mark is seldom if ever removed.[52]

The horror of bureaucratic power when it is out of control is that the individual finds himself in a situation with no escape. Once he has passed through the gates—and he may not even be sure when, where, or how he went through them—there is no exit. In the novel *Catch-22*, the point was made in the setting of the American military bureaucracy in Italy during World War II. If you were crazy and didn't know it, you kept on doing your job. If you were being driven crazy by your job, the conditions around you, and the people with whom you had to deal, and you sought help in getting a release from duty on these grounds, you obviously had enough presence of mind to make an attempt to extricate yourself from the situation. This meant that you were not really crazy yet, so there was no reason for granting a release from duty on the grounds of insanity.

Joseph K. finds himself in a similar situation. At last he comes upon a portrait painter who appears to have some influence with the judges on the court. He hopes that this man can help him remove the terrible uncertainty by having his case brought to a conclusion. The painter proceeds to tell him of three possible outcomes. The first is definite acquittal: The individual is free of the court and all records of the alleged crime and proceedings are destroyed. Of course, no one remembers such an outcome ever occurring and the painter has no control over such a thing. This leaves two other alternatives: ostensible acquittal and indefinite postponement. The first demands temporary concentration of energy, he is told, while the other "taxes your strength less but means a steady strain."

> *"First, then [says the painter], let us take ostensible acquittal. If you decide on that, I shall write down on a sheet of paper an affidavit of your innocence. . . . Then with this affidavit I shall make a round of the Judges I know, beginning, let us say, with the Judge I am painting now, when he comes for his sitting tonight. . . . Well, then, if I get a sufficient number*

[52] See R. D. Laing, *The Politics of Experience* (New York: Pantheon, 1967).

*of Judges to subscribe to the affidavit, I shall then deliver it to
the Judge who is actually conducting your trial. . . . The Judge is
covered by the guarantees of the other Judges subscribing to the
affidavit, and so he can grant an acquittal with an easy mind, and
though some formalities will remain to be settled, he will
undoubtedly grant the acquittal to please me and his other friends.
Then you can walk out of the court a free man." "So then I'm
free," said K. doubtfully. "Yes," said the painter, "but only ostensibly
free, or more exactly, provisionally free. For the Judges of the
lowest grade, to whom my acquaintances belong, haven't the
power to grant a final acquittal, that power is reserved for the highest
Court of all, which is quite inaccessible to you, to me, and to all
of us. . . . [With ostensible acquittal the] whole dossier continues
to circulate, as the regular official routine demands, passing on
to the higher Courts, being referred to the lower ones again,
and thus swinging backwards and forwards with greater or smaller
oscillations, longer or shorter delays. These peregrinations are
incalculable. A detached observer might sometimes fancy that
the whole case had been forgotten, the documents lost, and the
acquittal made absolute. No one really acquainted with the
Court could think such a thing. No document is ever lost, the Court
never forgets anything. One day—quite unexpectedly—some Judge
will take up the documents and look at them attentively, recognize
that in this case the charge is still valid, and order an immediate
arrest. I have been speaking on the assumption that a long
time elapses between the ostensible acquittal and the new arrest;
that is possible and I have known of such cases, but it is just
as possible for the acquitted man to go straight home from the
Court and find officers already waiting to arrest him again. . . ."
"And the case begins all over again?" asked K. almost incredulously.
"Certainly," said the painter, "The case begins all over again,
but again it is possible, just as before, to secure an ostensible
acquittal. One must again apply all one's energies to the case and
never give in." [53]*

K. was looking rather crestfallen at this point. The painter suggested
that postponement might be a little better received:

*"Shall I explain to you how postponement works?" K. nodded. . . .
"Postponement," he said, gazing in front of him for a moment as*

[53] Kafka, *The Trial*, pp. 196–99.

*if seeking a completely accurate explanation, "postponement
consists in preventing the case from ever getting any further than its
first stages. To achieve that it is necessary for the accused and his
agent . . . to remain continuously in personal touch with
the Court. Let me point out again that this does not demand
such intense concentration of one's energies as an ostensible acquittal,
yet on the other hand it does require far greater vigilance. You
daren't let the case out of your sight, you visit the Judge at
regular intervals as well as in emergencies and must do all that is
in your power to keep him friendly. . . . As against ostensible
acquittal postponement has this advantage, that the future of the
accused is less uncertain, he is secured from the terrors of
sudden arrest and doesn't need to fear having to undergo—perhaps
at a most inconvenient moment—the strain and agitation which
are inevitable in the achievement of ostensible acquittal.
Though postponement, too, has certain drawbacks for the accused,
and these must not be minimized. In saying this I am not
thinking of the fact that the accused is never free; he isn't free,
in any real sense, after the ostensible acquittal. There are other
drawbacks. The case can't be held up indefinitely without at least
some plausible grounds being provided. So as a matter of form a
certain activity must be shown from time to time . . . the
accused is questioned, evidence is collected, and so on . . . all
that it amounts to is a formal recognition of your status as
an accused man by regular appearances before your Judge. . . .
Both methods have this in common, that they prevent the
accused from coming up for sentence." "But they also prevent an
actual acquittal," said K. in a low voice, as if embarrassed by
his own perspicacity. "You have grasped the kernel of the matter,"
said the painter quickly.*[54]

The situation described by Kafka is rarely the result of human intentions. Most often, the individual is simply caught by forces that he
has unleashed but does not understand—"mindless, impersonal forces
that pursue their own, non-human logic," as Charles Reich puts it.
What we cannot understand we cannot control. Inevitably, those forces
come to dominate the individual.[55] In the middle decades of the
twentieth century, bureaucratic power is one of those forces.

Charisma is the third category of power discussed by Weber. People

54 Ibid., pp. 200–202.
55 Reich, *Greening of America*, pp. 12–13.

follow the charismatic leader because they believe that he is specially
called, ordained by fate or other such powers to perform his task. "If
he is more than a narrow and vain upstart of the moment, the [charis-
matic] leader lives for his cause and 'strives for his work.' " [56] He rises
above the bonds of tradition and law. Such leaders often gain a following when crises have weakened the forces of tradition and bureaucracy
or rapid social change has rendered them obsolete and their dictates
no longer apply. Charismatic power becomes dangerous precisely when
it is unchecked by the counterforces of bureaucracy and tradition, for
then the behavior of people with an absolute belief in a leader is restricted only by the bounds of the leader's imagination and whatever
power his opposition can muster.

Charismatic leadership is characterized by a mass base and a direct
rather than a mediated relation between leader and follower. The
charismatic leader

> *is not content with gaining and maintaining control merely over
> the machinery of government—the police, administrative offices,
> legislature, and courts. He consciously seeks to gain control
> over the individual citizen, not just by the threat of force but perhaps
> more significantly by appealing for affirmative and enthusiastic
> devotion.*[57]

Charismatic and referent power are similar, somewhat overlapping
categories; the former implies a more complete union than the latter,
depending not only upon a partial, narrowly restricted identification of
follower with leader but on "the construction by a leader and his associates of an image of him as infallible, omniscient, and incorruptible
and on a positive, active response to this kind of image-building by
those who are predisposed toward such leadership." [58]

A moderate degree of charisma, a substantial degree of tradition,
and a modicum of bureaucracy and law may help a society over hurdles
that it might not otherwise be able to surmount without a leader
capable of inspiring confidence in times of crisis. Unchecked charisma
can unleash furies of inestimable magnitude upon the body politic.
Such an adjustive, moderate degree of charisma checked by combination
with tradition and bureaucracy is exemplified by the presidency of

[56] Gerth and Mills, *From Max Weber*, p. 79.

[57] James C. Davies, "Charisma in the 1952 Campaign," *American Political Science
Review*, 48 (December 1954), 1083.

[58] Ibid.

Franklin D. Roosevelt. Roosevelt entered the White House at a time when traditional values had been severely challeged by a depression of major proportions. Shaken loose from the bonds of tradition and law, restive forces were beginning to emerge in the land. The potential for violence was great, the ground fertile for the machinations of the demagogue. Roosevelt was able to use charismatic power to effect changes in the laws and the bureaucracy without upsetting the ship of state. A less scrupulous individual might have used his power in another fashion. Arthur Schlesinger, Jr., describes the situation on the eve of Roosevelt's inauguration:

The fog of despair hung over the land. One out of every four American workers lacked a job. Factories that had once darkened the skies with smoke stood ghostly and silent, like extinct volcanoes. Families slept in tarpaper shacks and tinlined caves and scavenged like dogs for food in the city dump. In October [1932] the New York City Health Department had reported that over one-fifth of the pupils in public schools were suffering from malnutrition. Thousands of vagabond children were roaming the land. . . . Hunger marchers, pinched and bitter, were parading cold streets in New York and Chicago. On the countryside unrest had already flared into violence. . . . Mobs halted mortgage sales, ran the men from the banks and insurance companies out of town, intimidated courts and judges, demanded a moratorium on debts. . . . In West Virginia, mining families, turned out of their homes, lived in tents along the road on pinto beans and black coffee.[59]

The time was ripe for a charismatic leader:

Capitalism, it seemed to many, had spent its force; democracy could not rise to economic crisis. The only hope lay in governmental leadership of a power and will which representative institutions seemed impotent to produce. Some looked enviously on Moscow [Stalin], others on Berlin [Hitler] and Rome [Mussolini]. . . . "Even the iron hand of a national dictator," said Alfred M. Landon [then governor] of Kansas, "is in preference to a paralytic stroke." [60]

[59] Arthur M. Schlesinger, Jr., *The Crisis of the Old Order* (Boston: Houghton Mifflin, 1957), p. 2.

[60] Arthur M. Schlesinger, Jr., *The Coming of the New Deal* (Boston: Houghton Mifflin, 1959), p. 3.

Roosevelt did not overturn the system, but he did inspire faith and confidence in his following—in the multitudes who listened by the newly developed radio, which now enabled a leader to communicate personally with millions of people, as Roosevelt was to do in his "fireside chats." He promised the people leadership, action, and inspiration; "the only thing we have to fear is fear itself," he shouted in his inaugural address. "Action, and action now" was called for, as well as discipline from everyone. "We must move as a trained and loyal army willing to sacrifice for the good of a common discipline, because without such discipline no progress is made, no leadership becomes effective." He also needed a chunk of the power and authority that had heretofore inhered in the laws and traditions of the existing governmental apparatus: "It may be . . . that an unprecedented demand and need for undelayed action may call for temporary departure from that normal balance of public procedure."

The successful charismatic leader is powerful and decisive. If Roosevelt was unable to solve pressing problems within the existing structure of power, then he would "ask the Congress for the one remaining instrument to meet the crisis—broad Executive power to wage a war against the emergency, as great as the power that would be given to me if we were in fact invaded by a foreign foe." He spoke of "the people"; he was their representative; he was to lead them out of the time of troubles that, he said, were not of their own making. "The people of the United States have not failed. In their need they have registered a mandate that they want direct, vigorous action. They have asked for discipline and direction under leadership. They have made me the present instrument of their wishes. In the spirit of the gift I take it." [61]

Schlesinger writes that Roosevelt received nearly half a million letters within a few days after the inaugural address. He quotes from some of them: " 'It was the finest thing this side of heaven' "; " 'It seemed to give the people, as well as myself, a new hold upon life' "; " 'Yours is the first opportunity to carve a name in the halls of immortals beside Jesus' "; " 'People are looking to you almost as they look to God.' " [62]

Thus, moderate charismatic power led to an adjustive solution to a crisis and the forging of a new electoral coalition within the existing political order. At other times and places, greater amounts of charismatic power have led to a much more sanguinary situation. The dictatorship of Adolf Hitler in Germany during the 1930s and '40s indicates that no matter what the state of technological development

[61] Schlesinger, Jr., *Crisis of the Old Order*, pp. 7–8.
[62] Schlesinger, Jr., *Coming of the New Deal*, p. 1.

and the form of the division of labor, in times of crisis people are always susceptible to the appeal of the charismatic leader who simplifies perceptions of the problems, identifies enemies or scapegoats, and proposes vivid, simple solutions.

Frequently, it is just when the individual feels alone and overwhelmed by forces beyond his grasp that he looks with favor upon the charismatic leader. Hitler expresses this well:

> *When from his little workshop or big factory, in which he feels very small, he steps for the first time into a mass meeting and has thousands and thousands of people of the same opinions around him, when . . . he is swept away by three or four thousand others into the mighty effect of suggestive intoxication and enthusiasm, when the visible success and agreement of thousands confirm to him the rightness of the [leader's] . . . doctrine . . . then he has succumbed to the magic influence of what we designate as "mass suggestion."* [63]

Charismatic power usually has its greatest impact on the masses, because it is grounded more in emotion than reason, more in a desire for revenge than in a pragmatic, dispassionate assessment of the social, political, or economic situation. Voters who respond to charisma have been found to be poorly educated and socioeconomically marginal. In Davies's study of the 1952 presidential campaign, for example, charisma-oriented individuals were identified by their response to questions eliciting a description of the candidates. One respondent labeled charismatic (charisma-oriented) stated, "Eisenhower is God-sent in our moment of strife. . . . He is a leader of men. . . . His ideals of right and wrong are much higher than most politicians." The individuals in the charismatic sample were found to differ significantly from noncharisma-oriented persons on a number of dimensions. The former were less tolerant of indecision, crisis, and ambiguity and were more likely to favor decisive action and to make categoric, closed-minded judgments. They were also more likely to seek support for their views from others, to follow the crowd—illustrated in Davies's study by their prevalent belief that everybody was going to vote for their candidate. They also tended to vote for the leader rather than the party; they were attached more strongly to the personality of the leader than to party philosophy, policy, and issue stance.[64]

[63] Adolph Hitler, *Mein Kampf,* trans. Ralph Manheim (Boston: Houghton Mifflin, 1943), pp. 478–79. See also Gustav Le Bon, *The Crowd* (New York: Viking, 1960).

[64] See Davies, "Charisma in the 1952 Campaign."

In emphasizing Max Weber's threefold classification, we made the point that any of these types of power carried to extremes makes it impossible for the political system to allow the full human development of its citizens. We may also note that political systems rarely employ a single variety of power; instead, all three are generally in force, with one on occasion counteracting the others. Elites, for example, may entrench themselves in the government administrative apparatus or successfully monopolize the paths to leadership that have been legitimized by the power of tradition. The masses, in turn, when they are discontent, may attempt to counteract the power of tradition and bureaucracy by rallying behind a charismatic leader.

SUMMARY AND CRITIQUE

The purpose of government is to authoritatively allocate values in ways that satisfy those able to compete for what they believe is their fair share. Citizens are willing to support governments that are able to meet their demands. With resources scarce, many people have to make do with less than they might desire. Hence government employs various forms of power and influence, which are used to constrain dissatisfaction. When agreement on allocations cannot be reached and some members of the population attempt to use unacceptable means to obtain their values, government makes use of its monopoly over the legitimate use of force.

The use of power frequently leads to its abuse. For example, traditional power may be abused by the placing of inept leaders in high position; the abuse of bureaucratic power may rob people of self-esteem even though they are living in a modern, highly industrialized society. The abuse of charismatic power may mobilize forces in the masses that cannot be easily restrained.

Understanding of the configuration of institutions performing political functions, and familiarity with the groups that possess significant amounts of power, enable us to better analyze the functioning of various types of political systems and the extent to which they are able to satisfy citizen demands. The concept of *system,* however, is not without its faults and ambiguities. While a necessary analytical oversimplification, it does leave some very important questions unanswered. What, for example, is to be done about those with pressing needs that only government can fulfill but who lack the resources with which to articulate them? Are these people and their demands simply ignored?

If a population is primarily deficiency-motivated, then most members of the electorate can be expected to devote most of their efforts to looking after themselves with little or no regard for others. Are their demands to be given the same consideration as those coming from growth-motivated people, who are more likely to have the good of the community in mind?

Does the systems conception allow for anything other than the relative power of contending interest groups to decide whose demands will be met? Is it not probable that the government will use its power to reinforce those policies that sustain a deficiency-motivated electorate and sanction those that are conducive to the emergence of the higher needs?

Where, according to the systems notion, is political direction or leadership to come from? If the organized interest groups reflect a deficiency-motivated majority, who is to do the planning necessary to preserve an acceptable quality of life? These are questions that need to be considered—for they are at the heart of the problems plaguing America today.

It may be that the analytical concept of system does not reflect the level of development of the population. The systems model, like democracy itself, needs a growth-motivated electorate in order to function adequately. The pathologies alluded to above are not really due to conceptual flaws in the systems model but to the fact that a basic prerequisite for its successful functioning has not been met. How do we fulfill this prerequisite? *Can* it be fulfilled?

One advantage of the systems conception employed here is that it views politics as a two-way interactive process rather than as a one-way noninteractive process. In this conception, the masses as well as the elites are crucial to the functioning of the polity. The elites may rule, but if they move too far from the needs and desires of the ruled the government will lose support and may fall victim to revolution.

Selected Bibliography

BACHRACH, PETER, and MORTON S. BARATZ, "Two Faces of Power," *American Political Science Review,* 56 (December, 1962), 947–52.

BENTLEY, ARTHUR F., *The Process of Government.* Chicago: University of Chicago Press, 1908.

EASTON, DAVID, *A Systems Analysis of Political Life.* New York: John Wiley & Sons, 1965.

EASTON, DAVID, *The Political System.* New York: Alfred A. Knopf, 1953.

GERTH, H. H., and C. WRIGHT MILLS, *From Max Weber: Essays in Sociology.* New York: Oxford University Press, 1958.

GOLEMBIEWSKI, ROBERT T., *Men, Management, and Morality*. New York: McGraw-Hill, 1965.

GOLEMBIEWSKI, ROBERT T., *Renewing Organizations*. Itasca, Ill.: F. E. Peacock Publishers, 1972.

LASSWELL, HAROLD D., and ABRAHAM KAPLAN, *Power and Society*. New Haven, Conn.: Yale University Press, 1950.

LOWI, THEODORE J., *The End of Liberalism*. New York: W. W. Norton, 1969.

MARCUSE, HERBERT, *One-Dimensional Man*. Boston: Beacon Press, 1964.

MARINI, FRANK, ed., *Toward a New Public Administration*. New York: Chandler, 1971.

OSTROM, VINCENT, *The Intellectual Crisis in American Public Administration*, rev. ed. University, Ala.: University of Alabama Press, 1974.

TRUMAN, DAVID E., *The Governmental Process*. New York: Alfred A. Knopf, 1951.

WEBER, MAX, *The Theory of Social and Economic Organization*, trans. A. M. Henderson and Talcott Parsons, ed. Talcott Parsons. New York: Free Press, 1964.

ZEIGLER, L. HARMON, and G. WAYNE PEAK, *Interest Groups in American Society*. Englewood Cliffs, N.J.: Prentice-Hall, 1972.

7

Components of the political system: a functional approach

As we noted in the last chapter, the political system performs a number of functions, including satisfying citizen demands and maintaining the order and regularity that are prerequisites for individual fulfillment of personal needs. Political systems come in a variety of shapes and sizes; despite the virtually infinite variety that exists, each system reduces analytically into a similar set of components, each designed to perform a part of the job necessary to make the whole work.

Thus, we have functions within functions—the major functions that the political system performs for the society as a whole, and the functions that are an integral part of the political system itself. In this chapter we will look more closely at the division of functions within the political system and their related components. The long-standing battle between democracy and authoritarian government, for example, becomes, in the end, little more than an argument about two ways of organizing components of the political system. Both forms of government perform the same functions for the population, and both must, by internal division of labor, establish a workable balance between the demands of the populace and the government's ability to distribute resources. The better the balance, the less the need for coercive power and the more smoothly the system runs.

Some form of power is always essential, however. Under the assumption of scarcity, politicians must decide which demands to meet, which to delay, and which to forget altogether. The demands of powerful segments of the population are usually attended to; the demands of the less powerful are not so compelling; the demands of the powerless are rarely listened to at all. The astute politician will nevertheless be alert to the potentialities of the situation; the powerless today may be the powerful of tomorrow, and this gives politics its dynamic quality, as does the need to employ power to put the resulting government policies into effect. (Remember that overemphasis of any one type of power may

militate against efficient performance and lead to new sources of opposition.) Political coalitions are seldom stable, and the true politician is
an expert at "walking on eggs."

Although the functions specific to the political system have been
divided according to a number of classificatory schemes, the scheme
elaborated by Gabriel Almond and James Coleman is particularly useful. Almond and Coleman divide the functions specific to the internal
division of labor into input and output categories of the political
system. The input functions are concerned with the receipt and proces-
sing of demands; the output functions with the elaboration and execution of policy to meet them. The functions are as follows: [1]

Input functions
1. Political socialization
2. Interest articulation
3. Interest aggregation

Output functions
1. Rule making
2. Rule application
3. Rule adjudication

Every political system has an array of institutions or social structures
that provide for regularized patterns of human behavior through which
one or more of the above functions are performed. The rule-making
function may be performed by the legislature in a democracy—for
example, the two houses of Congress in the United States—or by a
council of the powerful, such as the Politburo under Stalin's regime
in the Soviet Union. The more primitive the society, the more numerous
are the functions performed by a single structure—for example, the
family; the more developed the society, the greater the division of labor
and hence, the fewer the functions performed by any single institution.

POLITICAL SOCIALIZATION

Political socialization is the process by which the citizen becomes aware
of the political system, its traditions and institutions, and how he is
expected to behave in regard to it. Successful political socialization is
a basic prerequisite for the effective functioning of the polity.

---

[1] Gabriel A. Almond and James S. Coleman, eds., *The Politics of the Developing
Areas* (Princeton, N.J.: Princeton University Press, 1960), p. 17. Political communication, eliminated here as an analytical category, is assumed to be a prerequisite for the
performance of all of the functions.

Its end product is a set of attitudes—cognitions, value standards,
and feelings—toward the political system, its various roles, and
role incumbents. It also includes knowledge of, values affecting,
and feelings toward the inputs of demands and claims into
the system, and its authoritative outputs.[2]

When political socialization is successful, the individual has learned the political system's basic values and beliefs. The world view that he has evolved in the process is consonant with the existing political order, and he is able to channel his motivating drives into paths that are acceptable within the existing state of society and politics. He therefore limits his demands to those likely to be carried out with the resources available to the policy makers, and he accords legitimacy to the government. He will thus remain loyal even though on occasion he may not receive complete satisfaction from government policies.

Political socialization is everything that the individual learns during his lifetime that has any effect on how he views the political system and acts toward it. Family, peer groups, church affiliation, union membership, and educational institutions are all significant in the individual's political socialization. The greater the consonance between the actions of the political system and the individual's beliefs in what is right, the greater his satisfaction with the organization and structure of the polity, and vice versa.

Group memberships are often a significant agent of socialization, incorporating in microcosm the decision-making procedures of the government and thereby facilitating the learning of behavior patterns that are matched by the behavior of politicians. Authoritarian child-rearing practices, for example, are not consonant with the demands of citizenship in a democracy, although the effects of such an upbringing may be mitigated by group membership later on. Consider the example of an individual who belongs to a recreational club. Bill Jackson (we shall call him) was the epitome of the working-class authoritarian. Strict almost to the point of brutality, he established his word as law in the family. He derived pleasure from issuing orders to his wife and children and criticizing when they were not executed to his satisfaction. The recreation club operated by democratic principles. Membership was open to all regardless of race or creed. All policy decisions were voted upon by the membership, and a constitution provided a written basis for the procedure. When Jackson was elected president of the club, he was forced to undertake a drastic alteration in his behavior and, over

---

[2] Ibid., p. 28. See also Herbert H. Hyman, *Political Socialization* (New York: Free Press, 1969).

time, in his belief about how the world operated. Although he was authoritarian at home and subject to an authoritarian routine at his place of work, a lumber mill, where he was forced to take orders from the foreman, his membership in a democratic group that represented his strong recreational interests acted to reduce significantly the cumulative effect of his family and work environment—to make the democratic political process familiar and, presumably, more meaningful to him.

Successful political socialization helps to create a common identity among members of a nation state.[3] This facilitates the development of a basic consensus on the limits of political behavior and the range of demands that can be pressed upon the political system. Consensus relieves the politician of the pressure that results when several powerful groups make competing, mutually exclusive demands, whereas if this identity does not exist, the institutions performing political socialization functions may perpetuate rather than eliminate acrimonious cleavages in the society. A consensus links both generations and social classes, making demands more predictable and allowing politicians to take action within the consensus to provide enough resources to meet them. Consensus also makes a serious miscalculation on the part of the elites less likely, for it brings the perceptions of the elites and the masses into closer accord. Under these conditions actions taken by policy makers are not likely to create the widespread alienation and apathy that foster the growth of charismatic movements that can lead to dissension and confrontations between elite and mass.[4]

How successfully the political socialization function has been fulfilled can be estimated by observing the cleavages in the political culture. As Gabriel Almond notes, "every political system is embedded in a particular pattern of orientation to political actions,"[5] a theme that we have been emphasizing by paying particular attention to the individual's beliefs and attitudes. This pattern of orientation is called *political culture,* "the system of . . . beliefs, expressive symbols, and values which defines the situation in which political action takes place. It provides the subjective orientation to politics."[6] Political socialization tends either to reduce or to perpetuate cleavages in the political culture. An analysis of political culture is therefore one way to get at some

[3] See Charles F. Andrain, *Political Life and Social Change* (Belmont, Ca.: Wadsworth, 1970), p. 55.

[4] See Robert K. Merton, *Social Theory and Social Structure* (New York: Free Press, 1968).

[5] Gabriel A. Almond as cited in Lucian W. Pye, "Introduction: Political Culture and Political Development," in *Political Culture and Political Development,* Lucian W. Pye and Sidney Verba, eds. (Princeton, N.J.: Princeton University Press, 1965), p. 7.

[6] Sidney Verba, "Comparative Political Culture," in Pye and Verba, *Political Culture,* p. 513.

measure of the effectiveness of the socialization process. Is the political culture homogeneous? Is there a basic consensus on the form and dynamics of the political system? Or is the political culture divided and fragmented? Where there is unity and agreement on the basic form, values, and operation of the political system, the political socialization function is adequately fulfilled. Where a society remains divided and in a state of disagreement over these fundamental issues, political socialization may work against the maintenance of enough consensus for government to function effectively.

In fragmented cultures there is usually cleavage within both the elites and the masses, dividing society into opposing camps in which portions of the elite as well as the mass will be found. Northern Ireland provides an extreme example of the failure of political socialization to remove a cleavage that runs through the center of the body politic—the division between Protestant and Catholic. Political socialization here perpetuates a distinction that is reinforced by the individual's learning experiences in the religious, economic, social, and educational sectors of society. Hence, the distinction is reinforced rather than extinguished. Londonderry Protestants still bait Catholics by annual parades and celebrations commemorating the lifting of a siege laid upon the city in 1689 by a Catholic, James II, shortly after he had been deposed as King of England by the Protestant William of Orange in the "Glorious Revolution." James had fled to Ireland, where he was denied a base of operations by the Protestant English landlords, many of whom holed up in Londonderry and kept their city from falling to him. The siege remains a living symbol of English hegemony and its failure is celebrated in Londonderry as is James's final defeat on the river Boyne celebrated by Protestants throughout Northern Ireland. Indeed, history has special significance in Northern Ireland, and the socialization process imparts a different—and slanted—perspective to each faction, thereby ensuring that the centuries-wide division will not be readily eliminated.

English-Protestant hegemony in Northern Ireland is built on a solid foundation of economic, social, and political discrimination aptly reflected in the words of Sir James Craig, head of the first government in Northern Ireland after its partition from the newborn Irish Free State (now the Republic of Ireland) in 1920:

> *I have always said that I am an Orangeman first and a politician*
> *and member of this parliament afterwards . . . all I boast,*
> *is that we are a Protestant parliament and a Protestant state.*[7]

[7] Liam De Paor, *Divided Ulster* (Baltimore: Penguin Books, 1970), p. 114.

"Orangeman," a term with an associated color (as opposed to the Irish green), is derived from William of Orange and describes partisanship with the Protestant English landlords against the native Catholic Irish. The Orange organizations began in the 1790s as a federated league of Protestants designed to counter Irish Catholic antilandlord societies—the latter in turn having evolved as a reaction to economic exploitation and the activities of local Protestant formations known as Peep O'Day Boys. The Peep O'Day Boys were bands of English Protestant emigrant laborers and tenant farmers who were in competition with the Irish. The Irish, long exploited and subservient, held something of an edge in that they would live at a lower level of subsistence than the Protestants and would therefore pay higher rents for land and would work for lower wages. The Peep O'Day Boys raided Catholic houses in the early morning hours, ostensibly to search for arms—which it was illegal for Catholics to possess—but also to remind the natives of English ascendancy.

The Orange movement was an attempt to formalize and extend the purposes and activities of the Peep O'Day Boys. At one point, in County Armagh "the formation of the Orange order was followed by a violent campaign by Protestants designed to drive Catholics from their homes . . . some thousands of refugees fled, abandoning their houses and holdings to be taken over by the Protestants." [8] The Protestant elites tended to "look the other way" when the Protestant masses in the Orange Order engaged in such activity. As one official put it as he watched a parade of unarmed Irishmen shortly after the order was founded:

> As for the Orangemen, we have a rather difficult card to play;
> they must not be entirely discountenanced—on the contrary, we must
> in a certain degree uphold them, for with all their licentiousness,
> on them we must rely for the preservation of our lives and
> properties, should critical times occur. [9]

The Orange Lodges have continued to the present as an important agent of Protestant political socialization, thus serving to reinforce and maintain the wall of ideological separation which runs through the political community of Northern Ireland. This fundamental division has made true parliamentary democracy impossible. As De Paor puts it,

8 Ibid., p. 38.
9 Cited in ibid., p. 39.

> *. . . normal parliamentary democracy could not function in a*
> *state where the citizens were divided, in the proportion of two to*
> *one, on the right of the state itself to exist, and where the same*
> *division, involving the same two main groups, affected religion,*
> *education, employment, housing, wealth and property, history,*
> *culture, and social life. A change of government was theoretically*
> *possible under the constitution but was not practically possible*
> *in a situation where every general election was a plebiscite, and*
> *where the ruling party had always taken the view . . . "a Unionist*
> *(Protestant, English allied) government must always be in power*
> *in Northern Ireland."* [10]

France provides another example of political instability due largely to the failure of political socialization. A peculiar set of circumstances created a society that is neither traditional nor modern, neither fully developed nor completely undeveloped, neither democratic nor aristocratic, but with elements of all of these. Taken together, they make for what Stanley Hoffman calls "the stalemate society," [11] a society with a divided political culture and a number of people living on the margins of economic and social subsistence. These people agree on but one thing: protection of their narrow interests. No major force in French society has the power or the electoral support necessary to retain the major government decision-making positions long enough to evolve coherent long-range policy.

Most modernized countries are characterized by corporate ownership of industry; a majority of the population in business, labor, or service industries; and those few remaining on the farm in possession of large holdings using modern equipment. A sizable proportion of France's population, however, is engaged in agricultural pursuits that provide little more than a marginal existence. Approximately half of the farmers own their land and one-third are tenant farmers or sharecroppers. The large farms that do exist are frequently held up by the Communists (a party of considerable power in France) as symbols of evil posing a threat to the tenuous existence of the small farmer who, lacking wealth, does possess some power in numbers when he can be motivated by negative appeals.

Industry also reflects individualism and concern with protection of the inefficient. Many industries are small and family owned. "While

[10] Ibid., p. 124.

[11] Stanley Hoffmann et al., *In Search of France* (Cambridge, Mass.: Harvard University Press, 1963), p. 11.

almost half the workers in Great Britain and the United States are employed in establishments of over 500 employees, only 27.3 percent of French workers are; 36 percent work in factories with less than fifty workers." [12]

While Britain has not had a political revolution since 1688 and the United States has had one constitution and a single attempted rebellion (the Civil War), "France, since 1789, has been three times a constitutional monarchy, twice an empire, once a semidictatorship, and five times a republic. Moreover, most of these changes have been effected by violence." [13] As a result, a number of political and intellectual divisions have emerged in addition to the economic ones: for example, clerical versus anticlerical, and republican versus monarchist or authoritarian—with each tradition grounding itself in the extremes of history. To condemn the republicans, monarchists point to the murder of the king in the French Revolution and the reign of terror that followed as heads rolled off the guillotine. The republicans can point to the coups and attempted coups that ended or endangered the republics as well as the scandals associated with monarchists and the military. The Dreyfus affair and the Boulanger episode are still cited although they occurred in the last decades of the nineteenth century, as both inflamed French society and solidified the intellectual traditions of republican against monarchist, military, and clerical groupings. The Dreyfus affair reeked of anti-Semitism and indicated that the French Officer Corps was willing to condemn a Jew on insufficient evidence for selling secrets to the enemy in what looked like an attempt to cover up for incompetence and intrigue within the military itself. The Boulanger episode, a comic-opera attempt at a takeover on the part of the dashing General Boulanger, Minister of War, who lost his nerve at the last minute with success in sight and wound up committing suicide on the grave of his mistress, "made royalists and clericals appear absurd. . . . But good republicans shuddered at the thought of what an able adversary might have done with the opportunities that Boulanger squandered." [14]

French labor is caught in a squeeze between the narrow, provincial views of the factory owner and the protectionist policy that keeps prices high and marginal, inefficient firms running. The Communists, who came inevitably to organize and represent a good portion of the workers, have an intellectual battle to fight in addition to the economic one. They remember the betrayal of the Paris proletariat at the hands of the

---

12 Gwendolen M. Carter and John H. Herz, *Major Foreign Powers*, 4th ed. (New York: Harcourt Brace Jovanovich, 1962), p. 491.

13 Ibid., p. 499.

14 Ibid., p. 503.

bourgeoisie after the founding of the short-lived Second Republic in 1848. At the time Paris was a hotbed of agitation and mob action. In June the Paris mob rose spontaneously in a mass action "born of desperation and exasperation, without known leaders or clear organization." [15] The newly formed government of the Second Republic, composed primarily of representatives of the bourgeoisie and small farmers and landowners attempting to protect their property from the excesses of the radicals in Paris, put down the rebels quickly and violently. Memories are long in France, and the Communists have not forgotten this and similar events indicative of the chasm that separates petty bourgeois from factory worker, and factory worker from everybody else in the society.[16]

The multiple cleavages and the resulting mutual suspicion and social fragmentation have led to a deep-seated distrust of authority, an overdose of individualism, and an unwillingness to work together for the achievement of common ends. The French conception of authority is reflective of people who distrust one another but are forced by events to live in geographical proximity. Hoffmann describes the French view of authority as involving the "coexistence of *limited* authoritarianism and *potential* insurrection against authority." Power is delegated

> *so that the drama of face-to-face personal relations [between opponents] can be avoided but only in order that, and as long as, the exercise of power from above remains impersonal [hence neutral] and curtailed both in scope (subject-matter) and in intensity (means of action) by general rules, precepts, and inhibitions.*[17]

Government in France, it could be said, is delegated authority almost by default or, perhaps, only by necessity. The socialization process has not been able to establish a basic consensus on the fundamentals of the political formula; hence "there was no agreement either on the objectives for which political power is to be used, or on the procedures through which disputes over such objectives can be resolved." [18] The result has been a swing from democratic to authoritarian regimes and back again— and the socialization process has been unable to build the consensus

---

[15] David Thompson, *Europe Since Napoleon*, 2nd ed. (New York: Alfred A. Knopf, 1962), p. 192.

[16] For example, see the analysis in Karl Marx, "The Class Struggles in France 1848–50," in Karl Marx, *Selected Works*, Volume II (New York: International Publishers, n.d.), pp. 169–295.

[17] Hoffmann, *In Search of France*, pp. 8–9.

[18] Ibid., p. 13.

that would bring the oscillations of the pendulum down to a reasonable level. Under conditions of democracy, the overdose of individualism and fragmentation in the French parliament leads to legislative *"immobilisme"*—an inability to act, a trait reflected in the title of a book by Herbert Luethy, *France Against Herself.*

As often happens in such cases, the country facing insurmountable political problems turns to the strongman, the man who possesses charismatic power and emphasizes values and traditions that no one can quarrel with. Decision-making power is then placed with him and the bureaucracy. With the deadlock in the policy-making process thus neutralized, some semblance of political stability returns, at least temporarily. If the socialization function remains inadequately fulfilled, however, the cycle will repeat itself; when the strongman leaves or is deposed, the old factionalism will loom up again.

Lucian Pye notes that four themes or dimensions tend to predominate in the description of political cultures: (1) trust versus distrust of individuals and political institutions; (2) unbridled acceptance of hierarchy, both social and political, versus an emphasis upon human equality and a tentative acceptance of hierarchy; (3) faith in the power of liberty to evolve stable political structures versus a belief in the need for coercion to perform parts of the task; and (4) primary loyalty and commitment to the national unit versus primary attachment to a subnational unit such as locality, economic position, or social grouping. Both France and Northern Ireland possess similar patterns on these dimensions, which indicate an unstable situation and therefore an inadequate fulfillment of the socialization function—assuming, of course, that the politics of integration and adjustment are more effective in achieving social goals than are the politics of disintegration and disruption.[19]

---

[19] In Pye and Verba, *Political Culture and Political Development*, pp. 22–23. Structural-functional theory, which we use in the main in this description of the functions of the political system, has been criticized for being "conservative": for tending to favor those institutions that uphold the status quo while downgrading those encouraging change in the social equilibrium. We are not making these assumptions. We *are* saying that, for attaining social goals, the politics of compromise and give-and-take are preferable to the politics of ideological intransigence. The reader should note that this is basically a democratic assumption. The dyed-in-the-wool authoritarian would prefer civil war, "do or die," to compromise. If the reader is similarly inclined he can still make sense of the discussion by simply reversing our value judgments—when we say that the socialization process is adequately fulfilled and therefore leads to an integrative, consonant fit between the politcal attitudes of all groups in the society and the assumptions and procedures of the political system, he can say that this means that the socialization function is *not* adequately fulfilled. For a discussion of functionalist theory see N. J. Demerath, III, and Richard A. Peterson, eds., *System, Change, and Conflict* (New York: Free Press, 1967). For a consideration of the functions performed by conflict, see Lewis Coser, *The Functions of Social Conflict* (New York: Free Press, 1956).

In both France and Northern Ireland the individual in the opposing group is distrusted. In France mutual distrust and suspicion are defining characteristics of the general culture.[20] A belief in individual equality, the idea that "I'm as good as they" or "I have my rights" is firmly established, as is a belief in individual liberty. In France this liberty is jealously guarded. In Northern Ireland infringements of their rights have long been resented by the Catholics. In both countries loyalty is focused more on the family, religious, economic, or ethnic group than on the national unit. (Recall Craig's words, cited earlier: " 'I am an Orangeman first . . . and a member of this parliament afterwards.' ")

Japan exhibits a more integrative political culture. For many years a semifeudal system controlled the lower classes of the social structure, the peasants and artisans. The government was tolerated as a legitimate part of the hierarchy, even though loyalty remained tied to the family. Equality was not a part of the feudal belief system. After the Meiji restoration the position of the emperor took on greater ideological significance. The virtues of the nation as an entirety were extolled and the government was able to finance industrialization from the output of the rural community by generalizing the allegiance given the family and the farm to the emperor, but without disrupting the peasant's traditional ties. In the nineteenth century, the threat of violent incursions against Japan by the technologically superior Western powers discouraged competing factions among the elite, which arose out of the Samurai, or warrior, class, from carrying their conflicts to the masses and thereby splitting the society. With conflict thus muted and a firm national image established, the transition from tradition to modernity was made possible. The socialization process emphasized literacy and education, the latter making much of filial piety and duty to emperor and country.

England shows a pattern similar to that of Japan after the Meiji restoration, with the exception that liberty is emphasized a bit more strongly. The monarchy has remained since medieval times, providing a strong element of continuity and tradition that knits together all parts of the society (with the exception of the Catholic Irish in Northern Ireland). Japan and England each possess a single common language throughout their island nations of relatively small dimensions. Water, a natural defense, has kept each relatively free from foreign invaders and the resulting introduction of foreign cultural and linguistic subunits. All of this has encouraged loyalty to the nation state, and political stability has been the result. From early on the English government has been looked to "as a source of benefits, if not for the whole population

[20] See Lawrence Wylie, *Village in the Vaucluse* (New York: Harper & Row, 1964).

then at least for some [of the powerful] groups." [21] All segments of the society have come to value liberty. The struggle for power, which pitted first the aristocracy and then the masses against the throne, has not always been smooth, but it has been carried out without the kind of social upheaval and drastic government alterations that ravaged France and split her into acrimonious pieces.

Significantly, the long tradition of the monarchy and a strong class structure, which until recently limited the voting franchise to those of wealth and birth (only in 1948 were property qualifications removed), has led to a population that defers to the authority of social station and academic achievement. Absolute equality is considered an impossibility by the Conservative party, and the Labor party would prefer to work at opening opportunities for the lower orders to advance on the basis of skills and education rather than declaring equality a practical goal and going all-out to achieve it. Trust in one's fellowmen (English policemen, "bobbies," are armed only with nightsticks) permeates the society, a trait Richard Rose contends can be "traced back to feudal conceptions of loyalty, which mixed personal honor and the obligations of office." [22] This trust extends to politics and is not broken lightly. In 1963 the "Profumo Affair" erupted over precisely that issue. Profumo, Minister of War in the government of Prime Minister Macmillan, was involved in a scandal involving himself, a Russian naval attaché, and a number of call girls.

No actual breach of military security was disclosed but the widespread public shock at the revelation of a Cabinet Minister who in denying the affair had knowingly lied to his Cabinet colleagues in private and to Parliament in public demonstrated anew the high degree of confidence the British citizen had in the rectitude of his public officials.[23]

Profumo resigned immediately and Macmillan resigned shortly thereafter.

England, like Japan, has become modern without throwing out the flavor and trappings of tradition. The old has at the same time been willingly adjusted to the new. England has been aided in this regard by the subservience of the church to the state—a relationship that was

---

[21] Richard Rose, "England: A Traditionally Modern Political Culture," in Pye and Verba, *Political Culture,* p. 93.

[22] Ibid., p. 95.

[23] Walter L. Arnstein, *Britain Yesterday and Today* (Lexington, Mass.: D. C. Heath, 1966), p. 368.

worked out in the sixteenth century during the reign of Henry VIII.[24] This meant that in subsequent reigns political problems would not become so readily involved with religious controversies—a combination always potent with rancorous conflict. The separation of church and state led to the efficient functioning of the socialization process. Historically, this meant that the English were able to preserve the coherence of their society in times of change. In contrast, France was torn asunder by revolution when the modernizing bourgeoisie and restive masses moved against the entrenched and unyielding power of king and church.

From these examples we can generalize distinctions between successful and unsuccessful socialization patterns. A distrust of government by the masses need not lead to instability if it is accompanied by a willing deference to authority or belief that the government has the right to coerce the recalcitrant citizen into conformity. A smooth evolutionary pattern, such as evidenced in the sketch of Japan, involved maintaining traditional patterns of deference while increasing the degree of trust and extending the horizons of the masses to include the nation as a whole. The unsuccessful patterns of political socialization manifest themselves as distrust of the individual (that is, of course, others), distrust of authority, and a strong belief in liberty (one's own, of course).

INTEREST ARTICULATION AND AGGREGATION

The interest articulation function involves the formulation of demands and their transmission from the society at large to the political system. This function is fulfilled by a number of structures, the most common being interest groups, political parties, the communications media, and mass movements—even leaderless events such as spontaneous riots, wildcat strikes, etc.

In most cases, interest articulation is prefaced by the recognition of common problems on the part of a group of individuals. If this recognition is too vague for common action, such individuals are said to constitute a potential, or latent, group. To become a group, in David Truman's use of the concept, individuals must "interact with some frequency on the basis of their shared characteristics." [25] Organized action —action in unison with a number of others to formulate and transmit their shared demands—is always more effective than unorganized action.

[24] See J. J. Scarisbrick, *Henry VIII* (Berkeley: University of California Press, 1969).

[25] David B. Truman, *The Governmental Process: Political Interests and Public Opinion* (New York: Alfred A. Knopf, 1951), p. 24. See also Mancur Olson, Jr., *The Logic of Collective Action: Public Goods and the Theory of Groups* (New York: Schocken Books, 1968), pp. 48–52.

Power is indeed enhanced by numbers, but only when the numbers act together to protect or further a common interest. The more specific the interest, the more uniform is the response and the greater is the power of the organization. As James Madison wrote in Article Number 10 of the *Federalist Papers,*

> *The smaller the society, the fewer probably will be the distinct parties and interests composing it, and more frequently will a majority be found of the same party; . . . and the smaller the number of individuals composing a majority, and the smaller the compass within which they are placed, the more easily they will concert and execute their plans of oppression. Extend the sphere and you take in a greater variety of parties and interests; you make it less probable that a majority of the whole will have a common motive to invade the rights of other citizens.*[26]

Interest groups are specialized articulation structures, "private associations . . . [that] promote their interests by attempting to influence government rather than by nominating candidates and seeking responsibility for the management of government." [27] They are more concerned with presenting singular demands than with combining or aggregating divergent demands; they occur on the boundary between the political system and the larger society. Unlike interest groups, political parties are integral parts of the political system, where they are involved with nominating candidates, taking responsibility for government policy, and performing aggregation as well as articulation functions.

There are several types of interest groups.[28] The most effective is the *associational* group, "a formally organized body made up of professionally employed officials or employees." [29] The professionals represent the membership on a full-time basis regardless of the electoral or political situation. Such groups frequently hire lobbyists, or professional "legislative advocates" as they are sometimes called, who attend the hearings of legislative committees and contact legislators, bureaucrats, and other government officials both formally and informally to bring their cause to the attention of political powerholders and, they hope, to encourage legislation in their favor. The National Council of Churches, the Amer-

---

[26] James Madison, *Federalist No. 10,* as cited in E. E. Schattschneider, *The Semi-sovereign People* (New York: Holt, Rinehart and Winston, 1960), p. 6.

[27] V. O. Key, as cited in Schattschneider, *The Semi-sovereign People,* p. 43.

[28] Ibid.

[29] Ibid.

ican Medical Association, the National Association for the Advancement of Colored People, the National Association of Manufacturers are examples.[30]

Groups supplement the work of political parties by keeping the demands of significant segments of the population visible in nonelection years, so that legislators are less likely to make laws that could alienate influential sectors of the society. Of course, group activity inevitably leads to a certain amount of bias on the part of government policy—a bias that tends to favor the elites over the masses, or the organized over the unorganized.

Organization, Schattschneider says, "is itself a mobilization of bias in preparation for action." [31] The opposite of mass apathy is elite organization and therefore a bias that works to the elite's advantage. Because elites have more education and a better knowledge of politics, as well as social and communicative skills, they are more likely than members of the mass to organize to represent their interests and to join existing interest groups. Further, they find it easier to get the attention of policy makers, most of whom share the elite's educational, economic, and social background.[32]

When an organization pursues its own interests in addition to its societally designated task, it is called an institutional interest group.[33] The military and government bureaucracy are two sectors of society frequently cited in this regard. In a discussion of the party apparatus in the Soviet Union under Stalin, Merle Fainsod points to the tendency of bureaucracy to act as an institutional interest group by concerning itself as much with its own preservation as with the task it is to perform:

The personal dictatorship of the leader [Stalin] has embodied itself in the Party dictatorship of the apparatus. Like Frankenstein's

---

[30] Cf. Henry W. Ehrmann, ed., *Interest Groups on Four Continents* (Pittsburgh: University of Pittsburgh Press, 1967); Lester Milbrath, *The Washington Lobbyists* (Chicago: Rand McNally, 1963); L. Harmon Zeigler and Michael Baer, *Lobbying: Interaction and Influence in American State Legislatures* (Belmont, Ca.: Wadsworth, 1969), p. 5; and L. Harmon Zeigler and G. Wayne Peak, *Interest Groups in American Society,* 2nd ed. (Englewood Cliffs, N.J.: Prentice-Hall, 1972).

[31] Schattschneider, *The Semi-sovereign People,* p. 30.

[32] Concerning the United States, see Charles R. Wright and Herbert H. Hyman, "Voluntary Association Memberships of American Adults: Evidence from National Sample Surveys," in *American Political Interest Groups,* Betty H. Zisk, ed. (Belmont, Ca.: Wadsworth, 1969), pp. 300–314. Regarding contacts and background similarities of lobbyists and representatives, see Zeigler and Baer, *Lobbying.* For a consideration of the educational, occupational, and regional bias of the Senate, see Donald R. Matthews, *U.S. Senators and Their World* (New York: Vintage Books, 1960).

[33] Almond and Coleman, *The Politics,* p. 33.

monster, the apparatus has acquired a momentum of its own, a
vested interest in its own survival which promises to outlive its
creator and to perpetuate his system of rule long after the forces
which shaped it have been forgotten.[34]

The U.S. military has pursued its goals through public relations ("the selling of the Pentagon") and through contacts between industry and the armed forces—examples are associations such as the Navy League and the practice of placing retired military personnel in civilian managerial positions in firms doing business with the government. The economic reliance of states on military bases and defense industries located within them provides another source of power for the armed forces acting as an institutional interest group, especially when the defense budget is being considered in Congress. In other nations, the military frequently enters politics more directly; in many Latin American nations the government is continuously subject to the whims of the armed forces, as the overthrow of the Allende government in Chile attests. In the Weimar Republic, Germany's unsuccessful first try at democracy, the fledgling government was compelled from the beginning to rely on the armed forces.

Another vehicle for interest articulation is the nonassociational interest group, a collectivity of people who are not formally organized but who possess such a unity of outlook and interest that their desires and demands, when expressed by members of such groups, are taken into account by the political authorities. Religious groupings (say the Catholic vote), racial minorities (for example, blacks and the black vote in the United States), linguistic subgroups (French-speaking Canadians with separatist sympathies), and regions are examples.

The U.S. South may be considered a regional nonassociational interest group; it comprises a collectivity in that Southern history and economics as well as social, educational, political, and even linguistic characteristics (the "Southern accent") have forged strong bonds among Southerners and have distinguished them from inhabitants of other parts of the country. Some argue that this is reflected in a unique brand of politics, which results from the region's

heritage from crises of the past, its problem of adjustment of racial
relations on a scale unparalleled in any Western nation, its poverty
associated with an agrarian economy which in places is almost

[34] Merle Fainsod as cited in Carl J. Friedrich and Zbigniew K. Brzezinski, *Totalitarian Dictatorship and Autocracy* (New York: Frederick Praeger, 1961), p. 32.

feudal in character, [and] the long habituation of many of its people to nonparticipation in political life. . . .[35]

That the South considers itself a distinctive region of America and is so viewed by the rest of America is illustrated by such phenomena as the Dixiecrat party and such popular labels as "the Solid South."

In the 1968 campaign, and especially at the Republican Convention, Richard Nixon went far out of his way to placate the South, as he did once in office. He paid close attention to Strom Thurmond, who had come to the Republicans from the regional Dixiecrat party. Thurmond was given veto power over the choice of vice-president, and Nixon attuned himself to the political outlook that could be called the "Southern ideology": states' rights, strict constructionists on the Supreme Court, local decision-making powers over public schools.[36] Thus, while the South was not an organized interest group, a voting majority with a unity of outlook and action ensured that region stronger representation than would otherwise have been forthcoming.

Anomic interest groups demonstrate the least-organized, most disruptive form of interest articulation: spontaneous outbursts of irate but unorganized or minimally organized people who share a sense of serious injustices and a demand for immediate action. Empirical studies of political violence by anomic interest groups reveal a *turmoil* dimension: "relatively spontaneous, unorganized strife with substantial popular participation, including political demonstrations and strikes, riots, political and ethnic clashes, and local rebellions." [37]

The lower classes are more likely than the middle and upper classes to adopt this form of action. In a study of civil strife in 114 nations and colonies from 1961 through 1965, it was found that working-class individuals (including farmers and the urban unemployed) were involved in 73 percent of the turmoil events as opposed to 61 percent for middle-class groups and 7 percent for the political elite and associated government employees (such as police and civil servants). The figure for middle-class participation is inflated because of student participation. Involvement in student demonstrations is frequently a transitory stage in an individual's development, usually ending at the completion of education, when the legitimate channels of interest articulation and political

35 V. O. Key, Jr., *Southern Politics* (New York: Vintage Books, 1949), p. 4.

36 See Garry Wills, *Nixon Agonistes* (New York: New American Library, 1971), especially chapter 6, part II, "Southern Strategy," pp. 241–56.

37 Ted Robert Gurr, "A Comparative Study of Civil Strife," in *Violence in America*, Hugh Davis Graham and Ted Robert Gurr, eds. (New York: New American Library, 1969), p. 544.

communication are discovered. Holding down a job and meeting the financial obligations that come with a spouse, a family, and acquisition of the material signs of middle-class status provide further political socialization and inhibit the earlier forms of interest articulation. The figures for the groups into which the former student is likely to move—the middle and professional class—are therefore interesting. While students are involved in 45 percent of the turmoil events, the middle classes are found in 8 percent of such events, professionals in 11 percent.[38] The student demonstrator of yesterday, therefore, is not likely to be on the barricades in the future. Success, a legitimate place in a world that he understands, and access to organized interest groups will see to that—as will the desire to please (or become) the boss and keep up with the Joneses.

In addition, the elites and aspiring elites are more likely to take a longer-range view of things, to solve problems on their own, and to feel responsible for their actions. "Throwing caution and responsibility to the winds" may be a diversion that is fun to think about, but it is seldom engaged in even when life becomes something of a bore. The middle-class dilemma is illustrated in a song sung by Roy Clarke:

> *Right or left at Oak Street*
> *That's a choice I make every day*
> *I don't know what takes more courage*
> *The stayin' or the runnin' away.*[39]

POLITICAL PARTIES AND INTEREST AGGREGATION

While interest groups function to articulate interests and channel demands, political parties are involved primarily in *interest aggregation:* collecting and combining interests. Interest-aggregation institutions develop platforms and programs, and sometimes ideologies, which, on one hand, limit the scope of demands, and on the other hand, modify those that come to the political system. Such modifications are an attempt to fit competing demands from powerful groups together in a package that will at least *minimally* satisfy each group while at the same time remaining within the boundaries of the possible given the resources available to the government. When interest aggregation is successful,

[38] Ibid., p. 555.

[39] "Right or Left at Oak Street," C. Williams–J. Nixon, Attaché Music Publishers, Inc.

no major group in the society will actively attempt to thwart the operations of the government. On the other hand, rancorous political conflict and the existence of conspiracies or open warfare against the government are signs that the interest-aggregation function is not efficiently fulfilled.

The political party, the institution most commonly involved with interest aggregation, is "any group, however loosely organized, seeking to elect governmental office-holders under a given label." [40] Implicit in this definition is some degree of organization linking leaders and followers, a stated program or set of appeals, and regularized procedures for selecting candidates and conducting political campaigns.[41]

Where parties do not exist, the interest articulation function may be fulfilled by a number of irregular mechanisms, described by William N. Chambers with reference to the United States as a

> *pluralistic, kaleidoscopic flux of personal cliques like those that gathered around the great magnate families in New York, caucuses of the sort that came and went in many New England towns, select and often half-invisible juntas in the capitals or courthouse villages in the Southern states, or other more or less popular but usually evanescent factions.*[42]

Political parties *formalize* the interest-aggregation function and provide durable links between elites and masses.[43] The absence of parties usually produces one of two conditions: Either the masses do not perceive themselves as active participants in the political process, or they are forcibly restrained from channeling their demands to the political system. Under the former condition, cliques composed of elites fulfill interest-aggregation functions; under the latter condition, conspiratorial parties bent upon the overthrow of the government are likely to develop.

In all cases, parties exist "whenever the notion of political power comes to include the idea that the mass public must participate or be

[40] Leon D. Epstein, *Political Parties in Western Democracies* (New York: Frederick Praeger, 1967), p. 9.

[41] See ibid. and William N. Chambers, *Political Parties in a New Nation* (New York: Oxford University Press, 1963).

[42] William N. Chambers, "Parties and Nation-Building," in *Political Parties and Political Development*, Joseph LaPalombara and Myron Weiner, eds. (Princeton, N.J.: Princeton University Press, 1966), p. 88.

[43] Epstein, *Political Parties in Western Democracies*, p. 9. Where political parties exist, the voter is able to hold someone responsible for public policy and thereby feel that he exerts a degree of control over politicians and political events.

controlled." [44] In few nations of the world can elites act with complete impunity—without any regard for the feelings and attitudes of the masses. With the awakening of democratic ideals and the extension of the suffrage in many nations of the world, political parties have become major aggregators of interest and mechanisms by which the masses can be controlled and rallied around the programs formulated by elites.

When the masses or some part of them are ready for representation by a political party of some sort but are not so represented, an outbreak of anomic interest-group action is the likely result. The "long hot summers" of the late '60s in the United States provide one example—young blacks were ready for representation. Another occurred in the Soviet Union under Stalin during the early years of the collectivization campaign of the late '20s and early '30s. The interests of the Kulaks, the middle class of Russian peasantry, were not taken into account when collectivization began. They killed their cattle rather than allow them to fall into the hands of the Communists at a time when the cities desperately needed food. The effects of this action have lingered even to the present time as less than maximum possible agricultural production.

Political scientists generally associate the rise of political parties with the onset of political crises—problems that demand alterations in the institutions of interest aggregation.[45] Joseph LaPalombara and Myron Weiner discuss three types of crises: the crisis of legitimacy, the crisis of integration, and the crisis of participation. Crises of legitimacy usually arise during the development of a new state and its evolution of new institutions of interest aggregation. Where traditional authority patterns have broken down, charismatic power appears as the major force by which aggregation structures are rebuilt—especially where the legal underpinnings of the old state were "identified with the interest of an imperial exploiter." [46]

In relation to the colonial period of the United States, for example, the structure of law and taxation prior to the Revolutionary War directly favored the interests of the English crown and disfavored those of the colonists—hence the cry of "no taxation without representation." In many of the newly emerging nations, former colonial powers occupy a position analogous to that of England in the American colonies. Under such conditions, the charismatic leader (such as a George Wash-

[44] Joseph LaPalombara and Myron Weiner, "The Origin and Development of Political Parties," in LaPalombara and Weiner, *Political Parties and Political Development*, p. 3.

[45] Ibid., p. 15, and the sources cited therein.

[46] Seymour Martin Lipset, *The First New Nation* (New York: Basic Books, 1963), p. 17.

ington) becomes a part of the interest-aggregating mechanism of the state. Later, after patterns of interest articulation and aggregation become clearly focused in a leader or group of leaders, parties emerge as formal, organized collectivities of interest that institute regularized patterns of representation and leadership selection.

The crisis of legitimacy is often associated with the crisis of participation and integration or nation-building. To overthrow a political system that no longer appears capable of meeting the demands of powerful groups in the populace, the collusion of the masses is usually needed, either to support the insurgents or at least to ensure their acquiescence to the changes the insurgents are attempting to bring about.

Thus, the masses must somehow be represented, and, in many instances, "politicized": made aware of political issues and their ability to affect the balance of political power. If everyone enters the political arena at once with expectations of great gain, a Pandora's box is opened, as raw, unarticulated demands impinge directly upon the policy makers. Once the insurgent leaders of a group bent upon change have found it necessary to widen the scope of conflict by building up support among the masses, new demands emerge that must somehow be taken into account. A crisis of participation follows as demands rapidly outstrip capabilities and the channels of aggregation are clogged by the "revolution of rising expectations." [47]

A crisis of participation may also emerge without direct elite intervention should ideas of liberty and individual rights lead the masses to believe that they have the right to intervene actively in the process of political decision-making.[48] The ideals of the French Revolution, expressed in the slogan "liberty, equality, fraternity," and carried forth on the bayonets of Napoleon in the early 1800s, led to a century-long ferment against subsequent regimes that restricted representation.

Political parties play a role in all of these crises. A crisis of legitimacy frequently results in a one-party system that brings all segments of the citizenry together. A nationalistic appeal aggregates diverse interests around a single rallying point that makes sectional or minority demands secondary to those of the nation as a whole. Where this is not possible and secession by minorities or sectional cliques is threatened, the one-party state frequently eliminates the opposition as an alternative. The civil wars in Nigeria and East Pakistan (now Bangladesh) indicate that

[47] See Schattschneider, *The Semi-sovereign People*. Schattschneider argues that the outcome of a conflict depends in essence upon the extent to which the populace is brought into the fray. Schattschneider argues that parties in a weak position will carry their case to the masses in an attempt to gain strength. The opposition may in turn be led to do the same thing. Politicization and widening of the scope of conflict follow.

[48] Joseph LaPalombara and Myron Weiner, "The Origin and Development of Political Parties," in LaPalombara and Weiner, *Political Parties*, p. 19.

aggregation through elimination is still an accepted—if extreme—alternative.

In the United States, long considered (ethnocentrically, perhaps) the perfect model of the successful evolution from revolutionary movement to stable democratic government, a tendency toward one-party aggregation was evident by 1800. The group in power, the Federalists, advocated control by the mercantile elite, a strong national government, and effective limitations on mass political participation. They were opposed by anti-Federalists, or Republicans. The Alien and Sedition Acts of 1798 were attempts to eliminate the opposition. The "wide latitude given the courts . . . allowed partisan federal judges to apply it with severity against Republicans for relatively innocent remarks. Fines or imprisonment, or both, were imposed on all Republicans actually tried under the Sedition Act." [49]

Crises of participation and integration are usually met by the proliferation of political parties and the transformation of elite cliques into organizations emphasizing mass appeal.[50] If this transformation fails to occur, the aggregation process cannot function adequately and the political system becomes unstable. In Weimar Germany, for example, the bourgeois parties of the center and right were able to maintain themselves without seeking the support of the masses because of their connections with the entrenched state bureaucracy, the military, and the East Prussian Junkers—an elite land-owning class. The masses, in turn, found that the avenues of aggregation were blocked by the interlocking power elites. Hence, they joined the Socialist or the Communist party, parties with a narrow ideological and economic appeal that threatened the socioeconomic position of the middle and upper classes. Bargaining and compromise between factions were therefore out of the question, and the resulting cleavage made it impossible for the government to operate within the accepted set of rules.

RULE MAKING

To fulfill their rule-making function, politicians must make conscious choices between alternatives, primarily in the legislative arena. In democracies the rule-making function is usually performed by a group of

---

[49] Morton Grodzins, "Political Parties and the Crisis of Succession in the United States: The Case of 1800," in LaPalombara and Weiner, *Political Parties and Political Development*, p. 311.

[50] See Otto Kirchheimer, "The Transformation of the Western European Party Systems," in LaPalombara and Weiner, *Political Parties and Political Development*, pp. 177–200.

elected officials who meet in formal session and register their preferences by voting. In nondemocracies the choices are usually made high up in the single-party structure, sometimes by vote, sometimes by a single leader, but always after alternatives have been weighed and the relative power of competing blocs assessed.

To analyze the rule-making function and its several aspects, political scientists have evolved the theory of political coalitions. Riker states that:

> *The interesting thing about conscious decisions by groups . . . is that, if groups are more than two persons, the process of making them is invariably the same. It is a process of forming coalitions. Typically some part of the authority-possessing group comes together in alliance to render a decision binding on the group as a whole and on all who recognize its authority. This decisive "part" may be more or less than one-half, indeed, it may be two persons or the whole group itself. But regardless of the number of persons conventionally believed to be decisive, the process of reaching a decision in a group is a process of forming a subgroup which, by the rules accepted by all members, can decide for the whole. This subgroup is a coalition.*[51]

Research in the theory of coalitions has led to a number of propositions concerning the behavior of politicians engaged in rule-making functions. At the outset we will have to assume a basic consensus about the set of ground rules within which authoritative allocations of values are made. (After all, no decision-making body can function until the procedures for making authoritative rules have been decided upon and put into effect.) Within the political ground rules, coalition theory outlines some general postulates concerning rule-making behavior.

Coalition theory begins by assuming that politicians are rational people. By this we mean that politicians attempt to maximize their gains and minimize their losses; in short, they attempt to win. If one of two alternatives promises more money, power, or both, the "rational" player will choose the outcome with the higher payoff. Riker thus elaborates on the "size principle"; for example, in the rule-making context under consideration here, other things being equal, politicians will attempt to form minimum winning coalitions—a coalition just large enough to pass a bill and small enough to ensure that no extraneous members belong to it. Ideally, this would include 50 percent of the

[51] William H. Riker, *The Theory of Political Coalitions* (New Haven, Conn.: Yale University Press, 1962), p. 12. Coalition theory is an offshoot of the theory of games developed by John Von Neumann and others. See John Von Neumann and Oskar Morgenstern, *Theory of Games and Economic Behavior* (New York: John Wiley & Sons, 1964).

voting members plus one. The smallest winning coalition is desired, so it is argued, so that the payoffs—the goods that come with winning—can be divided among the smallest possible number of legislators.

In arguing that large coalitions usually break up into smaller, minimum winning ones, Riker cites examples from the international arena. Upon defeat of the Axis powers in 1945, the Soviet Union and the United States left the coalition of powers that had united in order to win the war, just as the allied powers in World War I had broken into squabbling camps after they had victory in their pocket. Overwhelming majorities are unstable because the benefits that must be distributed to all are much less for each member than if distributed within a minimum winning coalition.[52]

Evidence of the size principle occurred in the electoral arena (the prelude to the development of coalitions in the legislative arena) with Nixon's strategy for the 1968 nomination and the subsequent campaign. With the breakup of the Democratic coalition, the Republicans had a good chance of forming a minimum winning coalition of electoral votes by emphasizing the South, Republican areas of the Midwest, and the evolving Republican West. The Nixon forces could overlook the liberal East, and keep Rockefeller, Lindsay, and Percy off the ticket. To include these areas in the coalition would only increase the size and the degree of conflict within it.[53]

The amount of information possessed by members of the legislature is also a factor in coalition theory: If there is perfect information as to the policy preferences of all participants in the bargaining process, coalitions tend to approximate the minimum size necessary for victory. In the absence of such information, coalitions may increase beyond 50 percent plus one as protection against losing by miscalculation.[54] The size principle is further refined by the concept of "ideological distance": [55] Decision-makers can be expected not only to attempt to maximize payoffs but also to favor potential coalition members who share their policy preferences. For example, short-term gain is not likely to lead to a minimum winning coalition composed of socialists and communists if the socialists could form a greater-than-minimum-winning coalition with a more conservative socialist grouping.

The size principle is further modified by the pattern of past political loyalties and resulting coalitions that have proven successful despite

[52] Riker, *The Theory of Coalitions,* chap. 3.

[53] Wills, *Nixon Agonistes.*

[54] Riker, *The Theory of Coalitions.*

[55] See Abraham DeSwaan, "An Empirical Model of Coalition Formation as an *N*-Person Game of Policy Distance Minimization," in Sven Groennings et al., *The Study of Coalition Behavior* (New York: Holt, Rinehart and Winston, 1970), pp. 426–44.

being somewhat larger than necessary. Here the desire to reduce uncertainty and a longer-term view of the situation outweigh the immediate gains to be made from a minimal winning coalition.[56]

Research on the preference orderings of legislators suggests that in few circumstances could rules be formulated to maximize the utility of a majority. It is not surprising that the process of formulating legislation leads to a set of policy decisions that do not satisfy the maximum expectations of the bargaining groups. Each must compromise. Small wonder, then, that democratic theorists have long emphasized the need for a pragmatic, give-and-take approach to rule making while powerholders in authoritarian or totalitarian societies must employ a considerable amount of coercion to put their programs into practice. Consider, for example, the situation depicted in table 1, which lists the preferences of legislators Johnson, Smith, and Wright for the three alternatives A, B, and C.

Suppose we present the alternatives two at a time, beginning with A versus B, and then the winner against C. In the first round A wins against B with two votes. A is the first preference of Johnson and the second preference of Wright, who votes with Johnson against Smith. For Smith, A is the worst alternative, B the best. For Wright, B is the worst alternative, A is not so bad. The first round ends with Johnson and Wright against Smith.

In the second round, A versus C, C wins with two votes and becomes the final alternative chosen. Here Wright is able to vote for his first preference, Smith for his second. Johnson votes for his first preference and loses.

Now let us alter the order in which the alternatives are presented. Instead of beginning with A against B, we will take B versus C first and

Table 1 *Preferences of Legislators Johnson, Smith, and Wright for Alternatives A, B, C*

Rank	Johnson	Smith	Wright
1	A	B	C
2	B	C	A
3	C	A	B

Source: James S. Coleman, "Foundations for a Theory of Collective Decisions," *American Journal of Sociology*, 71, no. 6 (May 1966), p. 619.

[56] See Barbara Hinckley, "Coalitions in Congress: Size in a Series of Games," paper presented to the American Political Science Association, Washington, D.C., September 1972.

the winner in that round against A. B versus C makes B the winner. Johnson prefers B to C and B is Smith's first preference. Wright loses this round. In the final round, A against B, B is eliminated because Johnson will vote his first preference and Wright his second, making A the winner. *Note that the final choice depended upon the order in which the alternatives were presented.*

Under the set of preferences outlined in table 1, the individual who can set the agenda and control the order of presentation exerts a considerable amount of control over the outcome. Hence frequently the most important question to ask in an analysis of rule making is who controls the agenda. Committee chairmen in Congress and the Party Secretariat in authoritarian systems like the Soviet Union's have such a capability. Those already *in the system* are at an advantage over those who are not. Because of the seniority system in Congress, congressmen from "safe" districts (in which a single party is dominant) will gravitate to powerful agenda-forming positions. In general, it is easier to make rules that support the status quo—that is, the policy favorable to those who control the agenda—than it is to radically alter the existing set of priorities.

An additional factor links rule making with the status quo: The alternative chosen is the first preference of a *minority*. In most cases of rule making, and in all cases where the preference ordering outlined in table 1 occurs, someone has to vote for less than his optimum choice to keep the least favored alternative from being chosen.

One reason for this "voting paradox" is that rule-making processes based upon "one representative, one vote" cannot take into account the *intensity of preferences*. One legislator may be extremely interested in an issue before the legislature, say the passage of a bill ensuring the continuation of price supports for agricultural produce, while another from a nonagricultural district may be only marginally interested. Yet the vote of one counts as much as the vote of the other. A recent example of the intensity of preference problem occurred during the Vietnam war. Males of draft age were directly affected by the continuation and progress of the war. They had only one vote apiece (assuming they were old enough to vote). Citizens whose lives and philosophies were untouched by the war also had a vote apiece. When someone who loses a vote feels that it is a life-or-death matter and sees that rule-making procedures do not adequately account for the intensity of his preferences, he will seek to either escape from the rule-making process or change it by going outside the accepted channels of policy making. Those who chose the first alternative emigrated to Canada or deserted from the armed forces; those opting for the latter alternative demonstrated, destroyed draft records, and in some cases joined organizations using violence to register the intensity of their preferences.

Intensity of preferences is registered in the legislative arena by the expenditure of resources, most notably one's power to vote on bills. Votes are exchanged in a process called logrolling: A legislator exchanges a vote for a bill that he is marginally interested in for another congressman's vote on a bill that he is intensely interested in. "Each has in that exchange expressed something about his intensity of preference." [57] The resources or power attached to one's vote increase with the significance of an issue and the alignment of legislators. When an issue arouses intense interest and the vote promises to be close, a great deal of bargaining will go on between the committed and the uncommitted, and the uncommitted will be able to extract a high price for his services. Money and organizational skill are additional resources that may be used to register intensity of preferences in the rule-making arena, as are interest groups that attempt to influence legislation. As with agenda control, however, these means are usually available to the elites, not the masses.

RULE APPLICATION AND RULE ADJUDICATION

Once made, rules must be put into effect, and any problems in their application brought to the surface and resolved. The last two functions are usually fulfilled respectively by the government bureaucracy and the judicial system.

Authoritative allocations of values that result from political activity are not confined to the rule-making process. Rule making only sets the stage on which bargaining over the specific nature of the allocations will take place. As Murray Edelman notes,

> *laws create a space in which to act. . . . In adopting this view the Greeks recognized that to draft a law is not to reflect a public "will"; it is only through subsequent bargaining and administrative decision-making that values find some sort of realization in policy.*[58]

Thus, even though the rule-making process may be such that the rules decided upon are rarely if ever completely satisfactory to a majority, implementation of the rules allows considerable leeway in execution, both symbolic and material. It is therefore in applying the rules and resolving disputes in concrete cases that the "authoritative

[57] James S. Coleman, "Foundations for a Theory of Collective Decisions," *American Journal of Sociology,* 71, no. 6 (May 1966), 620.

[58] Murray Edelman, *The Symbolic Uses of Politics* (Urbana: University of Illinois Press, 1967), p. 103.

allocation of values" finally takes place. Indeed, the actual meaning of a legal statute is simply "what its administrators do about it." [59]

The administration of laws usually reflects the intentions of the legislature that passed them when there is basic agreement on the service to be performed and the clientele groups are well organized. Veterans' organizations, for example, have received considerable benefits for their members without rousing the ire of public opinion because they are well organized and favorably received by the citizenry. In this instance, and in others where the allocations intended in the rules are realized by the actual distributions, the "groups which were strong enough to secure passage of the legislation continue to be dominant in the process of its execution." [60]

Administrators, like legislators, are subject to the power of the organized groups. If the rule-making arena and the rule-application and -adjudication arena are sensitive to different balances of power, interpretation of the law will reflect this difference. Regulatory agencies like the Federal Communications Commission and the Interstate Commerce Commission have, over time, come to reflect the interest of the groups they were supposed to regulate rather than speaking boldly for "the national interest." [61] The result is a "life cycle of regulatory agencies." Legislation for the agency is usually agreed upon during a time of crisis that brings together a group of people with diverse interests and somewhat contradictory group memberships. For example, economic depression resulting in part from the stock market crash of 1929 led to the Securities and Exchange Commission, and the crisis of World War II led to the Office of Price Administration.[62] In both instances, Franklin Roosevelt acted as a catalyst in developing group cohesion. He was abetted by the tendency of people to coalesce when the magnitude of a threat to well-being surpasses the intensity of internal discord.[63] As long as the threat is imminent and a charismatic leader is active, regulation will be effective. When the crisis is past and the leader has gone, unity

[59] Ibid., p. 139.

[60] Truman, *The Governmental Process*, p. 441.

[61] See Marver H. Bernstein, *Regulating Business by Independent Commissions* (Princeton, N.J.: Princeton University Press, 1955); Avery Leiserson, *Administrative Regulation: A Study in Representation of Interests* (Chicago: University of Chicago Press, 1942); Emmette S. Redford, *Administration of National Economic Control* (New York: Macmillan, 1952); Edelman, *Symbolic Uses of Politics;* and Truman, *The Governmental Process.*

[62] See Redford, *Administration of Economic Control.*

[63] See Coser, *The Functions of Social Conflict.* Note that prior to the 1973 war the Arabs were not able to unite successfully against the Israelis; their hatred of Israel was less than the intensity of inter-Arab distrust and rivalry. The picture may be changing now.

and active support of regulation decline. Of the OPA and price controls David Truman says:

> *The program was viable only through constant efforts, primarily on the part of the administrators, to maintain some cohesion among supporting elements and by continual adjustments with organized interest groups whose dominance in the administering process was a constant possibility. The latter, in fact, rendered the program unadministerable when the cohesion of the supporting groups was ruptured by the ending of the war and by the death of the popular leader.*[64]

With a narrow perspective of interests and a short memory, the public is able to remain attentive for only a short time. Once the initial goal is accomplished, it lapses into apathy and isolation from public affairs. The cry for a "return to normalcy" that elected President Harding after the idealism and exhaustion of World War I is an example, as is the rapid decline of the Anti-Saloon League after the passage of the Prohibition Amendment.[65] Passage of legislation demanded by an aroused public united behind a few crusaders usually signals a precipitous decline in interest and organization. The administration of the law then devolves upon people who find that their only sources of information and support lie with the narrow, highly organized interests they are ostensibly supposed to regulate. The public is unable to maintain its fervor for regulation when it comes to the specific administrative problems of relating generalities to the concrete and the often unglamorous aspects of specific cases, with their minute details in an attempt to follow rules of equity and due process.[66]

The passage of regulatory legislation itself, Edelman argues, is a symbolic reward for the masses; "where public understanding is vague and information rare, interests in reassurance will be all the more potent and all the more susceptible to manipulation by political symbols." [67] A visible structure for administering the law frequently serves to keep the masses quiescent. Thus, because the masses believe they are being taken care of, statutes designed to protect the "public interest" may, in fact, work the other way. Although they

[64] Truman, *The Governmental Process*, p. 442.

[65] See Peter H. Odegard's delightful study of the League in his *Pressure Politics* (New York: Octagon Books, 1966).

[66] See Martin Shapiro, *The Supreme Court and Administrative Agencies* (New York: Free Press, 1968).

[67] Edelman, *Symbolic Uses of Politics*, p. 38.

*function as reassurances that threats in the economic environment
are under control, their indirect effect is to permit greater claims
upon tangible resources by the organized groups concerned than
would be possible if the legal symbols were absent.*[68]

As public furor fades after the passage of enabling legislation, the
administrator finds himself facing the power of entrenched, highly
organized interests. A recent example involved the National Highway
Traffic Safety Administration. For several years, a large auto maker had
been manufacturing vehicles with defective engine mounts. When the
mount failed, the engine lurched to one side, severing a brake line and
jamming the throttle open. The result was a rapidly accelerating car, no
brakes, and, on some models, a steering gear that locked when the
driver attempted to stop the car by turning off the ignition. The first
complaint came to the HTSA in 1969, followed by approximately 500
more. Not until October 1971, after consumer advocate Ralph Nader
"openly attacked the agency's director . . . for his inaction" was any
action taken. The main reason for the delay appeared to be the power
the auto makers could bring to bear against the agency. As one official
put it, "We are the flea trying to find out what makes the elephant
lame." The auto maker, he continued, "has more press agents than our
30 investigators." The agency was afraid of losing cases in the court of
law and the court of public opinion unless the defect could be proven.[69]
This attitude of extreme caution changed only when the charismatic
Nader publicized the situation.

Especially in the emerging nations, the rule-making institutions and
the administrative sector differ significantly. Conflict between traditional
groups and tribes and the modernizing, Western-educated elite frequently
paralyzes the legislative process, especially when the general population
is not accustomed to the workings of democracy and has not yet ac-
corded legitimacy to the democratic rule-making institutions. Under
these conditions the administrative apparatus of the state—the civil
service and the military—assume a greater role. Frequently, as a result
of the training programs of the former colonial power, they possess a
monopoly of talent in policy execution, and rule-making functions
either devolve upon them by default or are taken over by them.[70] The
overthrow of Salvador Allende and the setting up of a military junta

[68] Ibid.

[69] *Newsweek*, 25 October 1971, p. 94.

[70] See Ira Sharkansky, *Public Administration: Policy-Making in Government Agencies* (Chicago: Markham, 1970), chap. 2, "Comparison in the Study of Public Administration."

in Chile is an example of this process. In such cases the division of function among rule making, rule application, and rule adjudication may be blurred, and while analytically distinct, are inseparable in practice. In Chile today, the military makes the rules, executes them, and adjudicates disputes, using considerable violence in the process.

Rule adjudication is the process of resolving disputes arising from the concrete application of statutes. Some court injunctions are issued against individuals whose behavior contravenes the rules they are engaged in applying; or an individual may intentionally break a rule he feels is unjust in order to make a test case and, he hopes, get the courts to force a change in the law. Independent regulatory agencies perform both administrative and adjudicative or quasi-judicial functions in that they may prosecute cases which are "then conducted before their own hearing officers and appeals are taken to their own commissioners."[71]

In some nations, particularly those with authoritarian or totalitarian forms of government, rule-adjudication takes the form of an internal struggle for power, after which the judicial system legitimizes the actions of the winner. Here courts are "star chambers," which extract forced confessions from the defeated opponents of the regime, thereby allowing the arbitrary decisions of the leadership to be clothed in the trappings of legality and justice. Examples include the notorious Nazi People's Court and the Moscow show trials of the 1930s in which party members accused of treason confessed publicly.

The functions discussed in this chapter are analytical and heuristic; they are abstractions from a very complex reality that are intended to be suggestive rather than absolute indicators of the structures and processes of politics. However, in addition to the descriptive material that suggests the utility of this scheme, there is some interesting additional evidence.

In a recent study analyzing the background of participants in the 1905 revolution in Russia, a statistical technique designed to locate unique clusters of individuals was employed. Five types of people emerged, and the types bear a close resemblance to the functions of government outlined in this chapter.[72] While all the individuals were by definition revolutionaries, the roles they adopted differed, as did the backgrounds of people playing different roles. Within a role type, however, the individuals appeared to be quite similar.[73] The typology is as follows:

[71] Shapiro, *The Supreme Court*, p. 5.

[72] Harlan J. Strauss, "Revolutionary Types: Russia in 1905," *Journal of Conflict Resolution*, 17, no. 2 (June 1973), 297–316.

[73] Ibid., p. 301.

Political Function	Role in 1905 Revolution
Political recruitment, socialization	Intelligentsia
Interest articulation	Propagandist
Interest aggregation	Party organizer
Rule making *	Upper-level politician
Authoritative functions (rule-application/ rule-adjudication)	Rebel-striker

Source: Harlan J. Strauss, "Revolutionary Types: Russia in 1905," *Journal of Conflict Resolution*, 17, no. 2 (June 1973), 310.

* The *Rule-making* function has been substituted here for what Strauss called the *Communication* function. It may be argued that communication, the ability to share meanings intersubjectively, is a basic prerequisite for the fulfillment of all of the other functions. As such, it may be a "given" in any political system that has indicated that it is able to persist through time.

The *intelligentsia* were upper- and upper-middle-class elites who were active in the Russian revolutionary movement at home and abroad. Their organizational efforts were directed at the nation as a whole, and they spread their philosophy through journalistic and propagandistic efforts rather than by way of overt violence. *Propagandists,* on the other hand, were "grass roots politicians." Eschewing violence, they spread the revolutionary word in face-to-face relationships with the masses, whose demands they articulated in revolutionary oratory. *Party organizers* brought the dissatisfied masses into the party and integrated their demands into the party program. They left violence to others, concentrating instead on the construction of a party apparatus. *Upper-level politicians* did not deal with the masses, but instead served as links between the old order and the new; they were the middlemen between the revolution and the regime. They assessed the progress of the revolution and the extent to which demands were likely to be legitimized by authoritative changes in the political ground rules. The *rebels* and *strikers* were on the firing line. The rebels enforced revolutionary policy; They made bombs, planned and executed assassinations, and the like. The strikers employed direct action in their attempt to put revolutionary policy into effect.

Strauss's study raises some interesting questions. Could it be that the revolution of 1905 came to the brink of success because the participants developed a division of political labor that mirrored the functions described in this chapter? Not enough is known in the social sciences to allow a firm conclusion, but the evidence is indeed suggestive.[74]

74 Ibid., pp. 310–12.

SUMMARY AND CRITIQUE

To satisfy citizen demands all governments must perform at least six analytically distinct functions: political socialization; interest articulation; interest aggregation; rule making; rule application; and rule adjudication. When any of these functions is not adequately fulfilled, some proportion of the citizenry will become dissatisfied and support for the government will erode.

By way of critique we might ask why six—and only these six—functions are involved in an analysis of politics. Why not three, or twenty-three? Can we state with certainty that these six functions are the minimum— or the maximum—that must be fulfilled for the government to work properly? Further, are these functions consistent across all political systems? Do governments of populations on the bare subsistence level share the same functions as the one that would operate in a hypothetical society full of self-actualizers? Indeed, in such a case, would these functions even be necessary—would government as we know it exist? If the functions apply with equal validity to systems as diverse as the American government and a nomadic tribe, then could it be, as Thorson maintains in *Biopolitics*, that they "explain everything and therefore nothing"?

Because it is difficult, perhaps impossible,* to empirically test broad analytical schemes like the one presented in this chapter, we must always guard against the tendency, perhaps unconscious, to reify them— to believe so strongly in a hypothetical construct that we take it to be real and lose our ability to perceive evidence to the contrary. Can we think of examples of successfully functioning political systems that did *not* fulfill any of the above functions? Can we think of other functions that were not included, but which bring about the downfall of a political system if they are not fulfilled?

The many different systems or configurations of government are all designed to fulfill the above six functions. The next chapter considers some of the major types of government and the forces that may lead a society to change from one system to another.

Selected Bibliography

ALMOND, GABRIEL A., and JAMES S. COLEMAN, eds., *The Politics of the Developing Areas*. Princeton, N.J.: Princeton University Press, 1960.

ANDRAIN, CHARLES F., *Political Life and Social Change*. Belmont, Ca.: Wadsworth, 1970.

BERNSTEIN, MARVER H., *Regulating Business by Independent Commissions.* Princeton, N.J.: Princeton University Press, 1955.

MERTON, ROBERT K., *Social Theory and Social Structure.* New York: Free Press, 1968.

PYE, LUCIAN W., and SIDNEY VERBA, eds., *Political Culture and Political Development.* Princeton, N.J.: Princeton University Press, 1965.

RIKER, WILLIAM H., *The Theory of Political Coalitions.* New Haven, Conn.: Yale University Press, 1962.

SCHATTSCHNEIDER, E. E., *The Semi-sovereign People.* New York: Holt, Rinehart and Winston, 1960.

ZEIGLER, L. HARMON, and MICHAEL BAER, *Lobbying.* Belmont, Ca.: Wadsworth, 1969.

8

Politics and crisis: political system types in the modern world

As there are different types of power, so, too, are there different political systems and relations between elites and masses upon which such systems are based. Robert Dahl notes that there is a "flood of typologies" describing the types of political systems in existence, present and past, and new typologies can be expected to emerge as quickly as old ones become obsolete.[1] Certainly the most famous typology originated with Aristotle. The scheme, although quite simple, has shaped political thinking ever since. Aristotle devised a sixfold scheme based on the number of people allowed to rule and the extent to which they ruled in their own interest or in the interest of the public at large, as table 1 indicates. Another scheme that summarizes thinking about types of political systems was designed by Bernard Crick (table 2).[2]

Table 1 *Aristotle's Classification*

Number of Citizens Entitled to Rule	Rulers Rule in Interest of: All	Themselves
One	Kingship (monarchy)	Tyranny
Few	Aristocracy	Oligarchy
Many	Polity	Democracy

Source: Robert A. Dahl, *Modern Political Analysis* (Englewood Cliffs, N.J.: Prentice-Hall, 1970), p. 49. See *The Politics of Aristotle,* trans. and ed. Ernest Barker (New York: Oxford University Press, 1962).

[1] Robert A. Dahl, *Modern Political Analysis* (Englewood Cliffs, N.J.: Prentice-Hall, 1970), p. 48.

[2] Bernard Crick, "The Elementary Types of Government," *Government and Opposition*, 3, no. 1 (Winter 1968), 3–20.

Table 2 *Types of Government and Their Characteristics*

	Autocratic	Republican	Totalitarian
Government seeks to bring order out of diversity by:	Authoritative enforcement of one of the diverse interests.	Letting diverse interests share in the government or the competitive choosing of the government.	Creating a completely new society such that conflict would no longer arise: it attempts to do this by means of the guidance and enforcement of a revolutionary ideology which claims to be scientific, thus comprehensive and necessary, both for knowledge and allegiance.
Role of the inhabitants (i.e., the masses):	Passive obedience and social deference ("suffer the powers that be" and "the rich man at his castle, the poor man at his gate . . .")	Voluntary and individual participation, hence partial and discriminating, never total, loyalty.	Mass participation and compulsory explicit enthusiasm (passive obedience is rejected as inadequate or suspect: "Who are those who are not the friends of the people but that they are the enemies of the people?")
The official doctrine:	Allegiance is a religious duty and government is part of the divine order.	Allegiance is demanded and given on utilitarian and secular grounds.	Allegiance is ideological; based upon an all-encompassing conception of man as a product of impersonal forces—whether racial or economic. Inner reservations must be exposed and punished just as surely as open dissent.
Typical social structure:	A highly stratified caste or class structure.	A large middle class or bourgeoisie.	Egalitarian in aspiration; but in fact a social structure mainly determined by political function.
Position of the political elite:	Self-perpetuating and exclusive (almost always fortified by myths of descent from the gods or great men).	A stable political class enjoying social prestige, but not exclusive. Subject to penetration by candidates from political and educational institutions designed to encourage mobility.	In theory a meritocracy based on perfect social mobility ("to each according to his needs, from each according to his abilities"). In practice a relatively small "inner party" with a relatively large "outer party."

Table 2 *(continued)*

	Autocratic	Republican	Totalitarian
Typical economic organization:	Agrarian, pre-industrial, usually aiming at self-sufficiency.	Market economy; capitalistic; or mixed capitalist/government control.	Centrally directed and mobilized war economy; or planned, centrally administered economy emphasizing rapid industrialization.
Attitude toward the law:	Law is customary and/or "god-given" and sacred. Law as applied is related to status; the lower the status the more arbitrary the outcome.	Law is made of both custom and legislatively made statute; the attempt is made to apply the law generally; i.e., outcome is not based on class, race or status.	Laws are the laws of history or race —they are greater than man and are interpreted and applied by the party ideologists.
Attitudes toward diffusion of information:	Proclamations, but no regular news: rumour and gossip as institutions exploited by both rulers and ruled; mainly oral communication.	Newspapers, periodicals not all under the control of the state. Effective operation of regime depends upon popular access to information and official access to accurate measures of opinion.	Mass-communications controlled by the state. The official encyclopedia preferred to books and novels. All art forms to be propaganda.
Attitudes toward politics:	Leaders are either above politics or politics is limited to the secrecy of the palace and the court. Conflict and opposition are tolerated so long as they do not become public and so long as no one appeals for support outside of the ruling class.	Politics is always tolerated; politics is conciliation; opposition can be public and is sometimes institutionalized.	Politics and opposition are seen as subversive and not just personal intrigue or conspiracy, but a symptom of social contradictions yet to be eradicated. Politics is a bourgeois sham.

Adapted with the author's permission from the more elaborate schema in Bernard Crick, *Basic Forms of Government: a Sketch and a Model* (Macmillan, 1973), pp. 74–81. We have not included his categories of "Attitudes to Knowledge," "Typical Institutions of Government," or "Theories of Property." (The book was sponsored by the journal *Government and Opposition*.)

Any classification scheme does some injustice to its subject; there are in fact as many types of government as there are governments. However, we gain nothing by using a classification scheme that is so specific that no generalizations can be made. Crick outlines three modal types that appear to be inherently stable when the type of political system coincides with the proper category on the other dimensions. Presumably, governments that fall in between these classifications will tend to be unstable and transitional, as is the case today in many of the underdeveloped nations:

> *Simply to take government in former British, Belgian and French Africa, their most common characteristic is chronic instability. The social systems seem largely independent of the political. The governments would like to transform society, sometimes even they have a totalitarian impulse, but they have no possibility of succeeding in that way. They are mainly autocracies, but rendered unstable by aroused economic expectations both in their elites and in their general populations—expectations arising from completely external factors and which cannot possibly be met internally.*[3]

The autocratic, republican, and totalitarian forms of government represent cognitively consonant configurations of social conditions, beliefs, and political structures. When the picture begins to change, for example, when an elite attempts to maintain an autocracy when an educated, economically significant middle class is emerging as the industrial revolution progresses, a great deal of dissonance will occur. The elites will miscalculate, the middle class will find itself frustrated, and instability is likely to follow.

An empirical analysis of political violence reinforces Crick's classification because nations falling between types of political system tend to be inherently unstable, as is true of many of the emerging nations today. Ivo Feierabend, Rosalind Feierabend, and Betty Nesvold argue that two basic patterns of values, two modal "value and belief systems" exist: a traditional and a modern. In general, Crick's *autocratic* system describes the traditional political system and his *republican* form por-

[3] Reprinted with the author's permission from Bernard Crick, *Basic Forms of Government: a Sketch and a Model* (Macmillan, 1973), p. 85.

trays the modern pattern.[4] At the midpoint of the progression from one to another, where the security of the past has been overthrown for the promise of the future that has not yet arrived, the "maximum possible mismatch" between social institutions and popular attitudes is likely.

On the *micro,* or individual, level the transitional midpoint is experienced as maximum discrepancy between *expectations,* the things he believes he is entitled to, and reality. This discrepancy between expectations and reality is called "relative deprivation." The individual feels deprived because he considers that something due him hasn't arrived; the term *relative* indicates that the extent to which the individual feels deprived depends upon his unique set of beliefs, values, and expectations. Individuals X and Y may live in the same part of town but X may believe that he has to accept an inferior position in life while Y believes that all people are created equal and should be given an equal opportunity to succeed. Should both hear a politician promise "equal opportunity after the revolution," only Y will suffer relative deprivation should the politician prove unable to deliver the goods on schedule.[5]

Relative deprivation is a significant concept because it is closely linked with frustration, of which it is an indicator. And frustration, as we have noted, is an instigator of aggression. When the institutions of society are unharmonious, when they work against each other and make it difficult for individuals to match their expectations with the reality, relative deprivation and resulting frustration are high, and a great deal of political violence and government instability can be expected. Figure 1 illustrates this situation.

As Feierabend, Feierabend, and Nesvold put it:

On the evidence, members of transitional societies aspire to the benefits of modernity, yet modern goals may be blocked by the

---

[4] Ivo K. Feierabend, Rosalind L. Feierabend, and Betty A. Nesvold, "Social Change and Political Violence: Cross-National Patterns," in *Violence in America: Historical and Comparative Perspectives,* Hugh Davis Graham and Ted Robert Gurr, eds. (New York: New American Library, 1969), pp. 606–67. Should complete consensus on the distribution of rewards ever exist in a technologically developed society, or should such a society be continuously threatened by its neighbors, the totalitarian form of government might be adopted. This point will be discussed later in the chapter.

[5] The literature on relative deprivation is voluminous. See Ted Robert Gurr, *Why Men Rebel* (Princeton, N. J.: Princeton University Press, 1970); and James C. Davies, "Toward a Theory of Revolution," *American Sociological Review,* 27 (February 1962), 5–19. For a critique, see Bernard N. Grofman and Edward N. Muller, "The Strange Case of Relative Gratification and Potential for Political Violence: The V-Curve Hypothesis," *American Political Science Review,* 67, no. 2 (June 1973), 514–39.

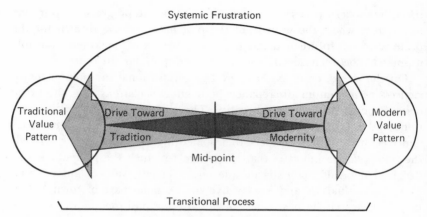

Source: Ivo K. Feierabend, Rosalind L. Feierabend, and Betty A. Nesvold, "Social Change and Political Violence: Cross-National Patterns," in Violence in America: Historical and Comparative Perspectives, Hugh Davis Graham and Ted Robert Gurr, eds. (New York: New American Library, 1969), p. 617.

Figure 1   Conflict Model of Transition from Traditional to Modern Value Pattern.

values inherent in traditional society. Any modicum of modernity introduced into traditional society will conflict with its traditions. The farther the process of transition progresses, the more likely and the more intense the conflicts between modern and established patterns. The situation may be depicted as a massive conflict, reflected in myriad individual psyches of different strata of the population and infecting different domains of the social process. It may lead to intergroup conflict between more traditional and more modern strata with conflicting social roles, structures, and expectations.[6]

The level of conflict and violence is reflected in data on political instability. The Feierabends used data on political violence gathered over an eighteen-year period (1948–1965). They assigned the following values to political events: 0 for regularly scheduled elections; 1 for dismissal or resignation of a cabinet official; 2 for peaceful demonstration or arrest; 3 for assassination of officials other than the head of state or sabotage; 4 for terrorism or assassination of the head of state; 5 for

[6] Feierabend, Feierabend, and Nesvold, "Social Change and Political Violence," p. 618.

guerrilla warfare; and 6 for civil war or mass executions.[7] An index of modernity was then developed by combining figures on per capita gross national product, caloric intake, telephones, physicians, newspapers, literacy, and urbanization.[8] The results are listed in table 3.

Modern countries are obviously more stable than either traditional or transitional countries, with only 17 percent of nations classified modern falling in the unstable category as opposed to 68 percent for transitional and 56 percent for traditional.[9]

The process of development is complex in its specific manifestations but relatively simple in broad outline. As a nation moves up the ladder of development, a greater proportion of the population comes in contact with significant aspects of modern life—automobiles, agricultural technology, and the like. The proportion of the population exposed to communications media also increases, as does the percentage of literates in the population. People begin leaving farms in favor of new, nonagricultural jobs in the cities. Urbanization increases, as does the number of those employed in nonagricultural occupations, while the percentage of the labor force employed in agriculture declines. The gross national product (GNP) increases.[10] The process generates considerable social and psychological dislocation.

Most of the people in the developing nations do not possess the "open-minded" outlook required by democratic institutions. Where such ideas or institutions exist, they are usually associated with a chronically colonial power. Further, traditional economic capitalism cannot be expected to appeal to the "uprooted, impoverished and disoriented masses produced by social mobilization" or the developmental process. For them, it is patently *not* true that "that government is best which governs least. They are far more likely to need a direct transition from traditional government to the essentials of a modern welfare state." [11]

The early history of the United States produced a type of government very different from that of today's newly emerging nations. At the time of this nation's founding, transportation and communications moved at a snail's pace by modern standards. In addition, a vast, rich, unexplored area provided a haven for those who were energetic but

[7] Ibid., p. 621.

[8] Ibid., p. 627.

[9] Ibid.

[10] Karl W. Deutsch, "Social Mobilization and Political Development," in *Comparative Politics: A Reader,* Harry Eckstein and David E. Apter, eds. (New York: Free Press, 1963), p. 583. This article also appeared in the *American Political Science Review,* 55, no. 3 (September 1961), 493–514.

[11] Deutsch, "Social Mobilization," in *Comparative Politics,* p. 586.

Table 3 *Relationship Between Modernity and Political Instability, 1948–65*

	I. Traditional	II. Transitional	III. Modern	
Unstable	Bolivia Burma China (mainland) Haiti India Indonesia Iraq Jordan Laos Malaya Morocco Philippines Sudan No.: 13	Brazil Colombia Costa Rica Cuba Cyprus Dominican Republic Ecuador Egypt Greece Guatemala Honduras Hungary Korea Lebanon Panama Paraguay Peru Poland Portugal Syria Thailand Tunisia Turkey Union of South Africa Venezuela No.: 25	Argentina Czechoslovakia East Germany France No.: 4	42 Total Unstable
Stable	Afghanistan Cambodia China (Taiwan) Ethiopia Ghana Iran Liberia Libya Pakistan Saudi Arabia No.: 10	Albania Bulgaria Ceylon Chile El Salvador Italy Japan Mexico Nicaragua Romania Spain Yugoslavia No.: 12	Australia Austria Belgium Canada Denmark Finland Iceland Ireland Israel Luxembourg Netherlands New Zealand Norway Sweden Switzerland United Kingdom United States Uruguay U.S.S.R. West Germany No.: 20	42 Total Stable
	23 Traditional	37 Transitional	24 Modern	84 Nations Total

Source: Ivo K. Feierabend, Rosalind L. Feierabend, and Betty A. Nesvold, "Social Change and Political Violence: Cross-National Patterns," in *Violence in America: Historical and Comparative Perspectives*, Hugh Davis Graham and Ted Robert Gurr, eds. (New York: New American Library, 1969), p. 632.

dissatisfied with the existing order in settled parts of the country. The sorely discontented could therefore "move west" and the government, kept some distance away by the transportation and communications difficulties, could not interfere with the everyday life of the people. All of this was conducive to the development of a philosophy of "rugged individualism" and a hands-off *laissez-faire* attitude on the part of the central authorities in Washington.

Under these conditions, gradual change was possible, as was a pragmatic, individual-rights policy based upon a humanistic and democratic heritage imported from England. By the Civil War, democratic attitudes had become firmly embedded in the thinking of the educated classes. At the same time the citizens were not exposed to a radically different —and better—alternative. They could not observe on a TV or movie screen that people of similar social station elsewhere enjoyed more of the good things in life. They therefore did not experience the degree of relative deprivation so prevalent today.

This is, of course, not the case in the emerging nations today. Instead of being able to move to the frontier where land is plentiful and a person can stand or fall by his own labors—labors that lead to the immediate reward of survival and well-being—individuals in newly emerging nations move to the cities where they find that the present is to be sacrificed for the future at precisely the time their appetites have been whetted for the benefits provided by a modern economy. For the industrial base needed for economic modernity can be built only if there has been some form of capital development. Because the capital is usually extracted from labor and agriculture, laborers must work long hours for low pay and perhaps even suffer a reduction in caloric intake as foodstuffs that would otherwise be available go into the export market. The farmer, in turn, must raise more and keep less for himself in order to create a surplus that can be turned into foreign currency. When people suffer a decline in their standard of living after hearing about the benefits of modernization, a truly democratic political alternative may be impossible.

Under these conditions two things are usually needed: inducements for the masses to concentrate on national rather than individual goals; and inducements to keep recalcitrants from challenging the leadership. Several factions competing for power, each parading a different set of national symbols and a different definition of national goals, would so fragment the masses that any appeal to national unity would soon be ineffective. Intensive propaganda is usually employed to keep people's thoughts in close accord with the policy of the leaders, while an efficient force of secret political police using terror tactics takes care of any potential political competition.

CRISIS POLITICS: THE TRANSITION
FROM DEMOCRACY TO TOTALITARIANISM

International crisis and the presence of an external threat often generate substantial increase in public support for leaders. As long as public faith in a political leader has not been greatly diminished before a crisis occurs, the result is usually an increase in popular support. In February 1961, prior to the Bay of Pigs invasion, a Gallup poll showed that 72 percent of the sample approved of President Kennedy's handling of the presidency. In May 1961, following the incident, 83 percent expressed approval. By midyear (July 1961) the crisis was past and his standing slipped to 71 percent. A similar rise and decline was registered with regard to the Cuban missile crisis: 62 percent registered approval before it occurred (in early October 1962) and 74 percent shortly afterward (November). In 1963 his standing dropped from a high of 76 percent in January, when the crisis was still vivid in the public memory, to 50 percent in November, when it may be assumed that the public had turned its attention elsewhere.[12] However, President Nixon's popularity slipped still further when he fired Special (Watergate) Prosecutor Archibald Cox, because his popularity was already low. Nixon was enmeshed in litigation over the Watergate tapes and had seen his vice-president Spiro Agnew resign following allegations of his role in a kickback scheme while he was governor of Maryland. Nixon's attempt to rally the public in the face of the Middle East war of 1973 therefore seemed defensive, self-serving, and hollow. Thus, at the time, nearly half of those sampled in one poll favored impeachment, a sure sign that any attempt to rally the public around him over the Middle East crisis would be extremely difficult.[13]

Crisis affects more than the relation between the masses and their leaders; and, once again, crisis politics tend to make any political system more closely resemble the totalitarian form. During an actual, imagined, or simulated crisis the population, including those fully imbued with democratic ideals, are inclined to place the "good of the nation" above the rights of the individual. The rights of people labeled as "threats to the nation" can therefore be easily disregarded, as can the procedural safeguards of their liberty. The government thus can employ terror and coercive tactics against any potential competitor without fear of arous-

[12] Figures from Gallup poll, *Public Opinion 1935–1971* (New York: Random House, 1972).

[13] NBC poll, reported by John Chancellor, 22 October 1973.

ing too much public support for the accused. The United States during the First World War provides a suitable example:

> . . . *during the conflict the demand for absolute loyalty had permeated every nook and cranny of the social structure. Independent agencies, such as the National Security League and the American Defense Society, together with the government-sponsored American Protective League, had converted thousands of otherwise reasonable and sane Americans into super-patriots and self-styled spy-chasers by spreading rabid propaganda which maximized the dangers of wartime sabotage and sedition. Supposedly, these agencies represented the nation's first line of defense against wartime subversive activity . . . actually they had become the repository of elements which . . . often used "Americanism" merely to blacken the reputation and character of persons and groups whose opinions they hated and feared.*[14]

In some states German was no longer taught in the schools and teachers lost their jobs for alleged unpatriotic statements; "in the nation at large men had been beaten and tarred and feathered for failure to buy war bonds or support Red Cross drives." [15] Conscientious objectors, many of whom were members of small religious sects, came in for particularly harsh treatment.[16]

Before the U.S. entrance into World War I, the public exhibited a significant ability to discriminate between anarchists preaching violent overthrow of political institutions and socialists advocating a moderate approach to political change by working within the system. The mind-closing effects of crisis are evidenced in the public reaction to deviants when the nation went to war:

> *Because of their universal opposition to the conflict, all radicals, regardless of their various persuasions, were lumped into the same category. The public mind suddenly lost its earlier ability to discriminate. As wartime fervor flamed hot . . . the general press, the courts, patriotic societies, government officials—the whole nation—regarded them all as traitors and sought to suppress them by force.*[17]

[14] Robert K. Murray, *Red Scare* (New York: McGraw-Hill, 1964), p. 12.
[15] Cited in ibid.
[16] See ibid., p. 13.
[17] Ibid., p. 32.

After the war, a population straining under the adjustment to post-war conditions, with their attendant inflation, unemployment, and uncertainty about the future, was ripe with frustration that could be exploited for its own purpose by the economic elite. Here "patriotism" could be turned against democratic principle in a classic case of elite manipulation. A sensationalist press helped set the stage by playing upon the patriotic fervor whipped up by the war and by arousing irrational fears of a "Bolshevik" takeover in the United States. Anarchist bombings were paraded as signs of a "conspiracy" and the Seattle general strike of 1919 was used by such opportunistic politicians as Mayor Ole Hanson, who brought out troops against people he proclaimed "want to take possession of our American Government and try to duplicate the anarchy of Russia."[18] An essentially false linkage between Bolshevism and labor was not difficult to establish in the public mind, and the connection was actively fostered in the publications of a number of private-interest groups financed by men like T. Coleman DuPont, J. P. Morgan, and John D. Rockefeller.[19] While membership in such groups was limited, publications and propaganda efforts were extensive. Patriotism became a euphemism for private property and economic conservatism while labor organization and the employment of the strike weapon were considered weapons in the arsenal of the Bolsheviks.[20]

The disclaimers of the American Federation of Labor and a quiet, peaceful passage of Independence Day 1919 after the press had blazed forth with headlines such as "REIGN OF TERROR PLANNED," "PLANS FOR WIDESPREAD VIOLENCE AND MURDER," and the like [21] did little to allay the public's fears, so strongly were the forces of selective perception at work. "In fact, by the fall of 1919 all strikes, regardless of their nature, had come to be considered 'crimes against society,' 'conspiracies against the government,' and 'plots to establish communism.' "[22]

With the public in this frame of mind, little was done to preserve the rights and liberties of the workers, and political fortunes were made by those who played on the prevailing mood. Calvin Coolidge, the

---

[18] Cited in ibid., p. 63. Murray notes that the radicals made much of the fact that "a few months after the Seattle episode Hanson resigned as mayor to tour the country, giving lectures on the dangers of domestic bolshevism—an activity which netted him $38,000 in seven months, while his salary as Mayor of Seattle had been only $7500 a year": ibid., p. 66.

[19] See ibid., pp. 85, 114, and *passim*.

[20] See ibid., chap. 7, "Labor and Bolshevism."

[21] Cited in ibid., p. 116.

[22] Ibid., p. 121.

lackluster governor of Massachusetts at the time of the Boston Police Strike of 1919, was catapulted to instant national fame when he ended the attempts of the strikers to attain a decent wage with the words: "There is no right to strike against the public safety by anybody, anywhere, any time." [23] All striking policemen were fired. Their plea for reinstatement was refused by the State Supreme Court.[24]

In the nationwide steel strike of the same year, the extensive intimidation and violence produced no outcry. At times there were nearly as many sheriffs as there were strikers.

> *In certain areas, union meetings were summarily broken up, picket lines were dispersed, and orderly participants were clubbed. In some small mill towns, the local mounted police rode over pedestrians on the sidewalks, injuring peaceful groups of men and women. When strikers attempted to defend themselves against such brutality, they were treated ruthlessly. For example, at Farrell, Pennsylvania, in a skirmish between strikers and police arising from the latter's oppressive curtailment of free speech, four strikers were killed and eleven badly wounded. The net result of such police activity was that in many areas civil liberty became a dead letter.*[25]

With few exceptions the press reported events in a highly selective fashion. It dwelt upon and magnified any shred of evidence of radicalism, and ignored the many provocations and transgressions perpetrated by the steel manufacturers, who were portrayed as bastions of law and order.[26] The results of the "Red Scare" hysteria of 1919 were strikingly similar to those of the McCarthy era in the 1950s. Teachers, professors, and clergymen suffered heavily, for, by the nature of their occupations, they are involved with ideas and issues, and discussion in and of itself implies something less than a full, enthusiastic, and unquestioning 100-percent support of the status quo. People in these professions found that "resultant public intolerance soon precluded the free exercise of . . . opinion and in many localities forced either a pattern of sullen conformity or arbitrary dismissal." [27]

The period 1919–1920 and its legacy of intolerance stands as an

---

23 Cited in ibid., p. 132.

24 Ibid., p. 133.

25 Ibid., p. 145.

26 See ibid., p. 146 and *passim*.

27 Ibid., p. 175.

example of the ability of crisis to divert a nominally democratic regime from the norms of democratic government. It also illustrates the penchant that masses and elites have for infringing upon civil rights and liberties when times become threatening and uncertain. Another example of the erosion of democratic attitudes and behavior during crisis occurred shortly after Pearl Harbor and U.S. entrance into World War II. There was a sudden, great hue and cry over the presence of native and alien Japanese on American soil. Heightened fear of sabotage and war hysteria eventually led to the mass evacuation of approximately 110,000 Japanese from their West Coast residences. Relocated inland, they lived for the duration of the war in an American version of the concentration camp. In the process of relocation they had to relinquish a hard-earned position of dominance in the California farm produce industry. They also had to sell or abandon most of their belongings. They received little in return, as is usually the case where the seller is desperate and the buyer is not.[28]

Once again, public opinion became hysterical and irrational, as is indicated by a quote from the *Los Angeles Times* of February 2, 1942:

> *A viper is nonetheless a viper wherever the egg is hatched. . . .*
> *So, a Japanese American born of Japanese parents, nurtured upon*
> *Japanese traditions, living in a transplanted Japanese atmosphere and*
> *thoroughly inoculated with Japanese . . . ideals, notwithstanding*
> *his nominal brand of accidental citizenship almost inevitably and*
> *with the rarest exceptions grows up to be a Japanese and not*
> *an American. . . .*[29]

Thus, clearly, democracy and crisis do not go together. The crises associated with rapid economic development make totalitarian forms of government attractive vehicles for modern technology and communication networks. At the same time, the actions of the masses undergoing crisis may in fact quickly transform a developed *democratic* nation into a *totalitarian* nation. The abuses of recent American administrations—reaching their extreme with Nixon, but not initiated by him—illustrate.

Long before the advent of the modern totalitarian state, Aristotle noted that certain forms of democracy have an affinity for the authoritarian forms of polity, oligarchy and tyranny. He described various types of democracy, all of which hold that "law is the final sovereign,"

---

[28] Alexander H. Leighton, *The Governing of Men* (Princeton, N.J.: Princeton University Press, 1968), pp. vii, 11–47.

[29] Cited in ibid., p. 18.

that is, the government is in the end subject to the laws of the land. Such democracies are governments of law, not of men, or, more correctly, not of one person or group of people speaking for "all of the people." Another type is a rule by the people rather than the law.

In his work on Aristotle, Ernest Barker writes of the "democratic citizen" in a society where the masses and not the law are sovereign: The member of the mass in such a society "looks with pride at his face . . . remembering that he is the forty-millionth part of a tyrant, and forgetting that he is the whole of a slave." [30]

Every totalitarian government, every dictator, every authoritarian leader backs his policy and his resort to intimidation and terror with the phrase "in the interests of the people." When "the interests of the people" are used as a rationalization for allowing a single individual to interpret, change, even to abolish the law, a democracy with sovereignty residing in the people has begun to be transformed to a tyranny (a single individual) or an oligarchy (a small group of leaders who are empowered to speak in the name of the people). When democracy ceases to be a rule of law that *all* including the elected leaders are subject to, then it becomes a rule of men playing upon the emotions of the masses; democracy then has ceased to exist. The masses are too easily swayed, they are too easily forced into voluntary submission, they are too willing to be led astray by the narrow-minded emotional appeal of the creator of crisis. It is with an obvious understanding of this situation that Archibald Cox, upon being fired by President Nixon from his job as Special Prosecutor of the Watergate case, stated that "whether ours shall continue to be a government of laws and not of men is now for Congress and ultimately the American people to decide." [31]

The Red Scare of 1919, the incarceration without trial of thousands of Japanese people during World War II, the arrest of thousands of demonstrators in Washington, D.C., in the 1970s and the subsequent dismissal of all charges for "lack of sufficient evidence" after things quieted down, as well as the absence of public outcry over these injustices, attest dramatically to the importance of the rule of law and the fragility of the balance maintained between democracy and totalitarian society.

Electronic technology allows the U.S. government to "bug" every citizen, if it so desired. This ability has been more than amply demonstrated by the Watergate scandal and the plethora of disclosures

[30] Ernest Barker, trans. and ed., *The Politics of Aristotle* (New York: Oxford University Press, 1962), p. 168.

[31] Cited in *Time Magazine*, 29 October 1973, p. 12.

associated with it, and by disclosures about FBI, CIA, and U.S. military domestic spying.

Long before Watergate, in *1984*, a brilliant novel written in the late 1940s, George Orwell revealed the fragility of democracy, indicating, as Aristotle had centuries before, that democracy can be transformed into authoritarian government—or, in today's world, a totalitarian government—by relying on little more than the basic principles of people and politics that we have outlined. (Orwell's novel will be discussed in some detail below.)

*TOTALITARIANISM AND MODERN SOCIETY

A major characteristic of a totalitarian government is direct political participation by the whole society. This does *not* mean that the population takes an active part in government decision making. Rather, the people *affirm* whatever the elite in power has done in the name of "the people." To accomplish such mobilization and obedience, all sources of counter organization must be eliminated and a closed-minded cognitive structure imprinted in the minds of the population. This usually involves both social and thought control: Not only must people be kept from organizing resistance, they must be kept from even *thinking* about such a thing. In Orwell's world of *1984*, the worst thing a citizen can do is commit a thoughtcrime—to actually think, or even to doubt, that the existing government is not the best one, that the existing policy is not the best one, that the leader, Big Brother, is not always absolutely correct.

Before a totalitarian government can be constructed, the thinking and organizing capability must be destroyed in precisely those people who, under nontotalitarian circumstances, are most likely to entertain the cognitive and behavioral predispositions of the middle and the upper-middle classes. These groups are least conducive to the maintenance of totalitarian government.

The middle classes have traditionally engaged in administrative, managerial, entrepreneurial, and technological pursuits. They occupy an important position in society and they possess a number of politically significant traits. To attain middle-class status a person must develop a sophisticated knowledge of modern society and social organization and, usually, much knowledge of people—how to deal with them, how to organize them, how to lead. At the same time, the middle classes are, in ways, ambiguous.

Although they are not on the bottom of the heap, they are not on the top of it, either. They frequently feel that while they put in the time and effort "getting the job done," someone else "up there" scrapes off the cream before they get to it. Thus, while they want to protect what they have gained through effort, education, and a little luck, they also want a bigger slice of the pie. And they possess the means of acquiring it; they form interest groups to assuage their feelings of being in a sometimes uncertain or precarious position between the anomic masses and the well-heeled elite. Upwardly mobile, they also join groups where they expect to gain information and contacts that may be useful in advancing their interests.

As a result of these multiple group memberships, the middle-class individual encounters a moderate amount of cognitive dissonance or cross-pressures. Economic group membership is likely to be counterbalanced by religious group membership, and both may be diluted further by membership in a community-service group that exposes him to people of different faiths and economic positions. All of this tends to foster an outlook that emphasizes moderation, compromise, and pragmatism, and this is conducive to the maintenance of open minds and a democratic form of government.

A further source of middle-class moderation is the extensive division of labor in a developed society. With a number of endeavors open to the middle-class individual, the interests of the middle class tend to crosscut one another, making for further compromise, because no single interest or faction is likely to attract middle-class unanimity. Hence, no single interest group or opinion leader is likely to achieve sufficient power to eliminate all competition. Thus, the interests of high-salaried government white-collar workers will compete with the interests of the middle-class corporate executive who is concerned with keeping government expenditures down to keep corporate taxes down. But the private executive may be forced to moderate this stand if corporate incomes depend on government contracts. The middle-class university professor may desire greater government intervention in major social problems, but he, too, may not favor the requisite increase in taxes, and will oppose government intervention in areas closer to home such as college curriculums and course content. And the executive, fearing possible nationalization of industry, may attempt to use private corporate efforts to solve problems such as industrial pollution which, if left unattended, will invite increasing government regulation.

To make matters more difficult for the potential authoritarian, the middle-class person is insulated by his group memberships from direct government contact and intervention, and is not so likely to be suddenly isolated and removed "one by one" without protest. In the Palmer raids of New Years's Day, 1920, a nationwide federal roundup of "alien" Communists, the majority of the 6000 arrested were poorly educated laborers. Many were recent immigrants. Some did not speak English. The radical groups to which they supposedly belonged scarcely deserved to be called organizations in view of the ideological dissension among the leadership and the lack of political sophistication among the following. The result would have been quite different if Attorney-General Palmer had suddenly started arresting middle-class executives, aspiring factory managers, journalists, lawyers, and college professors—along with some executive members of the National Council of Churches. The isolated mass man is susceptible to intimidation when he confronts government directly, because he is not used to exercising his political rights, knows little about government and the law, and is accustomed to accepting rather than questioning the existing order of things. The group orientation of the middle-class individual makes him much more visible to his peers. Should individual members of the middle class suddenly disappear, questions would immediately be raised and opposition quickly organized.

Further, attitudes and opinions that are anchored in a group context, as they are in the middle class, are more difficult to change than are attitudes and opinions that are not so anchored. People who belong to voluntary groups that represent their attitudes might therefore retain views that counter government propaganda much longer than people who do not belong to such groups. Thus, even though the masses may be swayed by government propaganda, the middle classes with their extensive group memberships usually prove much less susceptible to the oversimplification and the infringement of individual rights that are the hallmarks of the totalitarian order.

Totalitarianism therefore must begin with a breakdown in the matrix of middle-class group memberships.[32] The breakdown may take one of two forms, although usually both forms will have played a role in the transition from democracy to totalitarianism.

First, the middle-class individual can be removed from his organized group matrix through a major economic crisis in which he loses his socioeconomic position and is reduced to the alienated, hand-to-mouth, day-to-day existence of the lower classes. The unemployed middle-class person tends to withdraw from membership in voluntary organizations because they throw his lowered socioeconomic position in sharp relief. If unemployment persists, he turns inward and becomes listless and apathetic. A corresponding loss of self-esteem may ensue, and with it a decline in feelings that he can influence government. Political

---

[32] See the classic statements on this general thesis in Seymour Martin Lipset, *Political Man: The Social Basis of Politics* (Garden City, N.Y.: Doubleday, 1963); Hannah Arendt, *The Origins of Totalitarianism* (New York: World, 1963); and William Kornhauser, *The Politics of Mass Society* (New York: Free Press, 1959).

beliefs, such as the belief in democracy, become tenuous without the anchor of supporting group memberships. The end result of such a crisis is an individual who used to support the democratic regime but now appears frustrated, anomic, and cast adrift from familiar moorings. As such he is easy prey for the demagogue.

Precisely this situation paved the way for Adolf Hitler. Many formerly middle-class Germans were threatened with proletarianization—a fate truly fearsome to Europeans living in a rigid class structure. The backs of the traditionally moderate, hard-working German middle classes were broken by the inflation of 1923–24. In January 1922 the cost of living index stood at 20 (1913–14 = 1); by January 1923 it stood at 1120; in December 1923 it reached the astronomical figure of 1,247,000,000,-000! [33] Paper mills and printing plants working around the clock could not meet the demand for paper money. Before long the cost of the paper was higher than the value of the money printed on it.[34]

> *The most disastrous results of inflation . . . were felt by the urban middle classes, especially fixed income groups and those living on savings and pensions. These classes suffered economic and psychic damage that left permanent injuries to the social body of Weimar Germany. As [German Foreign Minister] Stresemann declared on June 29, 1927, "The intellectual and productive middle class, which was traditionally the backbone of the country, has been paid for the utter sacrifice of itself to the state during the war [World War I] by being deprived of all its property and by being proletarianized."* [35]

The result was predictable. "The mad days of inflation brought . . . a wave of political and social malcontent [sic] and cynicism, and a class of proletarianized burghers who became the happy recruiting ground for all the nationalistic and racialist movements that came to undermine the republic." [36]

With the New York stock market crash of 1929 many of the short-term loans that had bolstered the shattered German economy from 1925 to 1929 were foreclosed, and a new era of economic gloom settled in. Cynical and fearful, the middle-class German voter embraced fascism.

[33] Figures from Statistisches Reichsamt, *Statistisches Jahrbuch für das Deutsche Reich* (Berlin: Verlag von Puttkammer & Muhlbrecht, 1925), p. 259.

[34] Koppel S. Pinson, *Modern Germany*, 2nd ed. (New York: Macmillan, 1966), p. 446.

[35] Ibid., p. 447.

[36] Ibid.

Almost overnight, the Nazi party emerged from near oblivion to become one of the largest vote-getters in the nation, while electoral support for the middle-class parties was virtually wiped out (table 4).

The second force tending to isolate the middle-class individual is unabating external threat to the nation requiring constant mobilization of the middle classes and requiring all groups, regardless of original purpose, goals, or creed, to take a nationalistic stand and "rally around the leader." Under such circumstances, existing groups become transmitters of orders from the government to the citizen, and cease therefore to provide any insulation between the two. Israel may provide an example; if the threat of Arab attack extended unabated and the population had to remain in a constant state of alert, political opposition probably would soon cease and private organizations would become adjuncts of the political and military leadership.

Samuel Huntington argues that if modern authoritarian governments use continuous crisis to mobilize pluralistic groupings behind a single-party state, "expansionist" foreign policies, as in Nazi Germany, may ultimately result in the government's downfall.[37] This, it can be argued, need not be the case if *all* protagonists on the international scene need an enemy and therefore have a stake in limiting the aims of expansion. Indeed, it has been argued that the Russians need Israel as much as, if not more than, does the United States. With the United States committed to maintaining Israel as a nation–state, the Arabs turned to the Soviet Union as an ally. This potential alliance, in turn, led the United States to seek improved relations with Arab states and a reduction of Soviet influence.

It is possible to imagine a single party coming to power after an intense economic depression and extensive war, during which time

Table 4   *Percentage of Total Vote Received by Fascist and Middle-Class Parties in the Reichstag Elections of 1928 and the Elections of 1930 and 1932*

	Election		
Party	*1928*	*1930*	*1932*
NSDAP (Nazis)	2.6	18.3	37.3
Middle-class parties	27.5	22.3	5.2

Source: Figures computed from table in Seymour Martin Lipset, *Political Man: The Social Basis of Politics* (Garden City, N.Y.: Doubleday, 1963), p. 139.

[37] See Samuel P. Huntington and Clement H. Moore, eds., *Authoritarian Politics in Modern Society* (New York: Basic Books, 1970), p. 12.

pluralistic social groupings have broken down and the population has mobilized behind the leadership of a single party. Under wartime conditions the party gains control of the mass media and restricts the travel of its citizens. Suddenly, however, peace appears to be at hand, the crisis begins to abate, and voices of political opposition are raised. The regime in power could extend the crisis by making it appear that things are getting worse rather than better. It could, for example, shoot down some of its own passenger planes flying close to the "war zone"; it could fire missiles on occasion into urban and suburban areas, publicizing fully the destruction and human pathos—blaming it all, of course, on "the enemy." Threats and counterthreats could be printed in the papers and the term "subversive" attached to anyone who actively sought to refute the official line.

Suppose, too, that the enemy is the Soviet Union or Red China, and suppose that both of these countries find that the prospects for peace are so good that they can now afford to expend more of their gross national product on consumer goods, having fully developed the means of production in order to prosecute limited but extensive wars with sophisticated conventional weaponry such as was used in the Arab–Israeli War of 1973. But we know, from earlier chapters, that as a person's standard of living improves, he moves up the Maslow hierarchy. With full emphasis on a peacetime economy, the Soviet and Red Chinese leaders might realize that as their respective populations move through the self-esteem level and approach self-actualization, they will desire to participate more fully in the political process. Further, with the extensive division of labor in the modern, war-developed economy, the populace will begin organizing to pursue their interests, and before long something akin to a pluralistic group structure will emerge among the increasingly participant-oriented citizenry whose moderation and independence will contrast greatly with the fanatic, "crisis-born" acceptance of authoritarian rule. This threat to totalitarianism is real, as Huntington points out:

The events of the 1930's led many people to question the future of democratic government. In somewhat similar fashion, the events of the 1960's led many people to question the viability of authoritarian governments . . . [for] authoritarian government could well be incompatible with a complex, highly developed, industrialized, modern society. Most rich countries are democratic countries. Is it not probable, even inevitable, as societies become economically well off and socially complex, that their political systems will also have to become more open, participant, responsive? [38]

[38] Ibid., pp. 3–4.

Faced with this *internal* threat, the three totalitarian powers now reach a similar conclusion: They need each other—not as friends but as enemies, or, at best, as temporary allies—to sustain an external threat that keeps their populations mobilized. They also need war or the threat of war in order to consume the products of a technologically developed economy. If these resources were not consumed on war materials, they would be available for raising the standard of living of the masses, with the results mentioned above. To forestall such an eventuality, the protagonists reach a tacit agreement. They will engage in limited, continuous warfare and a constant state of mobilization, including occasional witch hunts for members of an enemy "conspiracy" within. This allows each of the ruling elites to label as "subversive" anyone who, being critical, threatens maintenance of the existing order. Once such a label has been affixed to such an individual, he may be removed with full public approval. Now each of the three totalitarian nations can settle down to the business of ruling a modern, technologically developed society. This is the situation that exists in Orwell's *1984*.[39]

Three major social groupings exist in the society of 1984: the elite inner party, the outer party, and the proles or masses. The inner party members make the major decisions that are carried out without deviation or question by the lower-ranking outer party. Members of the inner party enjoy the accoutrements of the good life; members of the outer party have lacked the comforts of peacetime prosperity for so long that they are almost forgotten. Outer-party members are under close scrutiny by the Thought Police, for they occupy a position akin to the middle classes in democratic society. They do much of the drudgery work, but at times the work is such that it might provoke thinking about why some of it is done. Once thinking and questioning begin, resistance becomes a potentiality and must be quickly discovered and eradicated. The Thought Police do the discovering and the Ministry of Truth does the eradicating. The eradicated individual ("vaporized" is the term used by Orwell) then becomes an unperson, someone who never existed.

The protagonist Winston, like other members of the outer party, holds a responsible position. The hours are long, the pay is low, and in the war-ravaged economy there is a shortage of everything from cigarettes to razor blades. He works in the Ministry of Truth. It is his job to alter, on direction from above, any historical record of unpersons or any differences between the present and past party lines that could throw even the slightest shadow of a doubt upon the validity of the current party line. Thus, any policy or terminology of the leader's that

[39] George Orwell, *1984* (New York: New American Library, 1959).

has become obsolete—or, in recent U.S. political parlance, "inoperative" —is removed from the record to make the current position appear to have always been the correct one. For "unpersons," he must ensure that their photographs, names, and anything that might possibly evoke a memory of them are systematically expunged from the printed archives of the state. After this is done, he must forget that he did it. After all, should he admit to himself that the party was altering history by falsifying the historical record, then the Ministry of Truth would really be the Ministry of Falsehood and the regime would in fact be ruling on the basis of lies, deception, and propaganda. Perhaps indeed the perpetual warfare might be intentionally perpetrated on the people by a political system that needed the atmosphere of continuous crisis to stay in power.

These would be truly dangerous thoughts. Should anyone—fellow party member or child member of "The Spies," the youth organization that is taught absolute obedience to the leader—see even one response to the words of Big Brother that suggests a glimmer of doubt, a frown of skepticism, or a blush of incredulity, that person would have the Thought Police at his door. Fortunately, Winston didn't have any children; his next-door neighbor had been turned in by his son, who heard him utter something disloyal about Big Brother in his sleep. But this only underscored the need to believe, in the innermost reaches of one's mind, that the party and the leader were always correct. To admit, even only unconsciously, that what appeared to be rewritten history was not really true or that the Party was not always right was to commit the terrible act of *thoughtcrime*. To harbor such thoughts at *any* level of consciousness or unconsciousness was to court a disaster like his neighbor's. Yet at the same time Winston had to remember what the old history was. For the Party would sometimes resurrect a "vaporized" leader when the Party line had changed and some gain could be made thereby. He would then have to recreate the individual and realter the record. To survive, one had to use—indeed, to train one's mind to believe in—*doublethink*.

Winston sank his arms to his sides. . . . His mind slid away into the labyrinthine world of doublethink. To know and not to know, to be conscious of complete truthfulness while telling carefully constructed lies, to hold simultaneously two opinions which cancelled out, knowing them to be contradictory and believing in both of them, to use logic against logic, to repudiate morality while laying claim to it, to believe that democracy was impossible and that the Party was the guardian of democracy, to forget, whatever it was necessary to forget, then to draw it back into memory again at the moment when it was needed, and then promptly to forget it again, and above all, to apply the same process to the process itself— that was the ultimate subtlety: consciously to induce unconsciousness, and then, once again, to become unconscious of the act of hypnosis you had just performed. Even the word "doublethink" involved the use of doublethink.[40]

All the while members of the Thought Police might be observing you at home, on the job, walking down the street. Telescreens, television-like devices, were placed at strategic outdoor locations in the neighborhoods where party members lived, in their offices, and in each apartment. The telescreen could transmit and receive simultaneously. It could not be turned off. It woke you up in the morning and went on all day and into the evening, transmitting the Party line and Party-approved programs. One never knew when his words and actions, even his facial expressions (one didn't want to commit a facecrime) were being observed.

How often . . . the Thought Police plugged in on any individual wire was guesswork. It was even conceivable that they watched everybody all the time. But at any rate they could plug in your wire whenever they wanted to. You had to live—did live, from habit that became instinct—in the assumption that every sound you made was overheard, and, except in darkness, every movement scrutinized.[41]

Enthusiasm was whipped up regularly for the party that ruled Oceania, as was blind, closed-minded hatred of the enemy, Eurasia. Every day the denizens of the Ministry of Truth and millions of other party members stopped their work and gathered in groups before a telescreen for the "two minute hate."

[40] *Nineteen Eighty-Four* by George Orwell. Harcourt, Brace & Jovanovich, Inc. Copyright, 1949 by Harcourt, Brace & Jovanovich, Inc. Reprinted by permission of Brandt & Brandt, Mrs. Sonia Brownell Orwell, and Secker & Warburg.

[41] Ibid., p. 6. The reader may be aware of a telescope-like device developed by the United States for use in the Vietnam war. It enables an observer to see in the dark. Even movements at night could be observed by the Thought Police, although such a possibility did not occur to Orwell when he wrote his novel.

The next moment a hideous, grinding screech, as of some monstrous machine running without oil, burst from the big telescreen at the end of the room. It was a noise that set one's teeth on edge and bristled the hair at the back of one's neck. The Hate had started.

As usual, the face of Emmanuel Goldstein, the Enemy of the People, had flashed onto the screen. There were hisses here and there among the audience. . . . Goldstein was the renegade and backslider who once, long ago (how long ago, nobody quite remembered), had been one of the leading figures of the Party, almost on a level with Big Brother himself, and then had engaged in counter-revolutionary activities, had been condemned to death, and had mysteriously escaped and disappeared. The program of the Two Minute Hate varied from day to day, but there was none in which Goldstein was not the principal figure. He was the primal traitor, the earliest defiler of the Party's purity. All subsequent crimes against the Party, all treacheries, acts of sabotage, heresies, deviations, sprang directly out of his teaching. Somewhere or other he was still alive and hatching his conspiracies: perhaps somewhere beyond the sea, under the protection of his foreign paymasters; perhaps even—so it was occasionally rumored—in some hiding place in Oceania itself.

The Hate rose to its climax. The voice of Goldstein had become an actual sheep's bleat, and for an instant the face changed into that of a sheep. Then the sheepface melted into the figure of a Eurasian soldier who seemed to be advancing, huge and terrible, his submachine gun roaring and seeming to spring out of the surface of the screen, so that some of the people in the front row actually flinched backwards in their seats. . . . But in the same moment, drawing a deep sigh of relief from everybody, the hostile figure melted into the face of Big Brother, black-haired, black mustachio'd, full of power and mysterious calm, and so vast that it almost filled up the screen. . . . The little sandy-haired woman had flung herself forward over the back of the chair in front of her. With a tremulous murmur that sounded like "My Savior!" she extended her arms toward the screen. . . .

At this moment the entire group of people broke into a deep, slow, rhythmical chant of "B-B! . . . B-B! . . . B-B!" . . . It was often heard in moments of overwhelming emotion.[42]

---

[42] Ibid., pp. 13–18.

The third group of people in totalitarian Oceania, the proles or proletarians, are left alone. Telescreens do not even exist in the working-class neighborhoods. The Party has nothing to fear from the masses:

> *Left to themselves, they will continue from generation to generation*
> *and from century to century, working, breeding, and dying,*
> *not only without any impulse to rebel, but without the power*
> *of grasping that the world could be other than it is. They could*
> *only become dangerous if the advance of industrial technique*
> *made it necessary to educate them more highly; but, since military*
> *and commercial rivalry are no longer important [the three nations,*
> *the only ones still extant, all being totalitarian and agreeing*
> *tacitly to keep their populations within their own borders and*
> *never eradicating each other because each must have an enemy],*
> *the level of popular education is actually declining. What opinions*
> *the masses hold, or do not hold, is looked on as a matter of*
> *indifference. They can be granted intellectual liberty because*
> *they have no intellect.*[43]

What leisure they have is spent drinking the cheap liquor the government makes available or in consuming some of the mental pabulum turned out by the Ministry of Truth, which contained:

> *a whole chain of separate departments dealing with proletarian*
> *literature, music, drama, and entertainment generally. Here were*
> *produced rubbishy newspapers, containing almost nothing but*
> *sport, crime, and astrology, sensational five-cent novelettes, films*
> *oozing with sex, and sentimental songs. . . . There was even a*
> *whole section . . . engaged in producing the lowest kind of*
> *pornography, which was sent out in sealed packets and which no*
> *Party member, other than those who worked on it, was permitted*
> *to look at.*[44]

There was also a lottery where the proles consumed what little money they had left. The state reaped huge profits from it, because only fictitious people won; but the proles never found out from the Party-controlled media. The continuous wars also kept their attention. News of great victories or, at times, threats of invasion brought them to their

[43] Ibid., p. 173.
[44] Ibid., p. 39.

feet when attention was flagging. Occasionally, if the Party thought the proles were looking for a little change in their drab lives, it would stage a hate rally or parade Eurasian prisoners through the street. Hate Week, for example, demanded much preparation and drained off quantities of whatever excess energy the proletarians possessed after a long day's work.

The preparations for Hate Week were in full swing, and the staffs of all the ministries were working overtime. Processions, meetings, military parades, lectures, waxwork displays, film shows, telescreen programs all had to be organized; stands had to be erected, effigies built, slogans coined, songs written, rumors circulated, photographs faked. . . .

A new poster had suddenly appeared all over London [now a part of Oceania]. It had no caption, and represented simply the monstrous figure of a Eurasian soldier, three or four meters high, striding forward with expressionless Mongolian face and enormous boots, a submachine gun pointed from his hip. From whatever angle you looked at the poster, the muzzle of the gun . . . seemed to be pointed straight at you. The thing had been plastered on every wall, even outnumbering the portraits of Big Brother. The proles, normally apathetic about the war, were being lashed into one of their periodical frenzies of patriotism. As though to harmonize with the general mood, the rocket bombs had been killing larger numbers of people than usual. One fell on a crowded film theater . . . burying several hundred victims among the ruins. The whole population of the neighborhood turned out for a long, trailing funeral which went on for hours and was in effect an indignation meeting. Another bomb fell on a piece of waste ground which was used as a playground and several dozen children were blown to pieces. There were further angry demonstrations, Goldstein was burned in effigy, hundreds of copies of the poster of the Eurasian soldier were torn down and added to the flames, and a number of shops were looted in the turmoil; then a rumor flew around that spies were directing the rocket bombs by means of . . . [radio] waves, and an old couple who were suspected of being of foreign extraction had their house set on fire and perished of suffocation.[45]

All of this suffices for the proles; as Orwell put it, they work, breed and die—without making waves. For that small minority of the proles who,

[45] Ibid., pp. 123–24.

by some accident of genetic inheritance, rearing, employment, or personality, aspire upward and perhaps to foment discontent, the future is bleak. "The most gifted among them, who might become nuclei of discontent, are simply marked down by the Thought Police and eliminated." [46] Such is life in the grim society of *1984*, in which the government—monopolizing more power than any actual, historical totalitarian government—was maintained, at least partially, by means of the constant brandishing of an external enemy. Orwell's "Goldstein" is simply a personification of the scapegoat used by demagogic governments to minimize dissent. In the late 1960s, student radicals became the "Goldsteins" of America, as did "outside agitators" in the civil rights drives in the South of the early 1960s, and "Communists" in the 1950s. If a single group—or person—can be portrayed as the source of evil, all measures are justified to repress the evil.

President Nixon apparently had an obsessive fear of discontent and encouraged clandestine domestic surveillance that differed from Orwell's Thought Police only in degree. To justify numerous alleged invasions of privacy, "national security" was invoked, in the name of which constitutionally guaranteed rights were violated.

THE DEMOCRATIC POLITICAL ORDER

The establishment of a democratic form of government necessitates direct confrontation of the apparent affinity between mass democracy and totalitarianism. The first item on the agenda of the democratic planner ought therefore to be the creation of a noncrisis atmosphere for the development of a democratic political order.

The second item on the planner's agenda should be setting the standard of living high enough that the mass public approaches the self-esteem level on Maslow's need hierarchy, thus ensuring that a sufficient portion of the population will support the postulates of equality and the *worth of the individual* that are a basic part of the democratic creed. Self-esteem, appreciation for the dignity and freedom of the individual, and a need for self-actualization, which manifests itself in part through the undertaking of civic obligations and willing participation in politics (at least to the extent of voting) are all characteristics of the open-minded democratic personality upon which stable democracies are based. Freedom from crisis and a decent standard of living are important not simply in their own right, but in the effect that

46 Ibid., p. 172.

they have upon the cognitive and psychological development of the population.

It appears that no population will be completely open-minded, respectful of the rights of other individuals, and the like. In addition, because the basic belief in freedom and individual rights makes a capitalistic economy consonant with (but not necessary for) a democratic form of government, competitiveness remains intrinsic in social behavior. If unchecked, the belief in unfettered freedom may run roughshod over the belief in basic human rights and dignity.

At the root of democracy lies a series of basic contradictions in creed and philosophy, which dictate a government based upon compromise and the search for a "middle ground." Many of these contradictions appear in the Declaration of Independence:

> *We hold these truths to be self-evident, that all men are created equal, that they are endowed by their Creator with certain unalienable Rights, that among these are Life, Liberty and the pursuit of Happiness.—That to secure these rights, Governments are instituted among Men, deriving their just powers from the consent of the governed. . . .*[47]

Liberty may at times conflict strongly with equality as one person's pursuit of happiness may infringe upon another's liberty; and equality in the eyes of the Creator may mean little on earth, where opportunities for self-realization may be inordinately dependent upon the socio-economic position and race of one's parents. Further, who are "the governed," and what is meant by "consent"? Should the voting franchise extend to the alienated, the cynical, the closed-minded, the person at his wit's end—or to an elite group of individuals intent upon pursuing pure economic self-interest at the expense of the less fortunate? Does consent mean a simple majority? Does it extend to decisions concerning the basic nature of the political system? (The basic democratic faith in humanity is in the end mitigated by the need to adhere to the laws of tradition—common law—and the writings of men now raised to mythical stature who, in the Constitution, erected a structure of government and a document that has the force of law—law that must remain "above men" if the political system is to remain democratic through good as well as bad times.)

---

[47] *Declaration of Independence*, reprinted in Martin Diamond, T. M. Fisk, and Herbert Garfinkel, *The Democratic Republic*, 2nd ed. (Chicago: Rand McNally, 1970), p. 605.

As numerous authors have noted, the *sine qua non* of democracy is a "balance between conflict and consensus," an "agreement to disagree." [48] This consensus amid diversity demands that the politically active population agree upon the basic ground rules of the political game. Conflict can thus be regulated and satisfactory decisions reached before any group becomes so frustrated that it attempts to radically alter the rules, forcing people to take extreme positions on issues so fundamental that compromise is no longer possible. Democracy, suffused with contradictions, requires a government where contradiction, opposing viewpoints, and compromise are necessary. All of this is, of course, conducive to cognitive cross-pressure and resulting moderation or "open-mindedness." If the philosophy of democracy were perfectly consistent, comprehensive, and holistic, it would lead to the rigid, narrow, closed-minded perspective that is not conducive to moderation, as in a world divided between the "totally good" and the "totally bad." Such a perspective is, as we have seen, associated with the extremes of authoritarian regimes rather than with the moderation of democratic government.

A price is paid for all this in the currency of time: Decision-making takes longer in a democracy than in a dictatorship. Democratic political institutions incorporate a balance of power; power is dispersed among branches of government, and the diverse views of many segments of the populaton are represented, frequently by individuals wielding decisive power at various crucial points in the structure of political decision making. This ensures that a number of viewpoints will be aired, compromises struck, and much time consumed. But impatience is not a democratic virtue, and this is another reason why a satisfactory standard of living is a prerequisite for a democratic political structure. A person with a well-stocked refrigerator, good health, money in the bank, and a good credit rating can let the government take its time in arriving at a decision that affects, say, his salary. He can quite literally "afford to wait." For the person who is barely subsisting, it is a different story. A pay cut or a day's work lost may mean severe hardship for himself and members of his family. He cannot afford to wait; he demands action *now*. The democratic politician who is "looking into the situation" cannot command his loyalty. The person who promises to get something done immediately, regardless of its long-term effects, can.

Democracies operate in an environment where individuals, and especially those organized in voluntary groups that represent their social and economic interests, compete for scarce resources. There is

---

[48] Charles F. Andrain, *Political Life and Social Change: An Introduction to Political Science* (Belmont, Ca.: Wadsworth, 1970), p. 180, and the sources cited therein.

usually agreement on the means of conflict resolution and disagreement on the actual allocation of values. Hence groups excluded from the allocations pertaining to one decision will attempt to get a more favorable outcome next time. The government, as Crick noted (see table 2 again), is supported on utilitarian grounds. It provides an expedient means to attain one's ends—ends that are limited and secular. Government is perceived neither as a vehicle through which a utopia is to be attained, nor as a device for ensuring conformity to religious values. (Indeed, where religion and politics are combined democracy is not feasible.) Democracy is designed to reconcile conflicts about limited goals. It cannot function where disputes arise over ultimate ends. Where such conflicts do arise, the basic ground rules are violated.

Democracy, then, is a form of government suited to a heterogeneous society divided into a number of organized segments that represent diverse but limited interests. It is particularly fitting to a society that is changing at a moderate rate, one rapid enough to necessitate efficient representational links between the rulers and the ruled, but not so rapid that major segments of society perceive intolerable threats to their social and economic existence.

Other characteristics of democracy include a solution to "the problem of succession by means of regular, open, and usually partisan elections, and which therefore legitimate the right of opposition." [49] Neither a legitimate opposition nor regularized procedures for succession exist in totalitarian political systems.

The major flaw in the practical performance of totalitarian political systems, with their centralization and "cult of personality" surrounding the absolute leader, is that, lacking regularized means of succession, the totalitarian state drifts with the vagaries of power struggles that develop whenever a dictator dies or is incapacitated.

Democracies, too, have basic weaknesses that under some circumstances could prove fatal. It is always possible that an aroused majority could, through legal, "democratic" means, vote the state out of existence or so alter the basic ground rules of government that democracy as we know it ceases to exist. Madison expresses his fears of this in Article 10 of the *Federalist Papers*. Louis Hartz puts his finger on another major flaw, one obliquely noted earlier in this chapter: In America, Hartz argues, there exists an unchallenged, unquestioned belief in Lockean natural law. The "inalienable rights of man" are, for example, accepted completely and without reservation. "When one's ultimate values are

---

[49] Douglas W. Rae and Michael Taylor, *The Analysis of Political Cleavages* (New Haven, Conn.: Yale University Press, 1970), p. 12.

accepted wherever one turns, the absolute language of self-evidence comes easily enough." [50]

Absolute language, absolute belief, absolute thought are indeed hall-marks of the closed mind. Thus, beneath the pragmatism, beneath the agreement to disagree on limited ends, lies a bedrock belief in demo-cratic ideology. And when this bedrock belief is challenged, emotional energies are released.

This then is the mood of America's absolutism: the sober faith that its norms are self-evident. It is one of the most powerful absolutisms in the world, more powerful even than the messianic spirit of the continental liberals which . . . the Americans were able to reject. That spirit arose out of contact with an opposing way of life, and its very intensity betrayed an inescapable element of doubt. But the American absolutism, flowing from an honest experience with universality [we could say lack of experience with anything contradictory to it], lacked even the passion that doubt might give. It was so sure of itself that it hardly needed to become articulate, so secure that it could actually support a pragmatism which seemed on the surface to belie it. . . . Because . . . [the American] never doubts his general principles, . . . he is able to dismiss his critics with a fine and crushing ease. But this does not mean that America's general will always lives an easy life. It has its own violent moments—rare, to be sure, but violent enough. These are the familiar American moments of national fright and national hysteria when it suddenly rises to the surface with a vengeance, when civil liberties begin to collapse. . . . Anyone who watches it then can hardly fail to have a healthy respect for the dynamite which normally lies concealed beneath the free and easy atmosphere of the American liberal community.[51]

English democracy, on the other hand, is not quite so vulnerable. Ancient, venerated institutions of a feudal and an autocratic past remain on the political landscape: the English monarch, the House of Lords, even the powdered and elaborately curled wigs worn by judge and barrister alike, bespeak a tradition different from those encountered in mass democracies. In addition, among the philosophies of monarch-ism, aristocracy, and democracy there have been struggles that at times

[50] Louis Hartz, *The Liberal Tradition in America* (New York: Harcourt Brace Jovanovich, 1955), p. 58.

[51] Ibid., pp. 58–59.

brought England perilously close to major upheaval. Their symbolic coexistence serves as a constant reminder that no single philosophy has a monopoly on truth; each has strengths that complement the others' (the staid aristocracy as opposed to the emotional masses; the pomp of the monarchy in contrast to the rabble-rousing of the crowd; the equalitarianism of mass democracy versus the haughtiness of royalty and upper classes, etc.). If each philosophy contradicts parts of the others, no one philosophy is likely to be rejected completely, nor will any one view be accepted unconditionally. Mass hysteria over a challenge to a basic tenet of democratic theory is therefore much less likely in England than in the United States; toleration of political deviation is also greater.

Perhaps it is a truism that not all democracies are completely alike. Frequently the stable two-party systems of England and the United States are compared with the unstable multiparty regimes on the continent: for example, France during the Fourth Republic; Germany during the Weimar years; and present-day Italy. Recently, however, political scientists, instead of looking at the number of parties, have concentrated on the cleavage structure or the degree of fragmentation characteristic of a given political culture. Arend Lijphart considers three types of democracy in these terms: centripetal, consociational, and centrifugal.[52]

Centripetal democracy "is the healthy type whose stability is based on a homogeneous political culture and is not threatened by normal interparty competition." [53] This high degree of cohesion and consequent stability may have several causes occurring individually or in combination. In centripetal *consensus* democracies, the degree of basic political division is minimal. In America, for example, both the Democrats and the Republicans have, since the Depression, realized the need for government intervention in the economy, although each approaches the issue from a slightly different perspective. In foreign policy both parties are virtually identical. Even the differences between Johnson and Goldwater, the two presidential contenders in 1964, were revealed by events to be more rhetorical than substantive. Centripetal *mechanically integrated* systems possess political cleavages and cultural differences, but the divergent interests are overlapping rather than mutually reinforcing.[54] The resulting cognitive dissonance leads to open minds and a balance of political power; moderation is an overall result. In centri-

52 Arend Lijphart, "Typologies of Democratic Systems," *Comparative Political Studies*, 1, no. 1 (April 1968), 3–44.

53 Ibid., p. 31.

54 See David B. Truman, *The Governmental Process: Political Interests and Public Opinion* (New York: Alfred A. Knopf, 1951).

petal *community* systems, political divisions that may be quite extensive are moderated by "overarching sentiments of solidarity." [55] The source of such sentiments can be nationalism, which is certainly part of the English secret of success and is symbolized by the monarchy; a unifying ideology; or an unquestioned political myth like individualism, as is the case in the United States.

Consociational democracies are stable political systems with as many as four or five political parties, each of which speaks for a membership with its own political and religious world view. Crosscutting cleavages —the major mechanism, according to traditional pluralist theory, for achieving the moderation necessary for effective democracy—do not exist. Further, in consociational democracies attempts are made to limit the political expression of party members. The obvious effectiveness of such democracies somewhat contradicts those who correlate the political stability of democracies with a small number of political parties. Significant exceptions are Holland, Belgium, and Austria. Holland provides an example.

The Dutch political system is composed of a two-house parliament with a cabinet form of government. The political culture is fragmented into five divisions with religion as a basic cause of cleavage; each major political party represents a separate religious or secular ideology, which is reflected in the organizational affiliations of party followers. In addition, the major parties possess their own newspapers and thereby provide additional reinforcement for a narrow, all-encompassing perspective.[56]

The country is divided into three blocs: Catholic, Protestant, and secular. This division is further strengthened through the process of education, because each bloc has its own schools. The Catholic People's Party is in command of the Catholic bloc, and can count on approximately 30 percent of the popular vote. Social class produces some intra-bloc crosspressure, because lower-, middle-, and upper-class Catholics belong to the party, but the overwhelming power of religion and Catholic education remains outstanding. Indeed, at one point in 1954, a "pastoral letter by the Roman Catholic bishops argued against membership by Catholics in non-Catholic unions and specifically prohibited affiliation with the Socialist union—a prohibition enforced by denial

[55] These three variations of centripetal democracy are described by Harry Eckstein, *Division and Cohesion in Democracy: A Study of Norway* (Princeton, N.J.: Princeton University Press, 1966), pp. 193–94; and are cited in Lijphart, "Typologies of Democratic Systems," p. 31.

[56] See the excellent analysis of Dutch political and social dynamics in Arend Lijphart, *The Politics of Accommodation: Pluralism and Democracy in the Netherlands* (Berkeley and Los Angeles: University of California Press, 1968).

of the holy sacraments." [57] This was a dictate that few church members would dare ignore.

The Protestant bloc accounts for approximately 20 percent of the popular vote, which tends to divide evenly between the Christian Historical party and its more orthodox and cohesive counterpart, the Anti-Revolutionary party.

The secular block is composed of two parties, each of which receives approximately 90 percent of its support from voters who are not attached strongly to either Protestant or Catholic faiths. The leftist-leaning Labor party draws its major support from the lower classes. To its right is the Liberal party, which represents upper-class business and white-collar interests. The former receives about 30 percent of the popular vote, the latter 10 percent. The remaining popular vote is divided among small, sometimes ephemeral parties.[58]

As a further element tending to splinter the political culture, the Dutch rely upon a system of proportional representation that allocates seats in Parliament on the basis of percentages of popular vote rather than the majoritarian, "win or lose" criteria used in the United States and Britain. As of 1956, a political pursuasion, party, or grouping that received 0.67 percent of the popular vote in an election was entitled to send a representative to the Second Chamber.[59]

Why does the Dutch political system remain stable without cross-cutting cleavages and with a Parliament composed of parties whose members possess holistic mental conceptions of the world that are inculcated and reinforced by their organizational affiliation? The answer is almost deceptively simple. Away from the public view, the elites cooperate, make compromises, and work out policy decisions. These decisions are then interpreted and communicated through party-controlled media to the mass membership of each bloc in terms of the ideology and symbols appropriate to it. Lijphart states that the top leaders of the major blocs "have played a pre-eminent role . . . in recognizing the problems and in realistically finding solutions in spite of ideological disagreements—a process in which the rank and file was largely ignored even to the extent of rigging an important election." [60] The actual process of decision making and the compromises struck between factions are usually kept secret by all parties concerned. The communications elite cooperates by refusing to "tell all." Members of

[57] Ibid., p. 39.

[58] Figures and description from ibid., pp. 23–26 and *passim*.

[59] Ibid., p. 162. For further discussion of proportional representation and other electoral procedures, see A. J. Milnor, *Elections and Political Stability* (Boston: Little, Brown, 1969), and the sources cited therein.

[60] Lijphart, *The Politics of Accommodation*, p. 111.

the media who are less guarded in their disclosures are apt to find that "access to . . . classified information is severely limited. . . ." [61]

The Dutch elites go to great lengths to keep any potentially divisive political disputes from reaching the masses. Since no single bloc has enough votes to form a majority in Parliament, and since the division of the population on basic religious and ideological grounds provides an electoral stability that makes a majority unlikely, the active emotional involvement of the mass public in political issues could lead to a serious conflict that might easily get out of hand. Some issues are simply kept secret, while proportional allocations of scarce resources such as radio and television time, the number of bloc members hired by the government, and the like defuse other potentially explosive issues. Other tactics, such as intentional obfuscation, are also employed by the elites when appropriate. This allows them to neutralize sensitive issues and explain compromises between blocs to the rank and file by using "complicated economic arguments and the juggling of economic facts and figures incomprehensible to most people." [62]

Obviously, the Dutch system can operate successfully only if the masses have faith in their leadership and defer to decisions made by elites. One reinforcement of this faith is the unwritten rule that all elites adhere to: Politics is not a game but a serious business, especially for a small nation with major cleavages. The ancient mercantile tradition of Holland and her precarious position between major European powers has infused the leadership with the idea that results rather than delay or avoidance of responsibility for political ends should characterize the political process. Ideological disputes are therefore not allowed to interfere with important political issues, especially if a major scandal like Watergate could so injure the faith of the masses in the elites that the resulting crisis of confidence would quickly lead to political chaos. Elite responsibility is deferred to by the masses.[63] In a question concerning the quality admired most in people, the Netherlands had the highest percentage of respondents who chose "respectful, doesn't overstep his place" (table 5).[64]

Two "keys to success" in consociational democracies emerge from this discussion: First, the political elites are willing to work within a framework of consensus on the value of maintaining the basic political structure, a consensus that demands that no elite member or bloc representative take his political problems to the masses; second, the masses defer to their social and political "betters." The masses, in turn, de-

---

61 Ibid., p. 133.

62 Ibid., p. 129.

63 See ibid., p. 123, and the sources cited therein.

64 Ibid., p. 145.

Table 5   *Percentage of Sample Choosing "Respectful, Doesn't Overstep His Place" as Most Admired Quality*

Netherlands	United Kingdom	Germany	Italy	United States
19	9	5	10	11

Source: Arend Lijphart, *The Politics of Accommodation: Pluralism and Democracy in the Netherlands* (Berkeley and Los Angeles: University of California Press, 1968), p. 148.

mand that the elites act responsibly, putting the job of governing and holding the nation together above the single-minded pursuit of personal or bloc interests.

It is probably no coincidence that successful consociational democracies are illustrated by small European nations, nations that at one time or another have been overrun by a stronger power. Vulnerability to outside threats thereby is an omnipresent "potential crisis" that minimizes centrifugal tendencies. Elites, thinking in a longer-range perspective than the masses, must therefore act to dampen the potentially explosive forces of internal political division.

We should note here that both successful forms of democracy—centripetal and consociational—have mechanisms that keep the masses separate from the political elites, thus insulating the political system against the effects of the cognitive and behavioral characteristics that we have used to describe the mind of the mass public. Where these separative mechanisms exist, in the form either of middle classes organized into counterbalancing groups, or of an agreement among elites to keep politics away from the deferential masses, democracy appears to be a stable, feasible political system. A democracy *without* either of these mechanisms is not likely to be stable. Rather, it will probably approximate the *centrifugal* type of democracy, illustrated by France under the Fourth Republic, the Weimar Republic in Germany, Spain during the years of the short-lived Republic (1931–36), and present-day Italy. Government instability; a fragmented political culture that deeply divides elites as well as masses; an inability of elites to compromise and form coalitions even in the face of crisis; and widespread apathy, despair, and frustration among the populace make such democracies particularly vulnerable to transformation into an authoritarian system, through the offices of the charismatic "man on horseback." Napoleon and de Gaulle in France, Mussolini in Italy, Hitler in Germany, and Franco in Spain came to the fore under conditions like those in centrifugal democracies.[65]

65 See Lijphart, "Typologies of Democratic Systems," p. 31.

AUTOCRACIES

As noted in table 2, autocracies thrive in an environment of deference, rigid social stratification, and an agrarian or semiagrarian economy. Autocracies are not "mobilization systems" as are totalitarian regimes, nor do they rely on extensive mass electoral participation for their support as do most democracies. Like consociational democracies, autocracies possess a set of elites who work out their compromises behind the scenes, away from the public, and always with an agreement to keep their quarrels to themselves and away from the masses.

Traditional power is the primary source of autocratic political support, along with a strong dose of bureaucratic power. Leadership may be embodied in a single individual or in a junta. The personality of the individuals involved is important but need not be the decisive factor,[66] as long as their actions symbolize the traditional values that uphold the society. A charismatic leader would be out of place in an autocracy;[67] in fact, because he could mobilize the masses in support of values that differed from tradition, such an individual poses a threat to the autocratic regime, and this ensures the quick demotion or demise of such a person.

The activities and person of Franco in Spain illustrate autocratic leadership and the desire to discourage any activity that runs counter to it. Franco, *Caudillo de España por la gracia de Dios* (leader of Spain by the grace of God), had ruled Spain for over thirty years, until his death in 1976; Benjamin Welles wrote in 1965: "no enemy, from Stalin down, has broken Franco's grip on power, and the Spanish people have grown so accustomed to his face that few can imagine an alternative. Many, in fact, prefer not to."[68] His career began in the Army, and he came early on to embody the values and virtues of the Spanish military tradition.

Anglo-Saxon democracy was unsuited to the Spanish temperament and would lead to Anarcho-Sindicalism, revolutionary Socialism —even Communism. It was the army's mission to defend Spain against her foreign foes and even against herself—though it might

---

[66] See Juan J. Linz, "An Authoritarian Regime: Spain," in *Reader in Political Sociology*, Frank Lindenfeld, ed. (New York: Funk & Wagnalls, 1968), p. 132.

[67] Andrain, *Political Life and Social Change*, p. 224.

[68] Benjamin Welles, *Spain: The Gentle Anarchy* (New York: Frederick Praeger, 1965), pp. 16–17.

*mean killing her. Such were the doctrines taught young Spanish
officers in Morocco prior to World War I, and Franco, by absorbing
them, rose rapidly in the estimation of his seniors.*[69]

Franco's discipline, military bearing, and aristocratic mien are legen-
dary, and many anecdotes surround them. As Commander of the Spanish
Foreign Legion in the twenties, so one anecdote goes, Colonel Franco,
inspecting his troops,

*halted before a particularly ugly trouble-maker, a German who
had been complaining of the food and other conditions. As Franco
listened coldly, the legionnaire, without warning, spat full in Franco's
face. Franco moved not a muscle. Slowly, he completed his round
of inspection and returned to his office. Then, summoning his
adjutant, he wiped his face with a handkerchief and quietly ordered
the legionnaire taken out and shot.*[70]

The image of Franco that was portrayed to the Spanish people was
one of paternalism, not charisma. He was aloof from the masses, appeared in public in elaborate military costume and received guests in
an atmosphere combining monarchical splendor with military bearing.
His "paternalistic despotism [was] based on the theory that the Spanish
masses are too turbulent to rule themselves and are better off with a
full belly and a muzzled mouth." [71] He, the military leaders around
him, and those allowed to move into positions of authority had

*. . . been conditioned to believe in the alleged evils of party
politics, liberal democracy, free speech, free thought, and free trade
unions. The need for a hierarchic elite of officers, priests, and
civilian conservatives as the only method of controlling Spain's
unruly masses has long been drilled into them.*[72]

Throughout, rapid change and any questioning of traditional values
were discouraged. People who dared to question Franco's policies might
be listened to and used if they could serve the purpose of the regime,

[69] Ibid., p. 18.
[70] Ibid., p. 19.
[71] Ibid., p. 13.
[72] Ibid., p. 66.

but they were not promoted.[73] The military, the police, and the Guardia Civil—a "paramilitary force that patrols the rural areas in pairs in eighteenth-century patent leather hats and gray cloaks"—were omnipresent reminders that the forces of tradition, stability, law and order were alive and well.[74]

Autocracies can function as long as the masses are quiescent, and as long as the elites can operate within the framework of traditional values and can monopolize the rights to political opposition and political organization. The masses are held in check by their position in the economy (where they put in long, tiring hours in semisubsistence agriculture, manual trades, and cottage industries), and by their deference to the elites. The deference of the masses to the elite is maintained by limiting access to institutions of higher learning and by actively engaging the population in a highly structured religion where salvation is contingent upon orthodoxy and adherence to the dictates of the ecclesia. In most autocracies, the church shares political power and influence with political and business elites. Where one religion predominates, such as Catholicism in Spain, the church performs a significant integrative function; it unites members of the major elite factions, and provides a sense of individual spiritual security for the individual in the mass while inculcating a deference that synchronizes the political culture with the autocratic government. Political stability usually results. In such systems the individual may occasionally find himself at odds with the political authorities, but rarely if ever does he find himself completely alienated, lost, and alone.

Autocracies also maintain a strong division between state and society. While the individual may be expected to "render unto Caesar that which is Caesar's," he retains considerable control over his individual economic and social freedom. Religious and legal codes remain in force, generally free from active interference by the political authorities. This strongly contrasts with totalitarian political systems.

WHICH POLITICAL SYSTEM IS BEST?

It is difficult to say that any one type of political system is the "best." When policy makers begin applying their own values and political preferences to people who possess different values, religions, and socioeconomic circumstances, even different world views, some gross errors of judgment are likely. After the "war to make the world safe for

[73] Ibid., p. 35.
[74] Ibid., p. 69.

democracy," President Wilson thought that "self-determination of peoples" would solve most of Europe's problems despite the unbelievable destruction and widespread impoverishment of nations wrought by the holocaust, which meant that democracy—at least centripetal democracy—was the alternative least likely to succeed. This was demonstrated by events in Germany and Eastern Europe during the '20s and '30s as one country after another adopted authoritarian government. In 1956, there was hope that the Hungarian Revolution would spark widespread revolt among the Russian people, leading ultimately to the overthrow of Soviet communism. The logic for such an opinion appeared to be an inherent belief that, given a free choice, anyone would choose democracy over any authoritarian alternative.

The ethnocentric idea that "democracy is best for everybody," if applied to nations regardless of their political culture, the distribution of closed minds in the population, the socioeconomic situation of the masses, and the reservoir of frustration existing in the society, is simply not realistic. For example, to say that the Dutch political system stifles political participation may be true, but it is also naive. For as long as major ideological differences divide the electorate, increasing mass participation will lead only to government instability. It would be better to admit that in some circumstances consociational democracy is the only nonauthoritarian political system feasible. Therefore, criticism of the political characteristics of such democracies, as compared to our own, is irrelevant. In fact, consociational democracies may be the *only* form of democracy realistically suited to a number of newly emerging nations. To reject consociational democracy out of hand because it does not resemble democracy in England and the United States may mean that the only feasible political alternative for modernizing elites in new nations is an authoritarian one.

Similarly, the attempt to impose a democratic political structure on a social and psychological context that is out of phase with it might lead to an experience of democracy so unpleasant that it could thwart the evolution toward such a political system for many years thereafter—despite subsequent social and economic changes that would make it a practical choice. The premature Spanish Republic, 1931–36, gave conservative and clerical segments of the Spanish population a glimpse of rampant factionalism, government instability, and extremist rabble-rousing that they are not likely to forget. As a result, many powerful groups had been determined to avoid making the same mistake again, even though enough socioeconomic change had taken place to support at least a consociational democratic regime before Franco's death.

The answer to questions concerning the best form of government must therefore be: "It depends." At times in a country's evolution the question "democracy or authoritarianism?" may have a uniquely in-determinate answer. A sophisticated political leader and his advisors may be able to take a consociational democratic path, while an equally sophisticated leader may just as feasibly move his country toward total-itarian rule. The only thing that appears certain is that failure will greet those who opt for a political system that is sorely out of phase with the social, psychological, and cultural conditions existing when the choice is made.

SUMMARY, CRITIQUE, AND CONCLUSION

Three major system types were discussed in this chapter: autocracy, totalitarianism, and democracy. Major emphasis was placed on the dynamics of change from one system type to another, with particular attention given to the transformation from democracy to totalitarianism. These two forms of government take on special interest in relation to the Maslow hierarchy. Democracy, we have noted, requires a population that is at least on the level of self-esteem. Totalitarian regimes are basically unstable in a modern technological context because the literacy and education required by modern productive processes raise the self-esteem of the citizenry to the point where demands for equality and political participation are likely to emerge.

Unfortunately, the cycle of human development can be cut short before full human potential is realized. If major calamity and crisis erupt before the masses have attained sufficient self-esteem, a democracy may give way to a totalitarian regime. Each totalitarian regime can then maintain itself by using the others as a threat, employing terror cam-paigns (ostensibly aimed at "internal agents" of external powers) against any individual who expresses independent thought. Totalitarian regimes in such a situation need no longer fear the effects of the modern pro-ductive process upon the psychological development of the population because the fruits of technology can be diverted into the production of war materiel. This ensures that full employment can be maintained in a modern economy where the standard of living is *permanently* held lower than is necessary if self-esteem is to emerge.

Throughout this book we have relied heavily upon a developmental conception of human needs as elaborated by the late Abraham H. Maslow. What evidence, both empirical and philosophical, validates such a conception in the real world? Concern for the individual lies at the root of democratic philosophy and the Judeo–Christian ethic, as it does of the major revolutionary philosophy of the nineteenth and twentieth centuries—Marxism. Erich Fromm notes that "for Marx the aim of socialism was the emancipation of man, and the emancipation of man was the same as his self-realization in the process of productive relatedness and oneness with man and nature. The aim of socialism was the development of the individual personality." [75] Although many may question Marx's assumption that revolution can attain such humanistic ends, few would deny that this philosophy has maintained substantial power and influence. This may be taken as evidence that the equalitarian ends sought by the revolution struck a deep, resonant chord in the need structures of great numbers of people widely separated by space and time.

The ends and means of human action and goal attainment embodied in the ideals of the Judeo–Christian ethic are additional manifestations of a willingness to believe in a humanistic philosophy (even though this philosophy is frequently distorted by secular authority). In the political context this ethic may be summarized as follows:

1. The political system and the actions of those within it must be psychologically acceptable to the individual; that is, they cannot generally threaten the individual.
2. The political system must allow man to develop his faculties.
3. The political system must allow the individual considerable room for self-determination.
4. The individual must have the possibility of controlling, in a meaningful way, those actions of the political system that affect him.
5. The political system should not be the sole and final arbiter of behavior; both the political system and the individual must be subject to an external moral order.[76]

Other goals derived from the Judeo–Christian ethic relate specifically to the individual and in effect mirror the basic Maslovian conception:

1. *Survival and physical well-being.* Each individual should have access to the conditions necessary for health, safety, comfort, and reasonable longevity.
2. *Fellowship.* Each individual should have a variety of satisfying human relationships.
3. *Dignity and humility.* Each individual should have the opportunity to earn a position in society of dignity and self-respect.
4. *Enlightenment.* The individual should have an opportunity to learn

---

[75] Erich Fromm, *Marx's Concept of Man* (New York: Frederick Ungar, 1961), p. 38.
[76] Adapted from the summary table in Robert T. Golembiewski, *Men, Management, and Morality* (New York: McGraw-Hill, 1965), p. 65.

about the world in which he lives. He should be able to satisfy his intellectual curiosity and to acquire the skills and knowledge for intelligent citizenship, efficient work, and informed living.

5. *Aesthetic enjoyment.* The individual should have the opportunity to appreciate aesthetic values in art, nature, and ritual, and through personal relations.

6. *Creativity.* The individual should be able to express his personality through creative activities. He should be able to identify himself with the results of his own activity, and to take pride in his achievements, intellectual, aesthetic, political, or other.

7. *New experience.* An important goal of life is suggested by the words variability, spontaneity, whimsy, novelty, excitement, fun, sport, holiday, striving against odds, solving problems, innovation, invention, etc. Each individual should have opportunity for new experience.

8. *Security.* Each individual should have assurance that the objective conditions necessary for attainment of the above goals will be reasonably accessible to him.

9. *Freedom.* Freedom is the opportunity to pursue one's goals without restraint.

10. *Justice.* The Christian law of love does not imply neglect of the self. The individual is to be as concerned about others as he is about himself—neither more nor less.

11. *Personality.* The preceding goals were stated in terms of the kinds of life experiences we wish people to have. These goals can be translated into the kinds of persons we wish them to be. Goals can then be regarded as qualities of human personality; accordingly, a desirable personality would be defined as one that is favorably conditioned toward the various goals.[77]

Much empirical research supports the Maslovian conception, but, as is true of many other concepts employed in this book, the supporting research did not originate with political scientists. Indeed, political scientists have traditionally been concerned with the "High Road" of "massive socioeconomic organization" as opposed to the "Low Road" of "patterns of organization appropriate for smaller units." Robert Golembiewski, summing up the situation over ten years ago, used Marx as an appropriate example:

Pessimism about the traditional pattern of organizing relatively small units—such as individual factories or multiplant firms—encouraged commentators to take to the High Road. Consequently,

---

[77] Adapted with minor alteration from ibid., where it had been derived from Howard R. Bowen, "Findings of the Study," in John C. Bennett et al., *Christian Values and Economic Life* (New York: Harper & Row, 1954), pp. 47–60.

attention has long been fixated upon these alternative macroscopic patterns for organizing such massive units as nation-states: capitalism, or socialism, or communism. . . .

Convenience also pointed to the High Road. For example, the armchair speculations of a Marx concerning the meaning of history would have been more complicated had he tempered his analysis of "class" with some rudimentary empirical observations. Instead Marx argued tightly that consciousness was determined by economic factors, and that class therefore was also based upon them. How, then, did a bourgeois product such as Marx become the tribune of the revolutionary proletariat? Marx's analysis, that is, did not cover even his own case. The High Road did not encourage such sensitivity to empirical data and, in many cases, the very neglect was raised to the dignity of a method. This does have a kind of intriguing convenience, but it pays a high price.[78]

The individual's level of development depends primarily upon the environment of the workplace. He spends most of his life there, and when day is done he brings it home in the form of work-related attitudes, emotions, and frustrations. But "macroscopic patterns of organization have no necessary connection with patterns of organizing work within an individual plant or firm. This macroscopic pattern can be equally oppressive under capitalism, socialism, communism, or any other *ism*." [79] It is therefore to disciplines more closely associated with the workplace such as industrial psychology and public administration that we must turn for empirical research relating to human needs.

For the sake of brevity and clarity we will focus on that stream of empirical research in industrial relations that goes to the heart of a distinction that we have maintained throughout this book—deficiency and growth motivation. The former, recall, involves the drive to satisfy the lower needs; the latter involves an individual's attempt to fulfill needs of self-esteem and self-actualization. In a seminal piece of work, Frederick Herzberg and associates sought to discern empirically when an individual was "exceptionally satisfied and exceptionally dissatisfied with his job." [80] Their research led to the discovery that two distinct sets of factors were involved: "the factors involved in producing job

[78] Golembiewski, *Men, Management, and Morality*, p. 18.

[79] Ibid., p. 20.

[80] David A. Whitsett and Erik K. Winslow, "An Analysis of Studies Critical of the Motivator–Hygiene Theory," *Personnel Psychology*, 20 (1967), p. 392. The original work is Frederick Herzberg, Bernard Mauser, and Barbara Bloch Sniderman, *The Motivation to Work*, 2nd ed. (New York: John Wiley, 1959).

satisfaction were *separate* and *distinct* from the factors that led to job dissatisfaction." [81] One set was made up of *hygiene factors:* those specifically related to fulfilling the lower, or deficiency, needs, involving such things as

> *supervision, interpersonal relations, physical working conditions, salary, company policies and administrative practices, benefits, and job security. When these factors deteriorate to a level below that which the employee considers acceptable, then job dissatisfaction ensues. However, the reverse does not hold true. When the job context can be characterized as optimal, we will not get dissatisfaction, but neither will we get much in the way of positive attitudes [toward work, the firm, etc.].*[82]

Job satisfaction emerged only when a second set of factors were included. "These factors were related to the doing of the task, to the feelings of psychological growth, and to more positive attitudes toward the work. Since these factors were also related to periods of superior performance and effort, they were labeled *motivators.*" [83] Motivators, or growth factors, included "achievement, recognition, work itself, responsibility and advancement." Recognition, Herzberg notes, here refers to "recognition for achievement rather than to recognition as a human relations tool divorced from any accomplishment." [84] The second set of factors is obviously related to Maslow's higher needs. It is evident from the original study which Whitsett and Winslow call "the most replicated study in the field," [85] and from those following that "at the psychological level, the two dimensions of job attitudes reflect a two-dimensional need structure: one need system for the avoidance of unpleasantness and a parallel need system for personal growth." [86]

The student of political science would do well to reflect for a moment on the implications of motivation–hygiene theory for the discipline. The political state has traditionally been concerned with hygiene factors—law and order, the economic well-being of the population, reduction of conflict between diverse interest groups, and the like. Yet motivation–hygiene theory indicates that, regardless of how well government does in these endeavors, we cannot expect it to be able to gain the active

[81] Frederick Herzberg, *Work and the Nature of Man* (New York: New American Library, 1973), p. 95.

[82] Herzberg, Mauser, and Sniderman, *The Motivation to Work,* pp. 113–14.

[83] Whitsett and Winslow, "An Analysis of Studies," pp. 392–93.

[84] Herzberg, *Work and the Nature of Man,* pp. 92–93.

[85] Whitsett and Winslow, "An Analysis of Studies," p. 393.

[86] Herzberg, *Work and the Nature of Man,* pp. 94–95.

support of the citizenry until the motivator factors are fulfilled—through, for example, public education of a high quality and broad availability; and a labor market that gives every citizen a fair chance to pursue a career that will be meaningful and challenging. The most a government addressed only to the hygiene factors can expect from all of its efforts, however strenuous, is simply a lack of dissatisfaction.

In this regard it is interesting that an empirical study by Knutson indicates that, for individuals who can be classified as "high self-actualizers," the relationship between social class and almost all of the antidemocratic characteristics associated with lower social class member-ship is reduced to statistical insignificance. That is, for individuals from the mass who attain self-esteem and higher, we can no longer predict with a high degree of accuracy that they will be cynical, powerless, fearful, distrusting, frustrated, overly dogmatic or—in a word—potentially antidemocratic.[87]

Finally, we should address the following issue: If the need hierarchy is indeed valid, reflected in the nature of man in the real world, then we should be able to observe specific, distinct consequences of the ability and the inability, respectively, to fulfill the higher needs. If fulfillment of the growth factors leads to satisfied, happy, and emotionally healthy individuals who are willing to actively support a democratic government and bear the responsibility that comes with political participation, then what of those who, for one reason or another, are not able to attain growth motivation?

Again we will draw briefly upon the work of Herzberg and his associates, who state that "hygiene factors can only provide for the ab-sence of mental illness, they cannot bring forth mentally healthy states. Motivator factors serve primarily to promote mental health while having little effect in producing mental illness."[88] The deficiency needs, they contend, range along a "continuum of pain-relief" while the growth needs involve a "dimension of emptiness-fulfillment." This does not contradict Maslow's theory, but, rather, supplements it; it implies that a person who is totally involved with fulfilling the lower needs is also in an emotional or spiritual vacuum. Living in such a vacuum, a de-ficiency-motivated person could choose a political alternative offered by a charismatic, authoritarian leader who promised to fill the vacuum with the "meaning" provided by a revolutionary "cause." We have noted that deficiency motivation and authoritarian movements seem to go together.

[87] See Knutson, *The Human Basis of the Polity*, p. 344.

[88] Frederick Herzberg; Yoash Wiener; Joseph Mathapo; and Lawrence E. Wiesen, "Motivation–Hygiene Correlates of Mental Health: An Examination of Motivational Inversion in a Clinical Population," *Journal of Consulting and Clinical Psychology*, 42 (1974), 411–19.

There are many points at which an individual's path to the higher needs can be blocked; and it could be argued that cognitive closure in a conspiratorial world view, below the level of self-esteem and self-actualization, might block one's way to higher need fulfillment. In line with motivation–hygiene theory, Herzberg and his associates have found evidence that "the disturbed individual attempts to derive a fulfillment experience through the satisfaction of the pain-avoidance needs—an affective experience that they cannot provide." In terms of this theory the roots of mental illness—meaning, in this book, the roots of authoritarian, antisocial, and antidemocratic behavior—are to be found in "motivational inversion." Here the emotionally unhealthy individual seeks an impossible fulfillment through deficiency rather than growth needs. Serious maladjustment is the result. This, of course, fits the image of the active–negative, portrayed in Chapter 4 as an individual out after ever-increasing quantities of power, which he views as a source of security. This person finds it impossible to gain fulfillment and satisfaction from his frenetic political activity despite prodigious efforts and despite victories that appear great in everyone's eyes but his own.[89]

In the context of modern America, this idea corresponds closely to an intuitive conception of the malaise in contemporary society by which the trappings of wealth, status, and economic security by themselves appear to be incapable of satisfying man's search for deeper meaning. The result of widespread motivational inversion can be seen as spiritual poverty amidst material plenty.[90]

Once poverty has been overcome, the desire for material wealth—the mercenary motive—diminishes as other needs require satisfaction. The correlation of personal happiness with money declines after a reasonable level of income has been achieved. Thus, in an industrial or post-industrial society, the middle and upper classes are ready to accept what now appears to be an inevitable decline in the rate of economic growth. However, the poor and working classes cannot be expected to adopt noneconomic values. "Locked into a situation where the escalator of growth will not give their rising expectations any satisfaction, they may be expected to react with bitterness and frustration such as to make them available for [the] paranoid style [of politics]. . . . The underclass is a menace to itself and to the nation."[91] A possible solution is redistribution of income, a choice painful to capitalist societies.

---

[89] See Brent M. Rutherford, "Psychopathology, Decisionmaking, and Political Involvement," *Journal of Conflict Resolution*, 10 (1966), 387–407.

[90] Herbert Marcuse, *One-Dimensional Man* (Boston, Mass.: Beacon Press, 1964).

[91] These remarks are heavily influenced by Robert E. Lane, "Social Trends in the United States," paper presented to the Second American Studies Conference, Taipei, Taiwan, 1976.

Name index

Subject index